The Other Victorians

Studies in Sex and Society

SPONSORED BY THE INSTITUTE FOR SEX RESEARCH
INDIANA UNIVERSITY
BLOOMINGTON, INDIANA

1. Steven Marcus / *The Other Victorians*

THE OTHER VICTORIANS

A Study of
*Sexuality and Pornography in
Mid-Nineteenth-Century England*

BY

STEVEN MARCUS

Basic Books, Inc., Publishers

NEW YORK

© 1964, 1965, 1966 by Steven Marcus

Library of Congress Catalog Card Number: 66–19926

Manufactured in the United States of America

DESIGNED BY VINCENT TORRE

To Gertrud

However strange it may sound, I think the possibility must be considered that something in the nature of the sexual instinct itself is unfavourable to the achievement of absolute gratification. . . . The erotic instincts are hard to mould; training of them achieves now too much, now too little. What culture tries to make out of them seems attainable only at the cost of a sensible loss of pleasure; the persistence of the impulses that are not enrolled in adult sexual activity makes itself felt in an absence of satisfaction.

So perhaps we must make up our minds to the idea that altogether it is not possible for the claims of the sexual instinct to be reconciled with the demands of culture. . . . This very incapacity in the sexual instinct to yield full satisfaction as soon as it submits to the first demands of culture becomes the source, however, of the grandest cultural achievements, which are brought to birth by ever greater sublimation of the components of the sexual instinct. For what motive would induce man to put his sexual energy to other uses if by any disposal of it he could obtain fully satisfying pleasure? He would never let go of this pleasure and would make no further progress.

SIGMUND FREUD

"The Most Prevalent Form of Degradation in Erotic Life"

Preface

I BEGIN this book with an account of its origins. I believe that it will add to the reader's understanding of what this work undertakes to do if he also knows something of how it came about. In the summer of 1961 I was teaching at the Indiana University School of Letters. It is a tradition at the School of Letters that each summer its several Fellows, or instructors, be conducted on a tour of the Institute for Sex Research. I was impressed by and interested in what I saw on this tour, and during the course of it found myself engaged in conversation with John H. Gagnon, one of the Institute's four research associates, trustees, or directors, as they are on different occasions called. This conversation was subsequently renewed, and then renewed again, and soon I found myself asked back to the Institute, speaking again with Mr. Gagnon and with the Executive Director, Paul H. Gebhard. At this point, a proposal was made to me. I was invited to return to the Institute to conduct researches in its library and archives. These had largely been amassed by the prodigious energies of the Institute's founder, the late Alfred C. Kinsey. They had also, I was told, gone largely unused and unexplored. It was the opinion of the Directors that the time had now come to begin to exploit this material, as it was also their belief that the time had now come to begin to open up the heretofore locked doors of the Institute, and to extend the use of its immense resources to scholars from other fields of study.

What the Directors of the Institute had in mind was a pamphlet, monograph, or book on one of the many subjects included in their collections. (As a more distant goal, if this project were successful, they envisaged a series of such monographic studies —written by a variety of scholars upon a variety of topics—of which the present study might be the first.) Our conversations in particular concerned writings about sexuality and writings of a sexual character published during the Victorian period.

My own interests appeared to have converged in that direction. I had just finished a book on Dickens, and before that, in collaboration with Lionel Trilling, had edited and abridged Ernest Jones's three-volume biography of Freud. It did not require a dialectician's cunning to make out that Dickens plus Freud might conceivably add up to an interest in writings about sex and sexuality in mid-nineteenth century England. I said that I would think the matter over, and returned to New York.

I thought the matter over, consulted with colleagues and friends, and after due hesitation decided to take at least a crack at the project. My hesitations and doubts had in part to do with the subject itself, with its dubiousness, its difficulty, its capacity to trouble and disturb. In all candor, however, I must confess that part of my reservations had to do with the Institute itself. Apart from my few conversations with Mr. Gagnon and Mr. Gebhard, what I knew of the Institute was got from a reading of its first two publications. Although like everyone else I was deeply impressed by the energy, the care, and the achievement of these works, and although I also believed that they had performed a genuine service to society, still I found myself often in sharp disagreement with a number of their assumptions, and found myself particularly opposed to certain parts of their intellectual attitude and to their intellectual style.[1] These latter seemed to combine an excessively hard-nosed and reductive kind of empiricism with an excessively aggressive skepticism toward ideas in general—sometimes it seemed to me that the distrust of theory, speculation, and ideas generated in these works became so strong that it was difficult to distinguish that distrust from anti-intellectuality. My own interests were to be found in literature, in the history of modern culture, and in ideas, especially those ideas that might be thought of as constitutive of the modern self. The instruments which I could hope to bring to bear on the material I was about to study were those of literary criticism, of the historical method, something of applied psychoanalysis, and something of social theory.

[1] Memorable expression was given to such reservations in Lionel Trilling's essay "The Kinsey Report," *The Liberal Imagination* (New York, 1950), pp. 223–242.

When I returned to Bloomington in 1962 to begin work on this project, my mind was troubled by doubts and reservations.

It gives me genuine pleasure to report that I was thoroughly mistaken, my doubts unfounded, my reservations unjustified. I have never worked in more congenial circumstances. I do not by this merely mean that the staff of the Institute were friendly, helpful, and encouraging, although they were certainly that. Nor do I mean that our interests and methods coincided, or that we met in happy agreement on all matters. I do mean that the air was full of ideas, that speculation was encouraged, and that my own insights, notions, guesses, suggestions, and suspicions were met with directly, on the same level at which they were offered. I should like to thank the members of the staff of the Institute collectively and individually.

My first debt at the Institute is to John H. Gagnon. During the first difficult months of research, when I was trying to set bearings in places where no bearings had been set before, he was particularly helpful. He was always willing to share with me his knowledge of the behavioral and biological sciences, to offer bibliographical suggestions, and to prevent me, by a knowing hint or two, from going headlong down blind alleys. Paul H. Gebhard took time off from his schedule of writing and administrative duties to discuss with me matters pertinent to my work. Wardell B. Pomeroy was especially helpful; during the earliest periods of my research, the idea sometimes crossed my mind that Mr. Pomeroy had privately undertaken to offer me a course of instruction in everything he knew—his open-handedness and accessibility were truly remarkable. Cornelia V. Christenson provided me with considerable help in matters pertaining to the archives and to certain historical questions.

Elizabeth Egan, the Institute's chief librarian, patiently searched for items, articles, and volumes, and as often as not directed my attention to things which I might have otherwise passed over. My thanks go as well to Mary Winther and Mary Louise Carter for being helpful in a variety of ways. William Dellenback, staff photographer, helped me with certain technical problems, and once, when it was desperately needed, with microfilm. Besides doing other things, Eugene Slabaugh worked a photo-copying machine overtime in my behalf, for which I am grateful. Bettie Silverstein and Joan Huntington typed the early chapters, and I am much in debt to the care and the precision of their work. For a number of favors and services I should also like to thank Alan Blaine Johnson.

Three further institutional debts must be acknowledged. The Council on Research in the Humanities, of Columbia University, the Indiana University Foundation, and the American Council of Learned Societies were all generous enough to award me grants for work on this project. These grants permitted me to set certain academic duties temporarily aside; and they permitted me as well to bring this work to conclusion sooner than I had originally thought possible.

At Indiana University, I should like to thank Michael Wolff and other editors of *Victorian Studies* for a number of useful and encouraging conversations. To Patricia Gagnon, my thanks for many kindnesses and much hospitality.

My friends Diana and Lionel Trilling deserve a special note of thanks. Discussions with them during the earliest phase of my researches were of great value to me. From the outset, the encouragement and advice of Irving Kristol helped to sustain me. I should also like to thank Meyer Schapiro for a number of useful suggestions.

I reserve my largest debt for the last. To my dear friend and wife, Gertrud Lenzer, I owe a debt to which I cannot give a full account. Our discussions of the subjects dealt with in this book were lengthy, intense, and argumentative. She brought her knowledge of the social sciences acutely to bear on the material I presented to her, and I cannot tell how many errors her sense of intellectual relevance and methodological rigor helped me to avoid. Without her example and her belief in me, this book would not exist in its present form, nor would it yet exist.

STEVEN MARCUS

New York
January 1966

Introduction

SOMETHING should be said about the "otherness" of the Victorians dealt with in this book. In part their otherness has to do with the nature of their interests; in part it has to do with the way they went about expressing those interests. At the same time, however, this otherness was of a specific Victorian kind, a kind that was of interest to the Victorians themselves and that remains of interest to us as we try to understand the past and ourselves in relation to the past. Their otherness connects them to us, but so does the fact that they were Victorians connect them to us as well. Connection is nevertheless not identity—and in the end these Victorians also remain both other to us and Victorian.

Moreover, the subjects dealt with in this work are not only those thought to have been "shocking"—or other—in the Victorian period; the way these subjects were regarded—and the way our notions of the Victorians continue to change, as the efforts of contemporary scholarship restore them for the first time to their full historical dimensions—are matters today of some surprise and wonder. That surprise and wonder, I might add, that sense of the presence of the other, should on the whole be taken as having a positive force.

The method pursued in this study may be simply described. It begins on the outside and then circles in. It opens with a discussion of the writings of the physician William Acton. These writings may be said to represent the official views of sexuality held by Victorian society—or, put in another way, the views held by the official culture. The second chapter is an analysis of the work of Henry Spencer Ashbee, or Pisanus Fraxi, the first, and most important, bibliographer-scholar of publications of a sexual and pornographic character. I try to demonstrate how, on the one hand, Ashbee is related to Acton, and how, on the other, he is deeply involved in the pornographic world or fantasy which he is attempting to subject to scholarly analysis. Chapters 3 and 4 are devoted to a discussion of the most important work of its kind from the period, the eleven-volume autobiography, *My Secret Life*. This work is important not only because of its authenticity—or because of the uses it may have as social or cultural history; it is also important because it helps to demonstrate the connection between an authentic account of sexual experience in the Victorian period and the fantasies and language of pornography. Chapter 5 consists of an analysis of four pornographic novels written during the period. In this section, I try to demonstrate something about the typical character and development of pornography; and I also examine these works in their relation to openly or legally published fiction. Chapter 6 is a brief account of an immense literature—the veritable flood of publications during the Victorian period of works devoted to describing the experience of flagellation. My account is curtailed for two reasons: the fantasy represented in this literature has already been analyzed; this mountain of material literally contains only a single fantasy, represented and re-represented almost to infinity, without significant variations. Its apparent want of intellectual interest, however, may conceal its social importance, and I ask a number of questions which point in the latter direction. In the last chapter, I sum up what has gone before and try to reach certain theoretical conclusions about matters entered upon at earlier points of the work.

The following book, then, consists of a series of related studies in the sexual culture—more precisely, perhaps, the sexual subculture—of Victorian England. For although I at first regarded this work as an exercise in literary criticism and history, or as a study of culture in the sense put to it by literary criticism, I soon found myself thinking of it—at least metaphorically—as an exercise in anthropology as well. The subculture to be studied was "foreign," distinct, exotic; at the same time it was a human subculture and consequently was relevant to our own humanity and culture. I could in addition fancy myself as being out "in the field": a new language or dialect had to be learned, preconceptions had to be rigorously put aside, and guidelines had to be laid down where none existed before.[1] To the exhilaration of being alone in an area where almost none had ever been before, there was added the anxiety that one had only one's own personal and very fallible sense of judgment to rely on. I have tried—as I trust the reader will see—to make very clear just where and how that judgment is being exercised; but there is no doubt in my mind that errors have inevitably crept in as well. It is no excuse of such errors to say that they are inevitable, and it is not pretending to anything more than ordinary truth to say that as I finish this work I look forward to the publication in the future of other studies, by other hands, which will amend, correct, enlarge, and go beyond such findings as I have been able to make.

[1] One of the chief difficulties attached to this kind of study has to do with the almost total absence of any kind of serious or reliable previous work. In this connection I should like to acknowledge two books which were of help to me, especially in matters of social history, M. J. Quinlan's regrettably forgotten *Victorian Prelude* (New York, 1941), and Norman St. John-Stevas' *Obscenity and the Law* (London, 1956). David Foxon's important and authoritative essays on the historical origins of pornography, "Libertine Literature in England, 1660–1745," *The Book Collector,* XII, 1, 2, 3 (Spring, Summer, Winter, 1963), 21–36, 159–177, 294–307, arrived too late to be of direct use to me. I am pleased to be able to report, however, that Mr. Foxon's conclusions and mine coincide, and that in general our lines of investigation and ways of thinking about this subject run in parallel directions.

Contents

The Other Victorians

Chapter 1: MR. ACTON OF QUEEN ANNE STREET, OR, THE WISDOM OF OUR ANCESTORS

I

Since this is a study of human fantasies, it may be useful to begin it by considering that official fantasy which in the mid-nineteenth century went by the name of scientific knowledge. I use the word "fantasy" not in a belittling or deprecatory sense but to describe the quality of thinking or of mind that one meets with in scientific or medical accounts of human sexuality in the English nineteenth century. This thinking, one soon learns, rests upon a mass of unargued, unexamined and largely unconscious assumptions; its logical proceedings are loose and associative rather than rigorous and sequential; and one of its chief impulses is to confirm what is already held as belief rather than to adapt belief to new and probably disturbing knowledge. And as we shall see it shares all these qualities in common with pornography itself. No doubt most people think this way about most things most of the time—that is to say, a good deal of our thinking consists of fantasy cast in the form of opinion or assertion; or, in another context, such thinking has the characteristics of what in the social sciences is called "ideology." Furthermore, no subject has had anything like the power to elicit such prepared responses as the subject of sexuality.

On the other hand, the Victorian era is very likely the earliest period in history for which such a study is easily possible. There is, in the first place, the question of the availability and extensiveness of published material. Then there is the fact that pornography and especially pornographic writing became an industry during this time—following, as it still tends to do, the course of development traced by the novel. In addition, the scientific spirit of the age found major expression in advances in the biological sciences and in medicine; and this, coupled with the strong social and reforming temper of the times, made for a situation in which considerable public discussion of sexual matters took place. Like ourselves, the Victorians were inclined to regard important issues as "problems." Behind this attitude, of course, is an assumption that "problems" are there to be "solved" and have a "solution"; conversely, one suspects that if so many things are held in the mind as problems, a certain problematical quality will be given to the whole. Sex has always been a problem in human civilization, but not until sometime during the nineteenth century, I think, did there emerge as part of the general educated consciousness the formulation that it might in fact be problematical—it is an idea that forms part of our inheritance. I can think of no more instructive illustration of these manifold tendencies, attitudes, contradictions and confusions than the writings of William Acton.

Though his name has long since been forgotten, Acton was something of a figure in his own time. In his virtues he was a truly representative Victorian: earnest, morally austere yet liberally inclined, sincere, open-minded, possessed by the belief that it was his duty to work toward the alleviation of the endless human misery and suffering which sometimes seem to be the chief constituents of society. Acton was born in 1813, at Shillingstone, Dorsetshire, the second son of a clergyman. In 1831 he was enrolled as apprentice to the Resident Apothecary to St. Bartholomew's Hospital, London, where he worked until 1836. He then traveled to Paris, where he devoted himself to the study of what was to become his life's work, diseases of the urinary and generative organs. In Paris he studied under and became a permanent disciple of the well-known American genito-urinary surgeon Philippe Ricord; during this period Acton also served for some time as an extern in the Female Venereal Hospital. In 1840 he returned to England, was admitted a Member of the Royal College of Surgeons, and began practice in his specialty. He was for some time, as well, Surgeon to the Islington Dispensary; and in 1842 became a Fellow of the Royal Medical and Chirurgical Society of London.

As a physician, it was said of him, Acton "was careful and safe . . . and had much technical skill," and it was not long before his practice became large. Sir James Paget, in his obituary notice of Acton, rather primly remarks that he "never used the opportunities of his large practice for an independent inquiry into the questions still remaining in the pathology of syphilis, and in the parts of general pathology which the study of syphilis may solve." He chose instead to become a writer, taking as his subject not only the diseases in which he was expert, but the social questions that were allied to them, such as illegitimacy and prostitution. (One of his papers, which I have not been able to obtain, is about "Unmarried Wet-Nurses"—the possibilities of this title seem positively Joycean.) His first book, published in 1841, was called *A Practical Treatise on Diseases of the Urinary and Generative Organs in Both Sexes,* and was successful enough to have gone through four editions by the time of Acton's death in 1875.

Acton first came before the public eye, however, through his writings on prostitution. He was one of the pioneers in the agitation, investigation, and discussion that finally led to the passage of the Contagious Diseases Act of 1866; this legislation provided that in certain areas where there were army encampments or naval stations or depots—such as Canterbury, Dover, Gravesend, Woolwich, and Aldershot—prostitutes be subject to periodical medical examination. Any woman who was found on examination to be diseased was hospitalized and treated at government expense; refusal to conform to the provisions of this act made her liable to be punished by imprisonment—this latter provision appears to have been largely unenforced or unenforceable. The first edition of this work was published some eight years before the Act was passed; the second, which came out in 1870, was much enlarged and revised, and incorporated Acton's observations on the workings of the new law. Its full, ringing title reads: *Prostitution, considered in its Moral, Social, and Sanitary Aspects, in London and other Large Cities and Garrison Towns, with Proposals for the Control and Prevention of its Attendant Evils.* And it is a very good book, certainly the best piece of work of its kind from the period that I have read. A brief examination of it will serve to introduce us to the quality of Acton's mind—at least to the quality of one side of it.

Acton's position can be straightforwardly outlined. Prostitution, he believed, was an inevitable, almost an organic, part of society. Efforts to repress or extirpate it have always ended in failure. At the same time, he argues, it would be "equally irrational . . . to imagine that this irrepressible evil can exist without entailing upon society serious mischief; though incapable of absolute repression, prostitution admits of mitigation. To ignore an ever-present evil appears a mistake as fatal as the attempt to repress it." The English habit of dealing with prostitution had been until then largely to ignore its existence; prostitution as it was practiced in England was, in the terminology of the times, free, private and clandestine, while on most of the Continent it was public, regulated, and licensed. Acton is too English himself, and too acutely aware of what the social possibilities in England were, to recommend the adoption of any system in which society through the agency of the State should appear to sponsor "immorality" by means of legalizing or licensing it. Yet he believes that it is "necessary to recognize its existence, and to provide for its regulation." Opposed by a combination of Podsnappery and religious extremism, by, as he puts it, "the dull stupidity that shuts its eyes to well-known evils, and by refusing to recognize accomplished facts and actual circumstances, endows them with a tenfold power of mischief, and which, while it justifies its inertness by religious theories, forgets the first practical duty of the Christian," Acton feels it necessary to come out strongly as "an advocate of RECOGNITION"—in capitals. (Which leads to the reflection that prostitution in Victorian England was the Red China of its day.) Acton's position then may be thought of as generally realistic, liberal, and Benthamite, a typical constellation of attitudes. He is concerned with the amelioration of a social evil, and for the intervention of government in a regulatory but minimal capacity. At the same time he feels it necessary to tip his hat toward the principles of personal liberty and *laissez-faire,* which had inevitably gotten involved in the discussion, and to "admit that a woman if so disposed may make profit of her own person, and that the State has no right to prevent her." Such an admission, of course, merely sharpens the horns of the dilemma on which this question—not to say Acton himself—is impaled, but we should recall that Acton is quite aware of the fact that it is a dilemma, and that all his choices are lesser evils.

One of Acton's chief purposes in this book is to humanize the prostitute, to educate or persuade his respectable audience to regard her not as some alien and monstrous creature but as a fellow human being. To this end he explodes the popular myth of the harlot's progress, demonstrating from his own professional experience that "such an ending of the harlot's life is the altogether rare exception . . . that the downward progress and death of the prostitute in the absolute ranks of that occupation are exceptional also, and that she succumbs at last, not to that calling, nor to venereal disease, but in due time, and to the various maladies common to respectable humanity." Moreover, he reports it as the general medical opinion "that no other class of females is so free from general disease" and that as a rule prostitutes are endowed with "iron bodies," with extremely resilient and resistant constitutions. He then goes on to institute this surprising comparison.

> If we compare the prostitute at thirty-five with her sister, who perhaps is the married mother of a family, or has been a toiling

slave for years in the over-heated laboratories of fashion, we shall seldom find that the constitutional ravages often thought to be necessary consequences of prostitution exceed those attributable to the cares of a family and the heart-wearing struggles of virtuous labor.

These remarks may help to illuminate another side of the complex hostility which all the respectable classes of society directed toward the prostitute. Still worse, he shows that "by far the larger number of women who have resorted to prostitution for a livelihood, return sooner or later to a more or less regular course of life." The major part of London's army of whores were, in other words, transients, and Acton asserts that "prostitution is a transitory state, through which an untold number of British women are ever on their passage." Their re-entrance into decency took place in a variety of ways: from finding work of some other kind, to opening small shops or lodging-houses, to emigration, and to marriage. This last route of escape seems to have been increasingly in use, and Acton calls attention to the frequency with which "the better inclined class of prostitutes become the wedded wives of men in every grade of society, from the peerage to the stable"; in addition, "as they are frequently barren, or have but a few children, there is reason to believe they often live in ease unknown to many women who have never strayed, and on whose unvitiated organization matrimony has entailed the burden of families." It stands to Acton's credit that, having said this, he goes on to assert that it is both the social duty and the social interest of the nation "to see these women through that state, so as to save harmless as much as may be of the bodies and souls of them." And all his recommendations for the treatment of prostitutes are in the direction of humanizing and rehabilitating them—though he is perfectly aware of how imperfect a success such efforts have achieved. As for those religious persons who opposed preventive and sanitary measures on the grounds that syphilis was "the penalty for sin," and that therefore syphilis should go unchecked and uncured because the chance of contracting it "is the strongest means of deterring men from being unchaste," he dismisses them with

something less than the contempt they deserved, arguing instead—and characteristically—that like other deterrents before
and since it didn't finally deter, which is true enough.

Acton is a rather gifted social observer. He notes, for example, that the world of prostitution is a "microcosm" of society at large, and that, chastity aside, it "exhibits, like its arche-
type . . . all the virtues and good qualities, as well as all the
vices, weaknesses, and follies." Prostitutes, he remarks, "maintain their notions of caste and quality with all the pertinacity of
their betters. The greatest amount of income procurable with
the least amount of exertion is with them, as with society, the
grand gauge of position." There is a nice edge to that last sentence. He also offers some shrewd observations on the reciprocal relation between prostitution and the demand made in the
respectable classes for money and position as the requirements
for marriage. And there is no doubt in his mind that the chief
cause of prostitution is "cruel biting poverty" and "the lowness
of the wages paid to workwomen in various trades . . . unable
to obtain by their labor the means of procuring the bare neces-
saries of life, they gain, by surrendering their bodies to evil uses,
food to sustain and clothes to cover them. Many thousand
young women in the metropolis are unable by drudgery that
lasts from early morning till late into the night to earn more
than from 3*s.* to 5*s.* weekly. Many have to eke out their living as
best they may on a miserable pittance for less than the least of
the sums above-mentioned." Is it any wonder, he asks, that
"urged on by want and toil, encouraged by evil advisers, and
exposed to selfish tempters, a large proportion of these poor
girls fall from the path of virtue? Is it not a great wonder that
any of them are found abiding in it?" It is a question that was
asked by Henry Mayhew and others before Acton, and that was
asked repeatedly during the age. And it is a question that takes
a good deal of answering—involving as it does the larger question of respectability and its social meaning. Acton reserves
some of his harshest comments for the respectable classes, although there is never any doubt of where his own allegiance

lies. And of course he disapproves of prostitution on moral grounds, reasoning that it offers satisfaction to only one part of man's inclinations at the expense of the rest. But he also—unlike many of his contemporaries—does not morally confuse prostitution with other kinds of illicit sexual relations, and asserts the need to "distinguish the indulgence of unlawful love from commerce with prostitutes; the one is the ill-regulated but complete gratification of the entire human being, the other affords gratification to one part only of his nature." However ambiguous the force of that term "ill-regulated," and however inadequate we may judge the vocabulary available to Acton, it seems clear that an effort to make the right kind of distinctions is going on.

Acton is also concerned for the state of the medical profession in England. When the first edition of this work was published in 1857, the London hospitals printed no statistical tables of their patients; by 1869 things had considerably improved, though it still remained impossible to form a reliable estimate of the number of prostitutes in London—figures ranging anywhere from 6,000 to 80,000 and above were offered. Nor was the exchange or gathering of knowledge from the private practice of physicians anything but primitive. "There is in our profession very little interchange of notes and statistics," he complains, "and no organized correspondence with any body or society, and I fancy no medical man could draw a sound deduction as to the greater or less prevalence of any particular disease from the state of his own practice." Such remarks call to mind Tertius Lydgate and George Eliot's description, in *Middlemarch,* of the state of medical practice in the England of an earlier generation. Indeed there are a number of correspondences between Lydgate and Acton, and in a curious way acquaintance with Lydgate has the effect, so to speak, of authenticating Acton, of filling him out, of making him seem less strange or out of the ordinary—which demonstrates how literature can sometimes help to retrieve the actuality of an unknown or forgotten person from the dust heap of history. Both Lydgate and Acton studied in France, and it is to France that

I I

-known and most popular work is called *The
nd Disorders of the Reproductive Organs.* It was
ned in 1857; within a year a second edition was
translation into French was made in 1863, from the
on; it went through a number of editions in America
ill being printed twenty years after Acton's death, an
ition coming out in Philadelphia in 1894. The cur-
this work seems to have been in accord with what was
ught of as qualified opinion, for the book received ex-
notices in the medical press. "In the work now before
d *The Lancet,* "all essential detail upon its subject matter
rly and scientifically given. We recommend it accord-
as meeting a necessary requisition of the day, refusing to
n that opinion which regards the consideration of the
s in question as beyond the duties of the medical practi-
er." The "topics in question" are sex, and *Functions and
orders* is an account of human sexuality, a subject which,
ton writes in his introduction, still needs "much elucida-
n." Until recently, he states, "many standard surgical writers
n the generative system have practically ignored the functional
spect of their subject; dealing with the whole of the wonderful
nd complex machinery of which they treat, as if the offices it
fulfills, the thousand feelings it affects, the countless social,
moral, and scientific interests with which it is so intimately
connected, were of little or no moment." Acton's purpose is to
supply this defect and to "investigate these subjects in the same
calm and philosophic spirit with which all other scientific inquiries should be approached." Furthermore, he writes in a
preface to the fourth, revised edition, he has devoted much care
to "the minute weighing of every sentence," hoping thereby to
achieve a precise and unobjectionable treatment "of a subject so
novel and difficult, and in many respects painful." I do not include these statements in order to play the easy game of "show-

Acton turns whenever he wishes to form a comparison. The
question of prostitution had received there consideration
"which has been denied to it at home; experiments have been
tried on the continent which we in England have hitherto de-
clined to make." And he counsels his readers to shake off national prejudice and extend to foreign institutions the "patient
and impartial examination that we would demand for our
own." And he turns first to France, he says, not only as England's "nearest neighbor," but "as the country that has always
led the way in the advance of modern civilization and the
growth of modern ideas." Matthew Arnold's "note of provinci-
ality" is not being sounded here, however remote from sweet-
ness and light Acton's subjects may be. But it must be remembered to his honor, as Paget said, that "he practiced honorably
in the most dangerous of specialties," and that "he wrote decently on subjects not usually decent."

As a writer, Acton has a kind of raw talent; his powers of
observation are often acute, but they, like his prose, are equally
often undisciplined and out of hand. Again the comparison
with Lydgate is in order. Here, for example, are some extracts
from Acton's account of a visit he made one "pleasant July evening" to Cremorne, the famous pleasure gardens in Chelsea.

As calico and merry respectability tailed off eastward by penny
steamers, the setting sun brought westward Hansoms freighted
with demure immorality in silk and fine linen. By about ten
o'clock, age and innocence . . . had seemingly all retired, weary
with a long and paid bill of amusements, leaving the massive
elms, the grass-plots, and the geranium-beds, the kiosks, temples,
"monster platforms," and "crystal circle" of Cremorne to flicker in
the thousand gas-lights there for the gratification of the dancing
public only. On and around that platform waltzed, strolled, and
fed some thousand souls—perhaps seven hundred of them men of
the upper and middle class, the remainder prostitutes more or less
pronouncées. I suppose that a hundred couples . . . were engaged
in dancing and other amusements, and the rest of the society, myself included, circulated listlessly about the garden, and enjoyed in
a grim kind of way the "selection" from some favorite opera and
the cool night-breeze from the river.

The extent of disillusion he has purchased in this world comes forcibly home to the middle-aged man who in such a scene attempts to fathom former faith and ancient joys, and perhaps even vainly to fancy he might by some possibility begin again. I saw scores, nay hundreds, about me in the same position as myself. We were there—and some of us, I feel sure, hardly knew why—but being there, and it being obviously impossible to enjoy the place after the manner of youth, it was necessary, I suppose, to chew the cud of sweet and bitter fancies; and then so little pleasure came, that the Britannic solidity waxed solider than ever even in a garden full of music and dancing, and so an almost mute procession, not of joyous revellers, but thoughtful, careworn men and women, paced round and round the platform as on a horizontal treadmill. There was now and then a bare recognition between passers-by—they seemed to touch and go, like ants in the hurry of business . . . the intercourse of the sexes could hardly have been more reserved. . . . For my part, I was occupied, when the first chill of change was shaken off, in quest of noise, disorder, debauchery, and bad manners. Hopeless task! The pic-nic at Burnham Beeches, that showed no more life and merriment than Cremorne . . . would be a failure indeed, unless the company were antiquarians or undertakers. . . . The *gratus puellae risus* was put in a corner with a vengeance, under a colder shade than that of chastity itself, and the function of the very band appeared to be to drown not noise, but stillness.

The younger portion of the company formed the dances, and enjoyed themselves after the manner of youth, but I may fairly say, without offence to the most fastidious eye or ear. . . . The officiating member of the executive, Policeman T, had taken up an amiably discreet position, where his presence could in no way appear symptomatic of pressure, and the chances seemed to be, that had he stood so posed until his interference was necessary on behalf of public order, he might have been there to this day.

Lemonade and sherry seemed to please the dancers, and the loungers indulged the waiters' importunity with a rare order for bitter-beer. A strongish party of undergraduates in drinking—all males—were deepening their native dulness in a corner with bottled stout, and more seasoned vessels struggled against depression with hot grog. In front of the liquor-bar . . . two rosy capitalists (their wives at Brighton or elsewhere) were pouring, for mere distraction's sake, libations of fictitious Möet, to the memory of auld lang syne with some fat old *dames de maison,* possibly extinct planets of the Georgian era. There was no drunkenness here to take hold of. As I have before recorded, there was among

the general compa
Let me try the ass
by women. I declar
anti-sociable habit o
to. Of the character
little moral doubt, but
by any great number of t
to the male visitors to in
No gentlemanly propositi
buffed, no courteous offer o
am firmly of opinion, that ha
ried in hopes of overtures fro
been there yet, with Policeman

This is a surprising bit of writi
of an occasion for "pleasure," th
alongside of is Dickens's description
don Sunday evening. The quality of
lar. It may also serve as a represent
prose: its virtues are self-evident; its s
tendency to garrulousness and repetition
made phrases or clichés—he clearly often w
passage is also characterized by a peculia
never quite certain of the source or location
frozen sadness. The depression is there in the
is also present in Acton, and not merely as a
he is observing but as something he has brough
and projects onto it. This inability to separate ou
what one must call the subjective and objective co
an experience indicates, I think, a dimmed conscio
further, a disinclination to examine the contents or n
one's responses. One thinks again of Lydgate; and th
"spots of commonness" which George Eliot ascribed
tincture the complexion of Acton's mind as well. Yet it
be too harsh to continue criticism of *Prostitution* along
lines. It could not have been an easy book to write, it stands
among contemporary works on this subject, and it represen
genuine effort of the humane intelligence.

Acton's best
Functions
first publis
called for;
third editi
and was s
eighth e
rency of
then th
cellent
us," sai
is clea
ingly,
join
topi
tio
Dis
Ac
ti
o

ing up the past" but to convey a sense of what Acton, and probably his readers, thought he was doing.

The full title of the work is *The Function and Disorders of the Reproductive Organs, in Childhood, Youth, Adult Age, and Advanced Life, Considered in their Physiological, Social and Moral Relations.* It is an admirably comprehensive designation, and the first comment on it must be that it is altogether misleading and inaccurate. The book is entirely about men and male sexuality. With the exception of two extremely short but significant passages not a word is said about women. The first implications of this discrepancy are to say the least odd: do women not have reproductive organs; or, alternatively, if they do, do they not have functions or fall into disorders? Moreover, Acton seems perfectly unconscious of the fact that he has anything to account for in this connection, and at no point does he feel it necessary to explain what in charity we may call the disproportions of his work—obviously there is nothing to explain. This kind of dislocated awareness serves to introduce us to the world of this book; it is a world part fantasy, part nightmare, part hallucination, and part madhouse. Yet we should recall that it was written by the author of that eminently sane work on prostitution—the operations of the mind are never simple, to coin a phrase.

Acton begins by describing the "Normal Functions in Childhood."

> In a state of health no sexual impression should ever affect a child's mind or body. All its vital energy should be employed in building up the growing frame, in storing up external impressions, and educating the brain to receive them. During a well-regulated childhood, and in the case of ordinary temperaments, there is no temptation to infringe this primary law of nature. The sexes, it is true, in most English homes, are allowed unrestricted companionship. Experience shows, however, that this intimacy is in the main unattended with evil results. . . . At any rate, in healthy subjects, and especially in children brought up in the pure air, and amid the simple amusements of the country, perfect freedom from, and indeed total ignorance of, any sexual affection is,

as it should always be, the rule. The first and only feeling exhibited between the sexes in the young should be that pure fraternal and sisterly affection. . . . Thus it happens that with most healthy and well-brought up children, no sexual notion or feeling has ever entered their heads, even in the way of speculation. I believe that such children's curiosity is seldom excited on these subjects except where they have been purposely suggested.

In short, the normal functions are non-functional. We need not linger over the fact that this passage is untrue; the quality of thinking present in it is of equal interest. In the first place, doubt is built into its very syntax. The conditional and the indicative are used almost interchangeably or as equivalents, and one of the effects of this is to suggest that "normality" is a precarious, wished-for, and achieved state as much as it is the state which in the common way of things is "normally" found. That is to say, the overt statement of this passage is expressed in terms which reveal a countering direction of thought or impulse. Secondly, "the simple amusements of the country" obviously exclude the sight of horses, cows, sheep, pigs, rabbits, and chickens. In order for this sentence to have passed unremarked, a good deal of collective amnesia must have taken place, and a good deal of folk-knowledge and traditional rural lore been repressed or denied. And the tenor of the entire passage makes it possible for us to guess at the audience to which this work is directed. It is precisely not an audience which has had an extensive living experience of rural life. Nor can it be an audience which has had—or which remembered—extensive experience of urban poverty, since childhood knowledge and experience of sex seem to have been both universal and universally acknowledged among the urban poor.[1] It is obviously directed at an audience composed of the urban middle classes, for only among those classes could there be found that combination of circumstances—living conditions, ideology, estrangement from traditional knowledge—which made possible a belief in the asexuality of childhood. (And as we shall see even this is untrue.) But

[1] In his book on prostitution, Acton himself points this out.

it is also an audience which has a need to read about sex, which is troubled by sexual ignorance and fear, and which has a consciousness of sexuality as a problem.

This is confirmed by what follows, for having spent a page and a half describing the "normal" asexual functions of childhood, he devotes the next twenty-odd pages to a discussion of sexual "disorders" in childhood, and communicates unmistakably the sense that childhood sexual play and childhood masturbation were both widespread and well-known phenomena. To be sure, he disapproves of these practices, but he does not deny their existence or prevalence. We are faced then with a double or contradictory consciousness. On the one hand, children are spoken of as pure and innocent and sexually quiescent; on the other, they are described as constantly threatened by horrid temptations, open to stimulation and corruption, and in danger of becoming little monsters of appetite. There is nothing to mediate between these two extreme states, no middle ground or connection between them. And the contradiction that children are both at once remains altogether unconscious.

The causes of this sexual "precocity" are legion. They include hereditary predisposition, "irritation of the rectum arising from worms," bed-wetting, irritation of the "glans penis arising from the collection of secretion under the prepuce," and, in boys who do suffer from such irritation, manipulation of the penis while washing it in order to reduce the original stimulus—these youngsters seem to have had it. Although Acton is not an advocate of circumcision, he finds the foreskin a dangerous nuisance for both sanitary and moral reasons. "It affords an additional surface for the excitement of the reflex action, and aggravates an instinct rather than supplies a want," he writes in a footnote. "In the unmarried it additionally excites the sexual desires, which it is our object to repress"—he is nothing if not candid. Other causes are flogging on the buttocks, as it was practiced in the large public schools, and indeed life at school in general. Just as in pornography no person, object, or idea is incapable of being enlisted in the cause of sexual activity, in Acton's view of the world almost no experience is exempt from the danger of prematurely awakening appetite in the young. And though Acton regards with apprehension what is pornography's *raison d'être,* in both the same process is taking place—the complete sexualization of reality.

Another important source of premature sexual activities is premature intellectual growth, and Acton reproves those tendencies in modern education whose aim is to foster intellectual superiority at the expense of more "wholesome" exercises. "For, as any one may observe," he remarks, "it is not the strong athletic boy, fond of healthy exercise, who thus early shows marks of sexual desires, but your puny exotic, whose intellectual education has been fostered at the expense of his physical development." There are more fantasies going on simultaneously in this sentence than one can easily count, and the logic of the statement is, to say the least, peculiar. Putting these to one side, however, we should note that such a passage raises a question which we shall be forced to raise repeatedly: what, at a given moment in the history of a culture, is the nature of "observation"; and correlatively what is the nature of "experience." As we shall have repeated occasion to see, both observation and experience are extremely selective—that is, extremely preconditioned—processes. Acton continues his observations by saying that the chief danger in early intellectual development is that boys will read works, especially "classical works," which are almost "certain to excite sexual feelings"; and although he has no wish to be "prudish or to believe that boys can or ought to be altogether kept from the risk of reading improper stories or books," the dangers of such a course must be faced.

> He reads in them of the pleasures, nothing of the penalties, of sexual indulgences. He is not intuitively aware that, if the sexual desires are excited, it will require greater power of will to master them than falls to the lot of most lads; that if indulged in, the man will and must pay the penalty for the errors of the boy; that for one that escapes, ten will suffer; that an awful risk attends abnormal substitutes for sexual intercourse; and that self-indulgence,

long pursued, tends ultimately, if carried far enough, to early death or self-destruction.[2]

The child is father of the man—and with a vengeance. With this passage we come upon the prevailing tone of this book; it is a characteristic Victorian tone. It is resonant of danger, doom, and disaster (to strike a Faulknerian note), and tells us of a world hedged in with difficulty and pain, a world of harsh efforts and iron consequences. In such a world reality is conceived of as identical with pain, and negative conscience is the ruling principle. It is a vision of life which is in every way the exact opposite of the vision of life in pornography, and is therefore its counterpart as well. And we can anticipate by saying that the closer such an account comes to being consciously held as official doctrine, the more inevitably will the extrusion from it of an under-world or under-life of pornography occur.

Acton has some suggestions to make about the prevention and cure of sexual activities in children. His first recommendation is that parents closely "watch their children," and this admonition is repeated so often that one begins to feel that were it taken seriously every middle-class Victorian home would have turned into a small Elsinore—and parents would have become, in Claudius' words, "lawful espials," terrorists of secret observation. As for the rest, Acton's suggestions are harmless enough; there is, we ought to recall, nothing of the quack about him. Boys should undergo a regimen of "gymnastic exercises regularly employed and carried to an extent just short of fatigue"—a nice distinction. He counsels the regular use of the sponge-bath, though showering and swimming are not without their dangers: it must not be forgotten, he says, "that the habit of remaining long in the water may be as great a source of evil as anything." Life at school presents such insuperable problems

[2] For a different, and more enlightened, handling of this subject by a contemporary French physician, see Raymond De Saussure, "J. B. Felix Descuret," *The Psychoanalytic Study of the Child* (New York, 1947), II, 417–424. At the same time, however, compare Bertram D. Lewin, "Child Psychiatry in the 1830's—Three Little Homicidal Monomaniacs," *The Psychoanalytic Study of the Child* (New York, 1949), III–IV, 489–493.

that Acton largely contents himself with generally supporting
Dr. Arnold's reforms: without a substantial raising of the
moral tone in schools, which can only be achieved through
marshaling "public opinion" on the side of virtue, little can be
done. On one point, however, he is insistent; every boy should
have a separate bed, for "evil practices are, I believe, most frequently learnt and practiced in bed." Obviously Acton does not
believe that the autoerotic can also be an autodidact. He then
closes this section by printing two letters, one from a clergyman, the other from "a member of one of the universities, who
was formerly at a large public school." These letters are so ab-
ject in their ignorance, and express such an agonized consciousness of shame and difficulty in discussing these topics, yet at the
same time are so serious and earnest in their desire for enlight-
enment and direction, that one is forced to withhold hasty
judgment on an undertaking like Acton's. These letters are representative, and what they reveal is a pitiable alienation on the
part of a whole class of men from their own sexuality. Acton's
work must be understood as both an expression of this condition and as one of the early efforts to overcome it.

If childhood has its sexual dangers and temptations, those
that beset youth "are increased tenfold" and are "infinitely
harder to overcome, infinitely more ruinous if yielded to." Although sexual desire in youth is a "natural instinct," and has its
own "beneficent purpose . . . mature and lawful love," the
young man is to be warned against fulfilling that desire. Indeed, "such indulgence is *fatal*. It may be repented of. Some of
its consequences may be, more or less, recovered from. But,
from Solomon's time to ours, it is true that it leads to a 'house of
death.' " There is a kind of exquisite hopelessness in that "more
or less." And what makes this bad situation even worse is that
the youth neither feels nor knows this. "He does not know that
to his immature frame every sexual indulgence is unmitigated
evil. He does not think that to his inexperienced mind and
heart every illicit pleasure is a degradation, to be bitterly regret-

ted hereafter—a link in a chain that does not need many to be too strong to break." We find ourselves here in a familiar set-ting; roughly speaking, it is the moral world of the Victorian novel. It is a world of nemesis, of unbreakable chains of conse-quences; it is a scene of incessant struggle against temptation, and in which the first false step leads irresistibly to the last. The fact that in the novel this style of thinking is largely applied—and often with great subtlety—to general moral and social be-havior is not immediately to the point; what is to be noted is that the same kind of mental process is going on in both. And that what in the novel made and still makes sense should in such a case as Acton's seem as good as insane is something of an indigestible paradox, no matter how we regard it.

Incontinence in all forms is harmful, but the "most vicious" form it can take is that of masturbation. Here is Acton's de-scription of a boy who habitually masturbates.

> The frame is stunted and weak, the muscles undeveloped, the eye is sunken and heavy, the complexion is sallow, pasty, or covered with spots of acne, the hands are damp and cold, and the skin moist. The boy shuns the society of others, creeps about alone, joins with repugnance in the amusements of his schoolfel-lows. He cannot look any one in the face, and becomes careless in dress and uncleanly in person. His intellect has become sluggish and enfeebled, and if his evil habits are persisted in, he may end in becoming a drivelling idiot or a peevish valetudinarian. Such boys are to be seen in all stages of degeneration, but what we have described is but the result towards which *they all* are tending.

This passage teaches us that masturbation was unquestion-ably at the bottom of all of Uriah Heep's troubles. But it teaches us other things as well. In the first place this description is a commonplace—scores of others from the period exactly like it might be cited. It occupied, therefore, the status of official belief, and this leads us to question both the relation between belief and experience or behavior, and the influence that belief can exercise on them. We can reasonably assume that masturbation was practiced among adolescents to about the same extent then as it is now—that is to say, it was as good as universal (Acton himself admits this). And we know too that most adolescents did not correspond to Acton's description of the masturbator, and that the largest part of them grew up to be what for want of a better word we must call normal males. Clearly then either an assertion of common sense founded upon experience must have occurred, or, what is more likely, the process of isolation was enlisted as a defense—the same process, say, which permits persons of genuine religious belief to transgress without excessive discomfort, and which permits us to hold contradictory feelings in the mind without an overwhelming sense of their contradiction. On the other hand, this description, however fantastic its confusion of cause with effect, cannot be written off as pure fantasy: it is based on observation. And there can be little doubt that in this period of history we confront a situation characterized not merely by extreme disturbance and guilt over masturbation, and sexuality in general, but by the emergence of those feelings into general organized consciousness in the form of such beliefs.

Of all the thousand natural shocks that flesh is heir to, masturbation seems the worst, and there is no doubt in Acton's mind "that it is the cause of disease." Among the multitude of afflictions that it can cause are impotence, consumption, curvature of the spine, and of course insanity. He then quotes from a contemporary treatise on "an inquiry into a frequent cause of insanity in young men" this description of certain inmates of an asylum for the insane.

> Engaged in no social diversion, the patients of this group live alone in the midst of many. In their exercise they choose the quietest and most unfrequented parts of the airing-grounds. They join in no social conversation, nor enter with others into any amusement. They walk alone, or they sit alone. If engaged in reading, they talk not to others of what they may have read; their desire apparently is, in the midst of numbers, to be in solitude. They seek no social joys, nor is the wish for fellowship evinced.
>
> The pale complexion, the emaciated form, the slouching gait, the clammy palm, the glassy or leaden eye, and the averted gaze, indicate the lunatic victim to this vice.

Apathy, loss of memory, abeyance of concentrative power and manifestation of mind generally, combined with loss of self-reliance, and indisposition for or impulsiveness of action, irritability of temper, and incoherence of language, are the most characteristic mental phenomena of chronic dementia resulting from masturbation in young men.

It might be difficult to find a more apt or prettier description of the romantic artist: the Ancient Mariner, the poet of "Alastor," Endymion, any one of Byron's early heroes fit this bill of particulars. This hardly indicates that these characters masturbated themselves into insanity; it does serve to show, however, how in a single culture one set of descriptive terms is forced into the service of representing a variety of states, in this case extreme states of mental alienation. One further fact that is noted but left unexplained is that these cases "chiefly occur in members of families of strict religious education . . . those who from this cause have become insane have generally . . . been of strictly moral life, and recognized as persons who paid much attention to the forms of religion." In addition, "in the acute attack resulting from this cause . . . religion forms a noted subject of conversation or delusion." Masturbation causes insanity; religion seems somehow connected with this process, but the connection goes unexplored—which can only lead us to conclude that the process by which causality is ascribed is often highly selective and tendentious.

If masturbation—and sex in general—causes all these horrors, how does the cause operate? With this we come to the informing idea of sexuality in the era before Freud. In the masturbating boy, "the large expenditure of semen, has exhausted the vital force." The continent boy, however, has "not expended that vital fluid, semen, or exhausted his nervous energy, and his youthful vigor has been employed for its legitimate purpose, namely, in building up his growing frame." Although Acton does not endorse the old formula by which it was calculated that an ounce of semen was equivalent to forty ounces of blood, he continually warns his readers that the semen "is a highly organized fluid, requiring the expenditure of much vital force in its elaboration and in its expulsion." The fantasies that are at work here have to do with economics; the body is regarded as a productive system with only a limited amount of material at its disposal. And the model on which the notion of semen is formed is clearly that of money. Science, in the shape of Acton, is thus still expressing what had for long been a popular fantasy: up until the end of the nineteenth century the chief English colloquial expression for the orgasm was "to spend."[3] It had not yet been displaced by the modern "to come"—a complex shift in metaphoric emphasis whose meaning is not at all clear. Furthermore, the economy envisaged in this idea is based on scarcity and has as its aim the accumulation of its own product. And the fantasy of pornography, as we shall have ample opportunity to observe, is this idea's complement, for the world of pornography is a world of plenty. In it all men are infinitely rich in substance, all men are limitlessly endowed with that universal fluid currency which can be spent without loss. Just as in the myth Zeus descends upon Danaë in a shower of gold, so in pornography the world is bathed, floated, flooded, inundated in this magical produce of the body. No one need ever worry again about husbanding nature's riches from expense.[4]

Behind these images we can make out two further ideas. One is a universal personal and cultural experience of poverty—and fear of it. The other is that the human body is a machine, and that sexual functions are essentially mechanical. Acton regards sexuality and sexual disorders as strictly physiological functions —there is no such thing yet as psychology, and the world he describes is pre-psychological in nature, as is the world of pornography. At this moment in history, then, scientific thinking about sex had attained the same level of intellectual development as pornography. And just as the advent of a genuine modern psychology was to spell an end to the kind of thinking represented in Acton's work, so we shall see psychology is the

[3] See "Th' expense of spirit in a waste of shame."
[4] See Chapters 4, 5, and 7 for further discussion of these matters.

one mortal enemy of pornography. Yet we should also observe that Acton's physiology is itself a fantasy; it is a fantasy physiology, and the fantasy expresses to the full the unconscious psychology that created it. It is a classic example of what Freud called "the return of the repressed."

What then is the prevention, cure, or solution for all these dangers? Acton's one recommendation is continence, which consists not only in sexual abstinence "but in controlling all sexual excitement." True continence, he writes, "is complete control over the passions, exercised by one who knows their power, and who, but for his steady will, not only could, but would indulge them." And he is under no illusion that such a practice will not be a trial, a sore and bitter trial, as he says. Continence in other words is a variant form of that essential nineteenth-century idea, Duty; and Acton gives to the word its full weight of difficulty, conflict, pain, and necessity. (Duty, or continence, may have been, as George Eliot said, "peremptory and absolute"; it never was, or is, easy.) The first requisite of continence is "that power of the mind over outer circumstances which we call 'a strong will.' " This sovereignty of the will, of man over himself, is of course "a matter of *habit*. Every victory strengthens the victor. . . . The whole force of his character, braced and multiplied by the exercise of a lifetime, drives him with unwavering energy along his chosen course of purity." These are admirable ideas, and one is right to take them as representative of an epoch of culture, in both its strengths and weaknesses. Placed as they are, however, in this context of darkness, danger, and fear, they appear more as gallant ineffectualities, resolute impossibilities than they do as practical solutions. For although the will is a form of consciousness and is consciously employed, its energies have historically been directed against consciousness itself—against intellect, introspection, self-examination, curiosity. Will is, in other words, a controlled consciousness which often contains within itself a fear of consciousness. And however much Acton is for the consciously willed direction of life, he is unequivocally against turning it inward; and he holds up Rousseau as a horrible example of what happens when a man "pries into his mental and moral character with a despicably morbid minuteness." This sort of "hideous frankness," he believes, can only lead to a perpetuation of the condition which it unjustifiably reveals.

Acton carries this idea one step further in his discussion of "nocturnal emissions or pollutions"—which are just about as undesirable, dangerous, and controllable as masturbation. If while he is awake a man "who has not debased and enervated his will is perfectly able to keep his thoughts entirely pure," then it is hardly less difficult for him to exercise the "power of keeping his dreaming thoughts pure, if he goes the right way to work." To those patients who complain that they cannot control their dreams, Acton delivers a properly authoritative reproach. "This is not true," he flatly declares. "Those who have studied the connection between thoughts during waking hours and dreams during sleep, know that they are closely connected. The *character* is the same sleeping or waking . . . if a man has allowed his thoughts during the day to rest upon libidinous subjects, he finds his mind at night full of lascivious dreams. . . . A will which in our waking hours we have not exercised in repressing sexual desires, will not, when we fall asleep, preserve us from carrying the sleeping echo of our waking thoughts farther than we dared to do in the daytime." Without pausing to analyze the confused mixture of half-truths, quasi-observations, wishful thinking, received ideas, and pure affirmative flummery in these remarks, we must ask ourselves what ideas lie behind these assertions and make them possible. Acton himself provides the answer, when he remarks the "very curious" disposition in the human system "to repeat an act and establish a habit." We notice this disposition "in children who wet their beds. Another instance is that of going to stool at a particular hour. Once establish the time of the bowels acting, and they act with regularity. So with emissions, if they occur one night they are likely to occur the next, and the next. The

secret of success is to *break the habit.*" The sexual hygiene of
continence is unmistakably founded on the idea of bowel control, and the connection of this with the fantasy of semen as
money is self-explanatory. At the same time, to regard the genital organization from the point of view of anal-economic regulation is to introduce another series of contradictions. It is to
assimilate the idea of money, or of life-giving value, to the idea
of waste, of dirt, of poison; and it is hopelessly to confuse the
two. In Dickens' later works, especially *Our Mutual Friend,* the
social ramifications of this process are memorably represented.
In Acton, however, these contradictions never emerge into consciousness, and the youth who has learned to control his sphinc-
ter should by the same token be able to constipate his genitals.[5]

III

If the youth has learned his lessons and has been lucky enough
to surmount or bypass the dangers that lurk on every side, then
he should reach adult life or manhood relatively undamaged.
At this time, he is able to experience "all those mysterious sensations which make up what we call VIRILITY." This distinctive
attribute "seems necessary to give a man that consciousness of
his dignity, of his character as head and ruler and of his importance, which is absolutely essential to the well-being of the family, and through it, of society itself. It is a power, a privilege, of
which the man is, and should be, proud. . . ." But this power
is as precarious as ever, if not more so, and the terrors of sex in
maturity are as threatening as they were before, and their numbers have if anything increased. Although Acton states that

[5] For a slightly eccentric but preternaturally learned and precise account of
the history of mechanical devices used to prevent masturbation, see Eric John
Dingwall, *Male Infibulation* (London, 1925), and *The Girdle of Chastity* (London, 1931). The reader may be interested to know that as late as 1921, in the
second edition of *Handbuch der Sexualwissenschaften* (Leipzig), p. 627, Have-
lock Ellis and Albert Moll were still able to recommend *"Onaniebandagen"* or
"Korsette"—little metal suits of armor fitted over the genitals and attached to
a locked belt—as prophylaxis for masturbation.

"the moderate gratification of the sex-passion in married life is generally followed by the happiest consequences to the individual," he obviously believes that few ever achieve this modest consummation. The consequences of sexual excess now include heart failure and loss of memory, and the rites of the marriage bed, though sacred, are perilous. Those who were continent before marriage become incontinent after it, intercourse is "indulged in night after night," and the result, at least for the man, "is simple ruin"—he goes bankrupt and is sold up. Such a man, however unconscious he may be of the fact, has been "guilty of great and almost criminal excess"—like the head of a company who has invested wildly in shares. Acton then cites a specimen case of this condition.

> A medical man called on me, saying he found himself suffering from spermatorrhoea. There was general debility, inaptitude to work, disinclination for sexual intercourse, in fact, he thought he was losing his senses. The sight of one eye was affected. The only way in which he lost semen was, as he thought, by a slight occasional oozing from the penis. I asked him at once if he had ever committed excesses. As a boy, he acknowledged having abused himself, but he married seven years ago, being then a hearty, healthy man, and it was only lately that he had been complaining. In answer to my further inquiry, he stated that since his marriage he had had connection two or three times a week, and often more than once a night! This one fact, I was obliged to tell him, sufficiently accounted for all his troubles. The symptoms he complained of were similar to those we find in boys who abuse themselves. It is true that it may take years to reduce some strong, healthy men, just as it may be a long time before some boys are prejudicially influenced, but the ill effects of excesses are sooner or later sure to follow.

This is all classically familiar material, but one is nonetheless prompted to wonder: if the consequences of sexual intercourse are indistinguishable from those of masturbation, then why marry? Moreover, the mental consequences are also the same. "Experience every day convinces me," he writes, "that much of the languor of mind, confusion of ideas, and inability to control the thoughts of which married men complain, arises from the sexual excesses they commit. This occurs not unfrequently from their marrying late in life, and still more often from their marrying a second time after having been widowers for some years." We may observe that the state of being a husband was already well on its way to becoming the condition of permanent crisis that it is today. The causes are naturally thought to be different—they are in fact reversed—but the state of emotions is remarkably similar.

In the passage I have just quoted, Acton uses the word "spermatorrhoea," a catch-all term which he defines as "a state of enervation produced, at least primarily, by the loss of semen." Along with tuberculosis, it appears to have been one of the virtually universal afflictions of the time; and it is allied to the various forms of impotence, which Acton deals with at some length. (One of the purposes of his work was to warn his readers against the innumerable quacks who offered to cure impotence by means of nostrums, potions, and magical drugs or machines.) Spermatorrhoea is itself a piece of magic, since it can be both cause and effect of almost anything. It can be the result of sexual excess, but then it can just as well be the result of intellectual excess, mental exertions having apparently the same consequences as sexual athletics. At this point, the Victorian doctrine of work, achievement, and accomplishment in the world turns around on itself, and the man who has created himself throughout a lifetime of unremitting concentration may find his success blighted by the very efforts that assured it. "The quality of the semen, and the exhaustion of the system which secretes it," Acton observes, "must have a great influence on the progeny. May not the fact observed by all ages, that the children of great men are not usually equal to their sires, depend, among other causes, upon deterioration of the impregnating fluid in the parent from the great mental demand upon him at the time impregnation took place?" In one respect, at least, self-help and self-abuse seem indistinguishable. At the same time, such a passage expresses a comprehensive Victorian attitude—that life is difficult, necessitous, and laced with tragic

contradiction. Whichever way it is regarded, life is terrible and
tragic—dark, complex beyond fathoming, incoherent, certain
of suffering, unavoidably to be endured. Yet beneath all the
fantasies (and being expressed through them), beneath all the
ignorance there is an emotion that sets the tone of this book and
all it represents. This emotion is fear—fear of sex in general and
particular: of impotence and of potency; of impulse and of its
loss; of indulgence and even of the remedies prescribed to curb
it. These fears, it may be said, are universal and exist in all societies or cultures; and all societies and cultures have devised
means of dealing with them. In the Victorian world, however,
what seems to have happened is that these fears have been
raised into consciousness along with certain of their contradictions; and it is the sense of irreparable contradiction that speaks
out most strongly from Acton's pages.

Thus, although spermatorrhea is a universal danger, it is no
more dangerous than its opposite, ungratified sexual excitement. To Acton, the "excitement of the sexual feelings when
not followed by the result which it should produce, is . . . an
unmitigated evil." This evil produces exactly the same dreadful
consequences for health as uninhibited sexual indulgence.
Young men are likely to become impotent as a result of prolonged sexual excitement which is for one reason or another not
gratified, and older men, particularly those who are married to
younger women, will pay the penalty of excited abstinence "by
becoming martyrs to paralysis, softening of the brain, and driv-
eling idiotcy." Whichever way one turns, then, things are terrible. Sex is thought of as a universal and virtually incurable
scourge. It cannot ultimately be controlled, and serves as a kind
of metaphor for death, as cancer does today. Some fifty years
after Acton, Freud was to discover that all thought was capable
of being sexualized, and that even the most abstruse intellectual
interests have a sexual origin and are endowed with a charge of
unconscious sexual energy. In the age before Freud, in the writings of such a figure as Acton, it is physiological sex which is
universal and universally protean; yet this very physiology illustrates the point of Freud's idea

What of woman in this world of torment and fear? As I mentioned before, women are discussed in only two places in Acton's book.[6] They appear in a section devoted to "Marriage," and at first sight seem to offer an escape from the nightmare of sexuality. "It is a delusion under which many a previously incontinent man suffers," writes Acton, "to suppose that in newly married life he will be required to treat his wife as he used to treat his mistresses. It is not so in the case of any modest English woman. He need not fear that his wife will require the excitement, or in any respect imitate the ways of a courtezan." This passage contains a cluster of interesting assumptions. It assumes, in the first place, and as a matter of public knowledge, that large numbers of Victorian middle-class men will have had mistresses—who were courtesans. It further assumes that the Victorian wife will not have sexual desires, and as a corollary adds that courtesans or mistresses are in themselves extremely sexual; both of these assumptions seem at least open to question. (It may be useful to note that modern "marriage manuals" reverse the formulation offered by Acton.) The operative word in the passage is of course "fear"; it further underscores the fantasy-conception of sexuality in Acton's work. But it also indicates to what extent this conception is both analogous to and the counterpart by opposition of the fantasies of pornography. In pornography, all women—including wives—are excited and behave like courtesans all the time. Since women are not like this, there is a natural temptation to conjecture that the persistence of the pornographic fantasy is somehow connected with this fact. It is indeed connected, but it cannot be accounted for by such a single, simple functional explanation.

But marriage alone is not enough of a safeguard—for either

[6] This represents a change from the older and pre-medical science writings about sex. In *Aristotle's Master Piece,* the most widely circulated work of sexual and proto-medical folklore in the English seventeenth and eighteenth centuries, the emphasis falls in the other direction, and considerably more space is given to the dispensing of information about female sexual functions than is given to describing those functions in the male. See also Otho T. Beall, Jr., *"Aristotle's Master Piece* in America: A Landmark in the Folklore of Medicine," *William and Mary Quarterly,* 3d Ser., XX (1963), 207–222.

man or woman. Pregnancy and childbearing seem to be the only reliable means of stifling sexual desire.

> If the married female conceives every second year, during the nine months that follow conception she experiences no great sexual excitement. The consequence is that sexual desire in the male is somewhat diminished, and the act of coition takes place but rarely. And, again, while women are suckling there is usually such a call on the vital force made by the organs secreting milk that sexual desire is almost annihilated. Now, as all that we have read and heard tends to prove that a reciprocity of desire is, to a great extent, necessary to excite the male, we must not be surprised if we learn that excesses in fertile married life are comparatively rare, and that sensual feelings in the man become gradually sobered down.

This is a representative passage of Acton's thinking. In the first sentence one can observe how belief or received opinion is offered in the form of observation, an unadorned instance of "ideology"—that is, of thought which is socially determined yet unconscious of its determination. The second sentence is a good example of the mode of reasoning one can expect to find in writings of this sort. The "consequence" is a consequence of nothing; or rather it is the consequence of fantasy or wish fulfillment, and the logic of the passage is the logic of intellectual daydream. It may be paraphrased in the statement that the best way of reducing or extinguishing sexual desire is to keep your wife pregnant. On the other hand, to the extent that this passage represents a genuine belief we cannot discount its source in attitudes or behavior or its reciprocal effect on them. Finally, if one compares the tone and content of such a passage—and of this book in general—with analogous ones in Acton's book on prostitution, it becomes clear that the earlier work is in point of humanity and generosity of feeling superior. And this leads one to suggest that we are confronted here by a disparity which is characteristic of the Victorian period—that during this time the development of social attitudes, of attitudes toward society and social problems, had outstripped the development of personal attitudes, of attitudes toward personal problems or conflicts, and of inwardness in general. Taken as a whole, the Victorian novel—as opposed to Romantic poetry on the one hand and the modern novel on the other—may be regarded as demonstrating a similar inequality.

Some pages further on, Acton recurs to women for the second and last time. He has, he says, "taken pains to obtain and compare abundant evidence on this subject," and goes on to epitomize his findings for the reader.

> I should say that the majority of women (happily for them) are not very much troubled with sexual feeling of any kind. What men are habitually, women are only exceptionally. It is too true, I admit, as the divorce courts show, that there are some few women who have sexual desires so strong that they surpass those of men. . . . I admit, of course, the existence of sexual excitement terminating even in nymphomania, a form of insanity which those accustomed to visit lunatic asylums must be fully conversant with; but, with these sad exceptions, there can be no doubt that sexual feeling in the female is in the majority of cases in abeyance . . . and even if roused (which in many instances it never can be) is very moderate compared with that of the male. Many men, and particularly young men, form their ideas of women's feelings from what they notice early in life among loose or, at least, low and vulgar women. . . . Any susceptible boy is easily led to believe, whether he is altogether overcome by the syren or not, that she, and therefore all women, must have at least as strong passions as himself. Such women however give a very false idea of the condition of female sexual feeling in general. Association with the loose women of London streets, in casinos, and other immoral haunts (who, if they have not sexual feeling, counterfeit it so well that the novice does not suspect but that it is genuine), all seem to corroborate such an impression, and . . . it is from these erroneous notions that so many young men think that the marital duties they will have to undertake are beyond their exhausted strength, and from this reason dread and avoid marriage. . . . The best mothers, wives, and managers of households, know little or nothing of sexual indulgences. Love of home, children, and domestic duties, are the only passions they feel.
>
> As a general rule, a modest woman seldom desires any sexual gratification for herself. She submits to her husband, but only to please him; and, but for the desire of maternity, would far rather be relieved from his attentions. No nervous or feeble young man

need, therefore, be deterred from marriage by any exaggerated
notion of the duties required from him. The married woman has
no wish to be treated on the footing of a mistress.

We need not pause to discuss the degree of truth or falsehood
in these assertions. What is of more immediate concern is that
these assertions indicate a system of beliefs. These beliefs are in
the first place associated with class: the "majority of women"
evidently fails to include "low and vulgar women"—this final
ascription might possibly include all working-class females.
These beliefs express yet again the notion that sex is a curse and
a torture, and that the only hope of salvation for man lies in
marriage to a woman who has no sexual desires and who will
therefore make no sexual demands on her husband. At this
point, we can observe how sexual responsibility is being projected onto the role of woman; she is being required to save
man from himself; and conversely if she is by some accident
endowed with a strongly responsive nature, she will become the
agent of her husband's ruin. In either event, she is being regarded as essentially a function of masculine needs, whatever
the direction in which those needs may run. That these needs
are in substance contradictory, that sexuality is a regular hell,
and that general impotence is a universal fear, not to say a universal condition, of middle-class men is the burden which Acton's book communicates.

We begin to see then how nearly related is the world which
Acton creates to the world envisaged by pornography. At all
points they touch either by analogy or by analogy through opposition, and sometimes by both at once. In both there is a similar split or divided consciousness; both are dominated by the
logic of fantasy and association rather than by the logic of
events or of consecutive thought. Both are also worlds without
psychology; they are worlds of organs and physiology in which
everything is convertible into matter. That is to say, both represent a primitive form of materialism. In pornography, this fantasy purports to be subversive and liberating. In Acton's work
it represents itself as grimly scientific and ineluctably tragic.

What is of largest interest, however, is that at this moment in history a human science—the investigation of sexuality—had attained approximately the same stage of intellectual development as pornography itself. Perhaps it might be more precise to say that it rested or remained fixed at that stage, and it is to the happenings of that enduringly arrested world that we must now begin to turn.

Chapter 2: PISANUS FRAXI, PORNOGRAPHER ROYAL

I

ON March 30, 1877, two hundred and fifty copies of a privately printed volume left the hands of an unidentified London printer. The manuscript of this work had been with him for almost two years, and its passage into print had been beset with unusual difficulties. The printing establishment was small, its "readers," such as they were, incompetent to correct the press of a complex and technical text, which was, moreover, written in several languages; and the compositor who set up the volume was himself familiar with only one language. As a consequence, the editorial reading of the work throughout its various stages of preparation devolved upon the author, and the extent of his thoroughness and care may be seen in the seven full pages of errata which he caused to be included at the end of the printed volume.

The title of the work is *Index Librorum Prohibitorum: being Notes Bio-Biblio-Icono-graphical and Critical, on Curious and Uncommon Books.* The volume is in large quarto and is printed on heavy, toned paper (it weighs almost four pounds). It has an engraved frontispiece and reproduces by photolithography occasional facsimile pages from works which it discusses in its text. It generously mixes inks and types of print: the title of each book noticed in the text is printed in red, the essential part of that title in Black Letter, and the names of authors, artists, and publishers in Small Capitals; in the index, authors' names are in Small Capitals, titles are in Old English, and subjects are printed in Antique; and throughout the volume, capitals, italics, and other faces, along with a variety of spacings and settings, are freely used. The work consists of an Introduction of seventy-six pages, a body of text four hundred and thirty-six pages long, a thirty-eight page list of "Authorities Consulted," and an Index of fifty-eight pages—all of this, including other minor additions, amounting to a mass of six hundred and twenty-one pages of print. Its author listed himself on the title page as Pisanus Fraxi.

The *Index Librorum Prohibitorum*—the title of course is humorously annexed from the Roman Catholic organ of censorship—is the first bibliography in the English language devoted to writings of a pornographic or sexual character. But the *Index* is itself only part of a work, for in 1879 there followed a second, companion volume, *Centuria Librorum Absconditorum,* and in 1885 Pisanus Fraxi completed his project with a third volume, entitled, *Catena Librorum Tacendorum.* This bibliographical trilogy is not only the first work of its kind in English; it is undoubtedly the most important, and probably the most important in any language. All later writings on this subject draw on its resources, either by reference, direct quotation, or outright cribbing; and half of the legends, rumors, and generally broadcast fantasies that have to do with pornographic writing can be traced, like the links of some bizarre chain letter, to their original source in these volumes. Such a weight of indebtedness is a result not merely of the knowledge of the writer and the comprehensiveness of his work but of the particular bibliographical form that he chose. These three volumes are not a simple listing of titles, dates, editions, and the like. For the largest majority of his entries, the author includes a description or summary of the contents of the work under discussion, quotes liberally, adds annotation and critical remarks of his own, and generally brings to bear whatever relevant or collateral information he possesses—which is always formidable. These volumes, then, cannot be regarded as a secondary source alone; they are primary material of the first interest, touching as they do on any number of points of social and moral history. They also serve to introduce us to a special kind of mind or person—the bibliophile of means, the wealthy collector of pornographic books.

Pisanus Fraxi was the pseudonym of Henry Spencer Ashbee.[1] Born in London in 1834, Ashbee was, according to the *Dictionary of National Biography,* "apprenticed in youth to the large firm of Copestake's, Manchester warehousemen . . . for whom he travelled for many years." Subsequently, the *D.N.B.* goes on, "he founded and became senior partner in the London firm of Charles Lavy & Co., of Coleman Street, merchants, the parent house of which was in Hamburg," eventually marrying Miss Lavy there. Toward the end of the 1860's, he "organized an important branch of the business at Paris . . . where he thenceforth spent much time." By this time Ashbee had "amassed a handsome fortune," and he was able thenceforward to devote his leisure to "travel, bibliography, and book collecting." He traveled widely—though accounts of where he went to and when differ—and wrote about his journeys. His collections included among other things "the finest Cervantic library out of Spain," various rare illustrated volumes, and a large number of works of art, these latter being largely water-color drawings by English eighteenth- and nineteenth-century artists. And his collection of various and assorted pornographic matter was according to all accounts the most elaborate and extensive ever to have been assembled by a private person.[2]

[1] Fraxi is a freely invented form of the Latin *fraxinus,* ash or ash-tree; Pisanus is a scatological pun.
[2] Note on terminology. I have decided in this work to use the word "pornography" as the general descriptive term for most of the material discussed. It is, I am aware, not altogether a satisfactory term, but it seems to me better than the ones usually used. The *D.N.B.,* for example, offers the quaint "Kruptadia," which is clearly impossible. The "curiosa" of booksellers is nothing but a blind. And as for the "erotic books" or "Erotica" which are in general currency, these seem to me little more than euphemisms which have through indiscriminate usage been hopelessly corrupted in the bargain, if indeed they ever meant anything. Most of the writing which is classified as "Erotica" seems to me in intention, in effect, and in fact pornographic, and I can find no sound reason for avoiding the term. When in the course of this study occasion arises to discuss a work which, though it deals with sexual matters, is not pornographic, notice will of course be taken of the fact.

Ashbee was closely acquainted with the notorious, and pathetic, Frederick Hankey, a wealthy Englishman who spent most of his adult life in Paris attempting to live out the fantasy that he was another Marquis de Sade—Ashbee spoke of him as "a second de Sade *without the intellect.*" Through Hankey, Ashbee met James Monckton Milnes (then, inevitably, Lord Houghton), whose collection of French pornographic writings, particularly those by Sade, was well known through the upper reaches of English literary society. What may be thought of as the Milnes-Hankey-Ashbee axis—or syndrome—forms one of those curious intersections of meeting that often occurred in Victorian England and that any understanding of the period must take into account. On Hankey's death in 1882, part of his small but highly specialized collection passed into the hands of Ashbee. Ashbee himself died in 1900. He bequeathed the bulk of his library of rare books—to the number of 15,299—to the British Museum. That institution, according to a French source, at first considered refusing the gift, but finally accepted it because Ashbee, having bequeathed to it at the same time his collection of all the editions and translations of *Don Quixote,* had placed it as a condition of this legacy that the British Museum conserve his erotic library as well. This library is presumably still there.[3]

At the opening of the *Index,* Ashbee announces his intention as "truth, the extension of bibliographical studies, and the accurate description of the works noticed in the following pages." Further on, he amplifies this statement. "The object of the present work," he writes, "is to catalogue, as thoroughly, and at the same time, as tersely as possible, books which, as a rule, have not been mentioned by former bibliographers, and to notice them in such a way that the student or collector may be able to

---

[3] Sources for material dealing with Ashbee's life are as follows: *Dictionary of National Biography* (Supplement), XXII, 79f.; Eugen Dühren, *Englische Sittengeschichte* (Berlin, 1912), II, 498–510; Guillaume Apollinaire, Fernand Fleuret, and Louis Perceau, *L'Enfer de la Bibliothèque National* (Paris, 1919), p. 21; James Pope-Hennessy, *Monckton Milnes* (London, 1951), II, 113–122; and Ashbee, III, l–liii. Ashbee, Pope-Hennessy, and the *D.N.B.,* though differing in matters of detail, seem largely reliable; the other two sources are of doubtful reliability.

form a pretty just estimate of their value or purport, without having recourse to the books themselves." The service thus performed is, to put it simply, rather ambiguous, and there is something slightly teasing, if not superior, about the last part of that sentence. It should be said, however, that this attitude is not typical of Ashbee; although, as we shall see, his shortcomings are considerable, he did not usually think of himself as resting upon an eminence—he is, after all, the sovereign of an underworld. And he is aware of it. "My object," he continues, "is to collect into a common fold the stray sheep, to find a home for the pariahs of every nation. I do not then hesitate to notice the catchpennies hawked in the public streets, as well as the sumptuous volumes got up for the select few, and whose price is counted in guineas. I embrace indeed that which should be avoided as well as that which should be sought." And since this is the first bibliography of its kind in English—and actually the first of its kind in any language—Ashbee's work is cut out for him.[4]

The difficulties to be overcome in this branch of bibliography are enormous, "everything connected with it being involved in obscurity, and surrounded with deception"—a situation that has since not substantially changed. "The author writes, for the most part, anonymously, or under an assumed name; the publisher generally affixes a false impress with an incorrect date; and the title is not unfrequently worded so as to mislead with regard to the real contents of the book." To discover the author

[4] In 1861 Jules Gay published the first edition of his *Bibliographie des ouvrages relatifs à l'Amour*. This work is by rights the first bibliography of its kind in any language. It was, however, a crude and unreliable catalogue, collected, as Ashbee observes, "from any and every available source . . . without thorough verification or digesting." It contains no critical apparatus, and though it was, so to speak, cleaned up and improved in later editions (the 2d edition was published in 1864, the 3d, in 6 vols., from 1871 to 1873), it cannot be thought of as existing in the same terms as Ashbee's magisterial performance. In 1875, the same year in which Ashbee completed the ms. of his first volume, there was published in Leipzig the first bibliography in German, Hugo Nay's *Bibliotheca Germanorum erotica*. This work, as Ashbee remarks, "gives information as to editions, places and dates of publication, etc., but contains no critical appreciations or extracts."

of a particular book is frequently impossible, and this is especially true of English, where "nothing has been done, and the task is now almost hopeless." Nevertheless, Ashbee has been able to discover the names of some modern authors and has traced the operations of the booksellers, a pursuit, he remarks, "equally interesting, but quite as difficult." Another difficulty has to do with the extraordinary range, diffusion, and quantity of works which fall into this category, and one of Ashbee's purposes in the *Index* is "to show through what widely spread ramifications erotic literature extends, and what a vast field has to be traversed. The field indeed, even in this restricted portion of bibliography, is so extended, and the books so numerous, that I have no hope of ever exhausting my subject." Furthermore, most of the books of this class are printed "either privately or surreptitiously, in small issues, for special classes of readers or collectors," and from the first must be thought of as scarce or uncommon. And they tend rapidly to become scarcer: "They do not usually find their way into public libraries . . . but are for the most part possessed by amateurs, at whose death they are not unfrequently burned; and they are always liable to destruction at the hands of the law. Their scarcity then . . . is very much in proportion to their age; and as society is constantly, so to say, at war with them, the natural course is for them to die out altogether." In the light of these remarks, one can more fully understand that blackmailing provision in Ashbee's bequest to the British Museum. Rather than permit his cherished collection of obscenities to be dispersed or destroyed, the old bibliophile, with appropriate Quixotry, would have allowed his entire library to go under: without institutional custodianship, it would very likely have been broken up and sold at auction. Ideals, it seems, can find expression even in such a morass as this.

In composing the *Index,* Ashbee had to contend with certain problems of method. He at first planned to classify his material by subjects but soon found this impracticable, "the titles of this kind of books being so specially deceptive." Consequently he adopted in the *Index* a strictly alphabetical arrangement, a decision which postponed rather than solved his bibliographical difficulties (and in any event the entire contents of the volume are recapitulated in the final alphabetical index). By the time he was ready with his second volume, however, Ashbee's sense of his project had both strengthened and refined, and the *Centuria* and the *Catena* are arranged according to subject. This arrangement is in itself of interest since it casts light not only on the field of study but on how Ashbee's mind regarded it. Volume II, the *Centuria Librorum Absconditorum,* may be roughly divided as follows. It begins with some fifteen pages noticing the works of Martin Schurig, an early eighteenth-century German physician and antiquary, who wrote a virtually endless series of historico-medico-sexual volumes, purporting to deal with the folklore as well as the actuality of sex. Like almost all writing of this kind, including that which is published nowadays, Schurig's work is itself folklore, though Ashbee is unable to consider it so. There follows some three hundred pages devoted to books of an "objectionable, immoral, or obscene nature" which also have to do with religion, particularly Roman Catholicism; this combination of anticlericalism with pornography is a characteristic mode of the genre. Forty further pages are given to noticing the eighteenth-century poem, "The Toast," and to a discussion of Rochester's writings. Then there are fifty pages concerning the obscene drawings and engravings of Thomas Rowlandson. The text of the book concludes with an extended notice-cum-discussion of French sodomy, English flagellation, and some further fragments of anticlericalism. Volume III, the *Catena Librorum Tacendorum,* is equally miscellaneous in its contents. It opens with thirty pages devoted to works "in various languages upon subjects relating generally to peculiarities of the sexes, or to their connection, criminal or otherwise, with each other." The succeeding thirty pages contain a discussion of the sexual life of Venice, of its prostitutes and courtesans in particular. The next three hundred pages are concerned with English pornographic fiction; the first two hundred and fifty of these pages deal with separately published individual works, the remainder with periodical publications. A short section is devoted to folklore, popular tales, and Spanish fiction. The text of the volume closes with almost one hundred pages of "Additions" to all the foregoing categories.

Turning retrospectively to examine Volume I, the *Index Librorum Prohibitorum,* we can say that these irregularly assorted categories by and large cover Ashbee's interests there, if we add to them his notices—which accumulate throughout all three of the volumes—of English collectors, writers, and publishers of pornography during his own time who were personally known to him. And we can say as well that these categories, with certain minor exceptions, just about exhaust the field itself.[5] They do so, however, rather accidentally, and demonstrate the extensive range of Ashbee's reading more than they do the success of his method. Although Volumes II and III represent an advance over the intellectually primitive alphabetical arrangement of the *Index,* the topical subdivisions of those volumes are arbitrarily placed and grouped; and the relations of the subdivisions are insignificant and manifest no particular order or direction. They provide Ashbee with a convenient way of displaying his reading, which is what he wants to do; they cannot be thought of as imposing a genuine intellectual order on the material, or as providing the distance which an intellectual instrument requires. On the other hand, to expect an absolutely original effort, and especially in such a field as this, to give us more than Ashbee has would be not merely arrogant and excessive but historically innocent.

Ashbee distinguishes himself from most previous bibliographers by virtue of the attention he gives to the contents of the books he examines. Bibliographers have hitherto, he remarks, confined themselves "to the outsides . . . of the books which

---

[5] Although Ashbee notices a considerable number of books of pornographic art, and never fails to discuss the illustrations to a volume, he cannot be said to have shown a systematic interest in this particular branch of his subject.

they have described, and have rarely penetrated further than the title page or the colophon." Such records are naturally useful as far as they go, "but the student requires to be informed of much more than this; he wants to get at the contents, and this with as little loss of time as possible; he must have an estimate of what is in the book, so that he may be able at once to decide whether he has to read it, or to leave it alone, and pass on to something else." To this end Ashbee has ventured further than any earlier bibliographer "in giving frequent and copious extracts . . . a few lines by the author himself being, in my opinion, a better guide for the appreciation of him and his book than a page of description from another pen." And he has further collected "the opinions of previous critics and bibliographers, so that the reader may estimate the books rather from their remarks than from my own." This quality of self-effacement is seldom met with outside of those minds whose command of their subject is inwardly so secure that they need not assert it.

The command Ashbee had achieved of his subject was equalled by the assiduity and thoroughness with which he treated it and prepared his work. This trustworthiness is indeed the hallmark of his reputation. In his Introduction to the *Index,* he lays it down as his invariable, and italicized, rule *"never to criticise a work which I have not read, nor to describe a volume or an edition which I have not examined."* And he follows this rule invariably throughout the first two volumes. Volume III contains an unimportant but interesting exception. At one point in his "Preliminary Remarks," Ashbee prints a footnote, three pages in length, which consists of a bare alphabetical listing of the titles of certain works of English fiction. He introduces the footnote with this explanation: "The books, all I believe, exist, or have existed, and most of them have passed through my hands at one time or another; as however they are not all before me now, I do not guarantee the titles given to be invariably correct." Several pages further on, Ashbee turns to acknowledge his indebtedness to a number of friends and asso-

ciates, now dead, who helped him in the work on all three volumes. Among these was one James Campbell (the pseudonym
of one J. C. Reddie), bibliophile, book-collector, and writer of
pornography, whose scholarship or expertise Ashbee implies to
have been the equal of his own. Campbell, unlike Ashbee, was
not a wealthy man and could not afford to publish his own
work. Shortly before his death, however, he presented Ashbee
with three manuscript volumes of "Bibliographical Notes," and
Ashbee states that he "found them of great service" in prepar-
ing the final volume. It is possible, therefore, that that long
footnote-listing, along with several other minor entries in the
Catena, are at least in part Campbell's work, which Ashbee had
every reason to trust. We can, on the other hand, take this small
and not fully substantiated exception as an additional indicator
of Ashbee's unique integrity in a world of thieves, brigands,
frauds, and liars.

As a final note on method, Ashbee raises the unavoidable
question for an undertaking such as his of the bibliographer's
tact and modesty. "In treating of obscene books," he writes, "it
is self evident that obscenities cannot be avoided. Nevertheless,
although I do not hesitate to call things by their right names,
and to employ technical terms when necessary, yet in my own
text I never use an impure word when one less distasteful but
equally expressive can be found." This statement is, as far as it
goes, a model of straightforwardness; whether it in fact answers the question raised is a matter into which we shall have
further occasion to inquire.

II

The various introductions and preliminary remarks to Ashbee's
three volumes amount to almost two hundred pages, a small
book in itself. In the course of these essays, Ashbee expresses
himself on a large number of topics related to the central interest of his work; and the ideas and attitudes he therein reveals

lead us a step forward in our consideration of that subject and of him. In the first place there is the inevitable problem of justification: how does one secure intellectual authorization for the study of matter so outlawed, vile, worthless, depraved, etc.? A convenient argument is close to hand—pornography is valuable because it reflects or expresses social history. "I hold that for the historian or the psychologist these books, whether in accordance with, or contrary to the prejudices and tendencies of the age, must be taken into account as well as, if not in preference to those in many other and better cultivated fields of literature . . . where shall we find a more truthful and striking picture of the rottenness and depravity of the old French *noblesse,* which undoubtedly hastened, if they did not produce the first revolution, than in the memoirs of the time, or in the novels of Mirabeau, de Sade, Andrea de Nerciat, Choderlos de Laclos, and others; or what history will make us so well comprehend the vices, follies, and venalities which disgraced the courts of our Georges, as the lampoons, scandalous biographies, and scurrilous periodicals with which that period abounded? Such writers undoubtedly reflected the times in which they lived, if they were not, as some historians maintain, the actual necessities and complements of their respective epochs." And he goes on to enlist both Buckle and Macaulay in his support, quoting at length from them passages in which they contend that the vices of a historical period are as important for its understanding as its virtues. There is, to be sure, a certain degree of truth in this argument, but it is a degree of truth decidedly easy to overestimate (nowadays this overestimation is tending to become part of advanced received doctrine). Pornography, like every other creation of the mind, is by definition historical; it is the product of a particular time and place. And it inevitably contains a certain amount of observation, some of it registered consciously, some unconsciously. Unlike the situation which exists in the novel, however, observation is incidental rather than organic to pornography—its governing tendency in fact is toward the elimination of external or social reality. And although on first inspection pornography seems to be the most concrete kind of writing—concerned as it is with organs, positions, events—it is in reality very abstract. It regularly moves toward independence of time, space, history, and even language itself. Furthermore, since it is by both internal, formal necessity and social convention isolated from social and historical actuality, it registers social and historical changes, if it registers them at all, more slowly and crudely than the novel or, for that matter, almost any other form of written expression.

How profound this confusion can become appears in Ashbee's second discussion of fiction. In the Preliminary Remarks to Volume III, he states that "fiction, of whatever description, always was, and still continues to be, one of the most influential branches of literature, and one of the surest sources whence to gather a picture of the times." He goes on to discuss different kinds of novels and novelists and then reaches this conclusion: "Now, Erotic Novels, falling as they generally do into the category of domestic fiction, contain, at any rate the best of them, the truth, and 'hold the mirror up to nature' more certainly than do those of any other description." In addition, "their authors have, in most instances, been eye-witnesses of the scenes they have described, as were a Furetière, a Restif de la Bretonne, or, to borrow but two examples from our own writers, a Defoe, or a Dickens; or even have, like a Marquis de Sade, themselves enacted, in part, what they have portrayed." The assimilation of all the varieties and degrees of this kind of writing to the Domestic Novel is ludicrous (it does, however, add a new dimension of meaning to the idea of the family romance). As for the argument on behalf of the superior "realism" of this kind of fiction, it can at best be entertained in a provisional and minimal way. But the whole case collapses when we see that all its claims are based on the belief that the writers of such fiction have in one way or another actually experienced the incidents they represent. In the overwhelming majority of instances this is the reverse of truth, and pornographic fiction cannot as a whole be thought of as a record of experience but must be thought of as a record of fantasy. Since these fantasies do actually exist, it is possible to say that in a certain sense pornography is a "realistic" representation of them—at least they are "realized" in pornographic fiction. But the question of "truth" or "reality" ends as a rule right there.

Much the same thing, it can be argued, is true of the novel itself. And we must allow a degree of credibility to this assertion. In the novel, however, the proportions are different, and the balance or intermixture of fantasy and experience infinitely more complex. Moreover, however realistic a novel tries to be it is always conscious of itself as a story, as something made up. Pornography tries precisely to subdue or extinguish this consciousness; it typically undertakes to represent itself not as a story or fantasy but as something that "really" happened—which serves to indicate at what a primitive level of fantasy it exists. In the degree that one accepts this combination of confusion and deception, in that degree is one involved in the pornographic fantasy itself. Ashbee, we can see, is fairly deeply involved.

Another sign of his involvement can be made out in a further intellectual error which the passage I have quoted commits. What Ashbee has done in it is to assimilate the entire category of obscene or pornographic fiction to the few exceptions within it, to those few works which tend to rise above the genre, or pretend to do so. This is to confuse critical judgment with phenomenological analysis; in addition, as we shall see, most of these exceptions are not exceptions at all but still operate within the conventions and standards of the genre from which they arise, and continue to refer to it more than they do to the novel or to anything else. We can conclude, therefore, that the justification of the study of pornography on the grounds of its direct importance or utility as social history is a slender and flimsy support indeed. Intellectually it almost involves more difficulties than it is worth.[6]

Other arguments of differing merit may be advanced, and

[6] These matters are taken up again in Chapters 3 and 6.

Ashbee resorts to most of them. He maintains, for example, that "no production of the human brain should be ignored, entirely disregarded, or allowed to become utterly lost"; the thought of taking this injunction literally staggers the mind, but one must grant to it a certain kind of ideal truth. Then there is what may be called the *argumentum pro bibliomania:* to the "real lover of books for their own sake, these unknown and outcast volumes . . . are infinitely more interesting than their better known and more universally cherished fellows, and acquire additional value for him in proportion to the persecution they have suffered, their scarcity, and the difficulty he experiences in acquiring them." We may take it as a working rule that such statements act as rationalizations for behavior harmless enough in itself but at the same time troubling enough to require distancing; and that they serve as screens for other motives. No great ingenuity is demanded to discover what these motives are, and Ashbee himself is intermittently capable of revealing them. "The desire to possess that which is forbidden," he lets drop in a footnote, "is as strong in the man as the child, in the wise as the foolish." That which is forbidden has naturally to do with sex; but when Ashbee turns his attention to justifying or discussing his own interests in this direction and asks himself the hypothetical question "why I have not turned my attention to works on subjects . . . more profitable," he is suddenly rendered impotent of thought. "I'll not answer that," he quotes in verse, "But, say, it is my humour; Is it answered?" This combination of a commendable though poignant candor with a disinclination or inability to examine the contents of one's mind or the nature of one's motives is familiar—we have already met with it in Acton. And we shall meet with it again repeatedly, it being, I believe, a characteristic mode of defense not only of pornography and the pornographic mind but of the stage of mental development which both may be said to have attained. And Ashbee is precise in his choice of the term "humour"; he is using it in the older historical sense, which signifies a mental disposition so deeply fixed or rooted as to seem

organic in origin. At the same time it describes a state of mind
having no apparent ground or reason, and a person "in his
humour" appears to those who observe him, and often to himself as well, as someone possessed by a capricious or eccentric
drive—which cannot be gratified since its demands are infinite.
He is, in other words, in subjection to himself, although he does
not experience it this way. In the Preliminary Remarks to the
Centuria, for example, Ashbee offers an apology to the reader
for his failure in this volume to reach "the goal for which I am
striving. I have not been able strictly to carry out my intention
of registering and branding exclusively worthless books. . . . I
have been attracted by masterpieces, and have neglected the un-
artistic; consequently in this volume less rubbish will be found
than in the *Index Librorum Prohibitorum."* The faintly plan-
gent note of regret is struck as Ashbee, looking back over his
second volume, suddenly recognizes that in it his "humour" has
been temporarily defeated or derailed by "higher" aims. It puts
one in mind of Noddy Boffin gazing wistfully over his shoulder
at the beloved dust-heaps he has had to relinquish.

Given over thoroughly to this pursuit, Ashbee is none the less
a Victorian. He makes it emphatically clear that he does not
"mean to say that books either blasphemous, immoral, indecent, or written to inflame the passions should be put into the
hands of young people, far from it," although, he counters,
such books "are necessary and profitable for the student to
know." Who that student is—he keeps turning up throughout
Ashbee's pages without ever becoming any less anonymous—
we all know well enough. And even here, Ashbee continues to
consider, such books should "be used with caution even by the
mature; they should be looked upon as poisons, and treated as
such; should be (so to say) distinctly labelled, and only con-
fided to those who understand their potency, and are capable of
rightly using them. The present work, of which the part object
is the labeling or pointing out such books, is not intended, any
more than the volumes of which it treats, for the young and
immature; and the hope is here expressed that it may be kept

out of the hands of those for whom it is not destined." From garbage or rubbish to potent poison; the language tells us that we are still in the world of William Acton, as do the attitudes of which that language is the vehicle. As for the hope which Ashbee expresses in the last clause, he had nothing to worry about: an iron law of nature determines it that such books pass only into the hands of those for whom they are destined.

It is difficult to decide to what extent the divisions in Ashbee's consciousness are the result of ordinary hypocrisy or of unconscious contradictions. On the one hand, he writes, "it is no part of my programme to preach or moralize." He does not commend the authors noticed, he asserts, nor does he praise their "lewdness, immorality, or irreligion. If I do not directly censure them . . . I at any rate merely lay their turpitudes or blasphemies before my readers as a truthful and unbiassed historian would do." That last sentence, we may note, is going in two directions at the same time, the "merely" making hash out of its original logic. But deflections of this kind are themselves the essential logic of thinking on this subject; they are its native mode or style of thought. So, Ashbee continues, "although the citations I produce are frequently licentious, being as a matter of course those which I have considered the most remarkable or most pungent," none of them and nothing in his work is "sufficient to inflame the passions." Indeed he asseverates, "My extracts on the contrary will, I trust and believe, have a totally opposite effect, and as a rule will inspire so hearty a disgust for the books they are taken from, that the reader will have learned enough about them from my pages, and will be more than satisfied to have nothing further to do with them." There is scarcely any point in analyzing the impossibilities of this utterance, particularly in view of what has immediately preceded them. The point to be noted is that the several elements in Ashbee's exposition—his "humour," the danger to both young and mature, his disavowal of moralizing, and at the same time the sanative moral effect he expects his work to have—are not simply contradictory; he is unaware of contradiction, and these conflicting tendencies exist side by side in his mind yet function autonomously and in isolation from one another. In addition to isolation, then, a whole series of unconscious displacements and denials are enlisted to make this kind of thinking possible or acceptable to consciousness. And as we shall have ample opportunity to observe, displacement and denial are among the chief *modi operandi* of pornographic writing.

These contradictions are the very tissue of Ashbee's intellect; they are to be found within single sentences as well as in adjacent passages. In his Preliminary Remarks to Volume III, the *Catena,* for example, Ashbee concludes his discussion of the value for social history of pornographic fiction with this statement: "Immoral, and amatory fiction then claims our study, and must unfortunately be acknowledged to contain, *cum grano salis,* a reflection of the manners and vices of the times—of vices to be avoided, guarded against, reformed, but which unquestionably exist, and of which an exact estimate is needful to enable us to cope with them." One hardly knows where to lay hold of this sentence, it is such a mess. To begin with, the grain of salt both cuts the ground out from under everything that has gone before and breaks the sentence into which it is inserted in half. It acts to nullify or neutralize (rather than to genuinely modify) the positive assertions that have preceded it, and in a characteristically ambivalent way allows the writer both to give and take at the same moment, to feel that he is making a daring pronouncement which is by a kind of magical simultaneity safely unexceptionable. And the last part of the sentence repeats the substitution of fantasy for reality, fuses past and present, and garnishes the whole with some sprigs of moral parsley. Similarly in Volume II, when Ashbee is representing the service his exhaustive study of "worthless books" will perform, he adverts to his Pylades, "the student," who must, he says, "consequently be grateful to the bibliographer who shall have taken the trouble to wade through this literary garbage, shall have estimated it at its real value, and shall give a terse but reliable account of it." Ashbee himself confesses that he has not been entirely able to achieve this object, although he has come closer to it than anyone previous to him. But the "real desideratum," he concludes, is for a "single work which, confining itself to the worthless and deceitful, points out what should be avoided." The reader can understand that in a vague, general way this sentence makes sense. But that it should be cast in the form of a tautology, that the categories it establishes are meaningless, and that the language itself dissolves beneath the slightest pressure of inspection suggest again that we are in the presence of a series of displacements. Such sentences are really about something else and have their referents elsewhere.

These processes may be observed in another context, as invading and conditioning Ashbee's scholarly virtues (it is not possible to make a strict calculation of the degree of causal influence exerted by such processes; they seem rather to act in the manner described in the social sciences as "independent variables"). One of these virtues is Ashbee's practice of giving "frequent and copious extracts" from the works noticed along with "the opinions of previous critics and bibliographers." This modesty and generousness, however, serve a double purpose, as we see a few pages further on when Ashbee declares: "I have not attempted to generalize or draw to a head the various and diverse material which I have manipulated; this is the province of the historian rather than of the bibliographer, and requires a more comprehensive grasp and an abler hand than mine." Here we can observe how Ashbee's virtues and predilections go together and how the former work as both mask and sanction for the latter. For Ashbee shares in common his dislike of or repulsion from generalization with pornography itself. Although, as I have said, pornography is paradoxically a highly abstract form of expression, it does not achieve its abstractness by means of its generalizing power. Generalization is in fact anathema to pornography, for what generalization does is to sum up or bring to conclusion a train of concrete instances; most of all it dispenses with the need for a further production of such instances, for a repetition of them. But it is precisely in repetition, in repetition sustained to infinity and beyond, that pornography and its allied phenomena live and move and have their being. Ashbee's indispensable virtues as a bibliographer, his tireless collection and production of instances, his indefatigable energy of quotation, his unbelievable scrupulosity of concrete detail all partake of the same impulses which both actuate his interest in pornography and are behind its creation. What Ashbee was able to do, then, was to take his obsession, transfer it without significant change or loss of form to a nearly related area, and put it to some further or secondary use. The process is a familiar one, the results in this case were unique.

III

Ashbee's three volumes are at once a monument of personal scholarship and a monument of his personal eccentricity. In point of fact, his eccentricity is so deep, radical, and unremitting that clinical terms seem more appropriate than the neutral and, within the context of English culture, virtually honorific ascriptions of oddity or eccentricity or whimsy. The chief characteristic of his writing is its pedantry. The long introductions to the separate volumes are largely composed of long, endless, and more often than not pointless and useless footnotes; there are in reality considerably more footnotes than text in each of them. These footnotes are made up of a variety of material, but the majority of them consist of quotations in an assortment of European languages. The quotations sometimes concern general bibliographical questions, sometimes general questions of literature and morals, and sometimes nothing in general. That is to say, the footnotes are there not because of their relevance to the text above them; they are there because Ashbee wants them there without regard to their content. These footnotes, as a consequence, take on a symbolic meaning, as does the shape of Ashbee's page. The kind of page that Ashbee continually seems to strive for, and that he frequently manages to achieve, consists of a single line of text from which there depends a page of footnote. Ashbee's persistence in this effort is so pronounced that one is tempted to go beyond common sense and see in it an unconscious iconography: beneath a very small head there is attached a very large appendage. But since this appendage principally contains the assertions of other men, Ashbee, employing a familiar maneuver of the unconscious, need not feel "responsible" for it.

Ashbee's mania for quotation is not, however, exhausted by these devices. He will stick in a few lines wherever a small blank space occurs, and he is happy to manufacture the opportunity to quote at length and liberty: Volume II, the *Centuria,* for example, opens with no less than six full pages of epigraphs. The functions of such a practice are not difficult to interpret. To use the words of other men instead of one's own is to attempt to arrogate their strength or authority; it is furthermore a primitive device of concealment, the words and ideas of others acting as a protective cover for one's own (children are inveterate quoters). In addition, a text which uses quoted material tends, in proportion to the thickness and frequency with which the quotations are sown, to become progressively less readable. Ashbee's own work, with its perpetual flood of quotations, with quotations interspersed with further quotations in several languages (his habit was always to quote in the original and never to translate), and with every page dotted with hiccoughing references and hieroglyphic citations, indicates that his own impulses in the direction of unreadability were quite strong. And we can understand this too as in part a defensive countermeasure: in a book which is written with the impulse to communicate "everything"—both in the way of knowledge and of sexuality—the countertendency to communicate nothing can be expected (just as children, again, who are on the point of communicating or who have just communicated some piece of sexual information to an adult will often spontaneously break into nonsense language). The difference between the impulse to "tell all" and the impulse to tell nothing is in such matters always difficult to maintain.[7]

Another distinctive element in Ashbee's practice is the inten-

[7] For an interpretation of similar and related phenomena, see John Rickman, "On Quotations," *International Journal of Psycho-Analysis,* X (1929), 242–248.

sity of his insistence on precision. He makes a point of empha-
sizing that throughout his work "all extracts given are tran-
scribed with every fault and peculiarity, whether of spelling or
punctuation; this should be borne in mind, so that errors which
belong to the original may not be attributed to me or my
printer." His justification of this absolute literalness is essentially cryptological. Error itself may be a source of knowledge,
"for by a peculiarity of diction, a special manner of punctuation, the omission or improper use of an accent, an author may
be detected, the genuineness of an edition determined, or even
in some instances the place and date of the publication fixed."
There is certainly a general kind of truth to this notion, and its
utility in other areas of bibliographical study has been proved.
On the other hand, we should not make the mistake of attributing to Ashbee an anticipation of *The Psychopathology of Everyday Life;* moreover, to my knowledge Ashbee never makes
any use of the practice that he so laboriously pursues. Once
again we find ourselves in the presence of behavior whose conscious justification has been displaced a considerable distance
from its primary motive. For if anything about this question is
at all clear, it is that Ashbee's chief source of gratification lies in
the mere fact of quotation, in the rigidly literal reproduction of
what he has read. There is certainly something ritualistic and
therefore something of an obsessional nature about this convention. And since, as I have implied, pornography itself is overwhelmingly ritualistic and obsessive, we can regard both the
structure and the content of Ashbee's bibliographical performance as being at least in part companion- or counter-obsessions.
Contrasts and analogies suggest themselves at once. Pornography is, for example, the most disordered kind of writing; not
only are the contents of pornographic writing "disorderly," but
the entire field, from the volumes themselves through all the
circumstances of publication and collection, amounts to a veritable model of disorganization and absence of control—it is, to
be sure, a "dirty" and chaotic state of affairs. Ashbee himself is
thoroughly implicated in this dark and dangerous business, but

onto it he has imposed what must have seemed to him the most inflexible and powerful kind of order. Accuracy, precision, literalness, reliability, absolute verification—all of these virtues can be seen as bearing with dialectical but equally irrational force on Ashbee's other interest. Yet because these virtues were not adequately beneath the guidance of reason, things did not work out exactly as Ashbee intended. For although he was able to reduce pornography to order and reintroduce it within the iron frame of scholarly and bibliographical control, the demands of that control were themselves remorseless and excessive. And the signs or symptoms of those demands, the fanatical quoting, the invariable literalness and precision, the infinitude of references, operate in the end not to master the subject but to reproduce on another level and in a symbolic way the original chaos and disorder they were intended to bring under command. This melancholy compromise will be familiar to anyone who has read much scholarship, in any field of study. Ashbee's work is only an extreme example of a representative instance.

Ashbee did not, naturally, think of himself in this way, and we can perhaps approximate the image he had of himself by examining his remarks on the writer he most praises and toward whom he expresses the strongest sense of affinity, Martin Schurig. "Of all the learned physicians or surgeons who have written upon the physical connection of the sexes," Ashbee writes, "no one has treated the subject so thoroughly, or brought together so many curious, interesting and extraordinary details." And it brings him particular pleasure, Ashbee remarks, to be able to bring "these little known, and less read volumes" before the "lovers of the curiosities of literature." Although physicians before Schurig had made inquiries into sexual matters and written about them, "the particulars, observations, and anecdotes given by Schurig far surpass any thing" that had previously been done. But it is not merely the freeness and boldness of Schurig's compendia which attract Ashbee, but the thoroughness of his scholarship: "Authorities are carefully and fully given; and citations are reproduced in the language and words of their authors. Each volume is furnished with a *Syllabus Autorum* and an *Index Rerum*, alphabetically arranged . . . and verified. It is this thoroughness, peculiar to erudite Germans, which renders their books so valuable to the student, although by the reader for mere amusement they may be thought troublesome and unattractive." Schurig was, in the words of a nineteenth-century French historian of medicine, the author of *"une série de vaste monographies, dans lesquelles il a rassemblé une mass considérable d'observations, puisées de toutes parts, et où il rappelle à pue près tout ce quie avait été fait avant lui."* He was, in other words, one of the first writers of what was to come to be known as *Sittengeschichten*, enormous tomes whose intentions, according to a contemporary German scholar, waver between the quasi-scientific and the pseudopornographic, whose pedantry is genuine but whose scholarship is spurious, and whose stupidity is invincible. These gala productions of the mind were once a speciality of German culture; they have now become a speciality of everybody and continue until today to be turned out in disconcerting quantity.

The titles of Schurig's books are in dog Latin and are very long. One can stand as a sample of the rest. *"MULIEBRIA Historico-Medica, hoc est Partium Genitalium Muliebrium Consideratio Physico-Medico-Forensis, qua Pudendi Muliebris Partes tam externae, quam internae, scilicet Uterus cum Ipsi Annexis Ovariis et Tubis Fallopianis, nec non Varia de Clitoride et Tribadismo, de Hymen et Nymphotomia seu Feminarum Circumsisione et Castratione selectis et curiosis observationibus traduntur. A.D. Martino Schurigio, Physico Dresdensi . . . MDCCXXIX."* Other, shortened, titles are, *Spermatologia Historico-Medica, Parthenologia H-M, Gynaecologia H-M, Syllepsilogia H-M,* and so on into the night. These titles, Ashbee observes, convey "but a faint notion, even to one of the profession, of the amusing and curious information" with which the volumes abound. Indeed it is impossible, he says, "without overstepping the limits of a bibliographical compilation . . . to give an adequate notion of the vast gathering of facts and

anecdotes embraced" within their pages. What Ashbee curiously fails to mention is that, in a manner customary to
the genre, the "facts and anecdotes" are by and large the
same from volume to volume: a few new details and incidents
are dredged up or invented, there is a certain amount of re-
shuffling of the material to satisfy the requirements of the
book's ostensible subject, but in the main the same old stories
and sexual fairy tales are recounted, with a straight face, for the
thousandth time. A scattered selection of a few of the topics
which Schurig rehearses will give the reader some idea of his
work. "Various names of the penis . . . The size of the nose
indicative of that of the yard . . . Writers who affirm that
Adam was a hermaphrodite . . . De Pudendi muliebris de-
nominationibus . . . Hair on the private parts so luxuriant
that it was cut off and sold . . . Sodomy committed in three
ways . . . Virgo a serpente amata . . . Salacium puellarum
instrumenta . . . Utrum mas an femina majorem voluptatem
sentiat . . . Cohaesio in coitu . . . Copulation prevented by
the excessive size of the clitoris . . . Bestiality with various
animals of both sexes, with mermen and maids, with demons,
and with statues . . . De gravidarum coitu . . . Imagination in
women." Ashbee also reproduces by photolithography a page
from one of Schurig's books. It is taken from a section in which
Schurig is "treating of the size of the male human member,"
and consists of a letter written in a seventeenth-century German
so illiterate as to be virtually indecipherable. The writer of this
letter is a woman, and as far as can be made out she is hysteri-
cally lamenting the fact that her husband—at any rate some
man—has a penis so enormous that coitus with him is impossible. The center of the page is neatly decorated with a perfectly
drawn circle whose diameter is two and a half inches or six and
a half centimeters, whichever side of the ruler you prefer to
read. Although Ashbee is willing to admit that "medical science has made vast progress" since Schurig's time and that
many of "his theories and notions have consequently been long
since exploded," he continues to insist that "his vast erudition

cannot be too much admired, nor can the value be underrated of the numberless pertinent *facts* which he has amassed, and for which he invariably gives his authorities." It is Ashbee who emphasizes the word "facts," and this leads us to suggest once more that we are dealing with a subject in which the idea of fact regularly ceases to have a signifiable meaning. In this context, fact almost invariably comes to mean that somebody wrote, said, or dreamt it; this regressive sense of reality is, I should suggest, a principal requirement for any prolonged involvement with this subject. It is, furthermore, a sense of reality quite compatible with the process of forgetting from one book to the next what one has read.

A final resemblance which Ashbee implicitly draws between himself and Schurig has to do with style. Schurig wrote in what Ashbee describes as "the macaronic style frequently used by the learned Germans of the time," an irregular mixture of Latin and German, which bears certain similarities to the macaronic verse from which the term is derived. Ashbee finds this style to have "real charm" and defends it against modern detraction by assimilating it to the style of *The Anatomy of Melancholy*. Ashbee's habit of interspersing his prose with quotations in a number of languages may be regarded as a latter-day equivalent of Schurig's macaroni.

As for Ashbee's own English prose, that is something else again. At certain moments of stress, as we have seen, its logic tends to break down and reveal behind it the logic of unconscious processes and associations. Its tone is often blurred and uncertain, as in the following. "For while in France, in Italy, and even in Germany," he writes in the Introduction to the *Index*, "some of the most esteemed authors have not hesitated to write licentious books, with us the veriest grubbians only have, as a rule, put their pens at the disposal of Venus and Priapus." On the one hand, this is a representative specimen of "period style"; one would not be surprised to find such a passage in, say, Bulwer-Lytton—the fake elegance, the tinsel periphrases, and the dead euphemisms are perfectly familiar. On the other, its archness, coyness, and donnish drollery are themselves compatible with a certain kind of pornographic style. The workings of that style can be readily demonstrated. In Volume III, Ashbee is noticing a work entitled *Love's Tell-Tale; or; The Decameron of Pleasure,* a slightly changed reprinting in 1865 of a work that first appeared about 1830. The first story in the book is called "Little Miss Curious's Tale," and Ashbee undertakes to summarize it for the reader.

> Between little Miss Curious, when in her tenth or eleventh year, and her father's servant, Henry, a friendship springs up. She watches him, and between the chinks of his bedroom door observes while he is allaying the ardour of his temperament in solitude. One day, while chasing a butterfly in the garden, little Miss Curious falls upon a stake, which penetrates the part destined for the reception of a more pliable instrument. Henry is at hand, carries his young mistress into a summer house, extracts the stake, and laves the wounded part. The ice is now broken—miss is no longer reserved before Henry, but allows him every possible freedom. He, however, restrains himself, and does not endeavour to snatch the last favour until one day, he surprises her in the summer house, asleep, with her person exposed, when, after a little gentle masturbation, he makes a partial attempt upon her virginity. The damsel wakes, and Henry hastily hides his member. Miss, however, determines to bring matters to an issue, and drags the now crest-fallen limb from its concealment. Her youthful fingers soon produce renewed vigor, and to her great satisfaction she watches at her ease that operation of nature which she had hitherto only indistinctly perceived through the cracks of the door. She now begs Henry to complete her education, which after obtaining her promise of secrecy, he does that same night in her own "little bed," she being only 12 years old.

This is, to be sure, not bad of its kind (providing that one forgets, as Dr. Johnson said, that a man could write like this forever if he would but abandon his mind to it). It is leisurely and smooth, and contains several literate touches. But beneath its surface one detects an endless searching for "new" terms or equivalents. For though repetition is a central formal attribute of pornography, this repetition is set within a context which also demands that it be accompanied by minute, mechanical

variations in both general arrangement and language—thereby
delivering it from the onus of "mere" repetition. Like the murder mystery and Hollywood movie, pornography is an extremely conventionalized form of expression. Departures from
the convention are confined to a limited number of formulae,
and anything more radical is likely to end in violation of the
convention and failure rather than in transcendance and transformation. Ashbee's prose, it can be seen, falls well within the
boundaries of the convention, and it is therefore not a prose we
can count on for its strong grasp on the actual. In the passage I
have cited, Ashbee's prose flows smoothly, without a halt,
bump, or interruption about the incident of the little girl falling
on the stake. What this indicates, simply, is that he has accommodated himself to the reality of the convention—in the pornographic fantasy, as in the comic cartoon, one can be destroyed
or dismembered without being hurt. To some extent, of course,
any experience of any art requires such an accommodation; in
pornography the degree of envelopment by the fantasy tends to
be larger, the submission of one's sense of reality to the fantasy
more peremptory and absolute. (It may be able to succeed in
this requirement because the threshold for such fantasies is in
most men quite low.)

This confusion of fantasy and reality, this interfusion of various levels of perception is not in Ashbee confined to those areas
I have already referred to. The process continues to generalize
itself and invade other parts of his intellect. In the end, Ashbee
is unable to resist his own impulses, and what began as investigation of a literature concludes as propaganda for a reality.
Ashbee devotes a great deal of space in his three volumes, for
example, to the extensive literature of flagellation. And he does
start some effort to sort out fantasy from reality, introducing
material from personal memoirs, letters, interviews with
friends as a kind of evidential check on the literature. But at last
he is overpowered by the literature, by the strength of the fantasy, that is by the strength of desire. "Women," he concludes,
"delight in administering the birch; and innumerable are the

tales of schoolmistresses whipping their pupils, mothers, and especially mothers-in-law, their children, and taking grim pleasure in the operation. Indeed women are more cruel and relentless than men. . . ." The logic of this passage is instructive. That children were beaten as punishment cannot be doubted; it is no less true that sexual fantasies of flagellation were widespread, as the enormous literature devoted to the subject demonstrates; and it is also true that a certain number of men acted out these fantasies, resorting in the main to prostitutes who would beat them or consent to be beaten. At this point, however, a shift in levels of reality occurs, and the masculine sexual fantasy is projected onto women. The elements of this fantasy are, very simply, that women instigate this practice, that they perpetuate it, and that they experience, as do the men concerned, a specific and directly felt sexual pleasure from it. There is no evidence in support of this contention, there never was any, and if Ashbee had been able to disentangle himself from the material that he reproduces in his pages he would have been able without much effort to make this out. But if we look back at the sentences I have quoted, we can see that the key term, logically and syntactically, is "the tales"—its placement and ambiguity allow the shift in reality to take place. Ashbee also accepts as fact the legend of "a female whipping club," of a group or "society of ladies who meet together for the mutual application of the birch." This fantasy has been, at least since the end of the eighteenth century, a permanent presence in the literature of flagellation. The club's place of venue may change, but all else remains the same; and when one meets with it in the latest jazzed-up versions put out by the Olympia Press it is like coming across an old if slightly frayed and tattered friend.

The tendency I have been discussing is generalized still further, and the most astonishing sections of Ashbee's work are the more than three hundred pages which deal with anticlerical literature. Ashbee himself is an anticleric of the simplest description; "every system of theology," he asserts, "has, sooner or

later, become alloyed with immoral doctrines, impure rites, or
obscene practices and customs." To have any real force, naturally, his anticlericalism must be directed at the "Church of
Rome"; and joined with these sentiments is a classic, uninflected rationalism. "Every reflecting mind must find it difficult
to understand how, in the present nineteenth century, a system
so false, prurient, and polluted, can still be believed in, can find
devotees ready to lay down their lives in its support, and even
make converts of men of knowledge, experience, and bright
parts. For, whether we consider the absurd miracles which are
even today being palmed off upon the credulous; the blunders,
crimes and follies of the infallible popes; the vices and hypocrisy of many of the clergy, both regular and secular; the duplic-
ity, lax teaching, infamous doctrines, and dishonest commercial
dealings of the jesuits; the scandalous quarrels which have
taken place between the different orders, and the irregularities
and licentiousness which have at all times distinguished monas-
tic institutions, both male and female; their useless asceticism,
puerile macerations, and their flagellations, at once absurd,
cruel and indecent; the gross oppression and horrid cruelties of
the inquisition; the terrible system of auricular confession, and
the abuse which has been made of it; the coarse, scurrilous,
abusive and licentious discourses . . . etc., etc., etc." This sentence is distributed across nineteen pages of Ashbee's text; the
top of each page contains one, two, or three lines; virtually
every word is superscribed with a footnote marking, and the
notes themselves take up the body of the page. Their contents
are what one might expect, as are the contents of the three hundred succeeding pages. To sum up in brief what cannot here be
entered upon at length, Ashbee's obsession with the sins of
Rome is the counterpart and analogue of his interest in pornography. What he experiences with direct sexual pleasure in pornography he experiences with the added pleasure of moral indignation in relation to Rome. For Roman Catholicism is a
pornographer's paradise, and there is, as they say, evidence to
back up every change. All priests are lechers, satyrs, and pimps,

all nuns are concubines or lesbians or both. The confessional is the locus of meeting of lubricity and piety. This perfect balance of outrage and envy is matched by a similar ambivalence of idea; the Church of Rome, like everyone's parents, is at once ascetically denying us the gratification of our impulses and hypocritically wallowing in a wholly sexualized existence, making love over the nasty stye. One thinks wistfully of what Newman could have done had he access to this volume when he prepared his *Lectures on the Present Position of Catholics in England*.

In the course of this extended assault on Rome, Ashbee treats in detail certain English works from the seventeenth and eighteenth centuries. These are mostly anti-Catholic narratives, confessions, and records of testimony given at trials; and they contain by far the best and most interesting writing of anything within Ashbee's three volumes, arising as they do out of the world of Bunyan and Fox and the folk tradition of English dissent, and retaining, even in their madness, some of that tradition's vividness of language and feeling. But Ashbee is too preoccupied with his indictment of Rome to consider that he has come across something that looks like literature. This is worth noting if only because one of Ashbee's explicit intentions is to apply critical judgment to the works he treats. The character of that judgment, when it is applied, is easily illustrated. In the *Index*, Ashbee notices a small volume of sonnets, *Les Amies, scène d'amour sapphique*, written supposedly by one Pablo de Herlagnèz. Ashbee comments, "These sonnets, 6 in number, are pretty, but display no great talent," and then adds, "The author's real name is Paul Verlaine." One has to admit that this is very easy hunting; besides, anyone could make such an error. A more representative instance of Ashbee's critical procedure can be extracted from his discussion of an eighteenth-century book of stories, *L'Année Galante*, which he doesn't regard very favorably. "The book is divided into 12 chapters," runs his comment, "each bearing the name of a month, for which there seems to be no *raison d'être*, as the adventures have no affinity to the season in which they are told." So much for the weather. And here is his descriptive evaluation of one of Rowlandson's obscene plates, *The Larking Cull.* "A bed room; toilet table to the left, looking-glass hanging on the wall to the right, a pot of flowers on a small table at the back, all prettily drawn. Two figures; the youth's member is very large, and unnaturally tapered at the end, a form particularly affected by Rowlandson. Pleasure is depicted on the faces of both actors." That last sentence rings in the ear as if it were a sepulchral admonition; one can almost hear Mrs. Wilfer saying it. As for his general critical idea of the history of English pornographic writing, Ashbee commits himself to the notion that since Cleland things have been going downhill. The reason for this deterioration is that later writers have been influenced by Sade "and have copied the cynicism, cruelty, and impracticable lasciviousness which he made the distinctive feature of his books. Thus, the nature of English erotic fiction has been changed, and its wholesome tone (if any book of the kind can be called wholesome) entirely lost." It seems to me that Ashbee's qualifications, intentions, and achievements as a critic are fairly captured by his use of the word "impracticable."

Ashbee may be regarded as coming under the class of minds described by Arnold in "The Literary Influence of Academies" —provincial, eccentric, Persian in their excessiveness, withal original. What makes Ashbee particularly susceptible to such characterization is that his subject is itself originally invested with those qualities and is thus designed to elicit the latent irregularities and distortions in the mind which undertakes to deal with it. We may also regard him as belonging to the group of English gentlemen-amateur scholars, private persons who turned a personal interest, hobby, avocation, passion, or mania to good account. These range from someone like Mr. Casaubon at one end of the scale to someone like the Fowler brothers at the other. Ashbee falls about in the middle: the nature of his interests pushes him in the direction of Mr. Casaubon, while the actuality of his achievement tends to raise him above his subject. Although in the preceding pages I have subjected him to rather severe analysis, my purpose in doing so was not disparagement. In the first place, I wanted to demonstrate in part how a mind like Ashbee's works and how, historically, the investigation of pornography is itself to a remarkable degree an example of the phenomenon being investigated. Secondly, a balance had to be redressed, since the few brief discussions of Ashbee's works which exist in English, French, and German are absurdly disproportionate in their uncritical praise. Such adulation, one may add, is a disservice to Ashbee, since it tends to obscure his actual accomplishment. Nevertheless, it would be unfair to close a chapter on him without giving the reader some further notion of that accomplishment.

I V

The one part of Ashbee's mind in whose sense of reality we can place unlimited confidence is that part which deals with the books themselves—with their external specifications, dates, titles, printing history, and variant editions; and with their internal specifications in the sense of an accurate account of their narrative contents. Connected with this is Ashbee's extensive knowledge of the pornographic publishing trade as it grew and flourished during the nineteenth century. Being the chief European collector of his time, he was naturally intimate with the workings of that industry and with the customs and practices of the entrepreneurs who gained their livelihood in it. The principal circumstance of that trade is its obscurity, and as we have seen, Ashbee himself often complains of the difficulties of amassing evidence or of finding out anything at all. Yet he has brought more light to this darkness than anyone else.

One of the first things to be learned from a study of Ashbee's volumes is that by the mid-Victorian period the pornographic scene had established itself in very much the same modes, categories, and varieties as exist today. Alongside of works which fumbled toward giving a scientific account of sexuality were grouped volumes describing the "rites" and "practices" of certain curious sexual and religious cults, volumes which purported to be anthropology of some kind, volumes of folklore, and a whole range of sex and marriage manuals of differing inflammatory intensity but uniformly equal ineptitude and disingenuousness. Fiction presented a familiar visage. From the outer circles in which there floated about stories, novelettes, and whole novels of a sentimental-witty-racy kind, known in the trade as "galanterie," one proceeded slowly and by gradually increasing degrees of openness in the use of language and description of events to the center, the hard core. Reprinting of old favorites went on apace, and there was a brisk trade in translations, re-translations, and back-translations—one of the tricks of the business being the creation of new works by a process that may be called progressive mutilation. The trick consists of re-translating a work exclusively from its last immediate translation, so that, say, by the time a work originally entitled *The Romance of Lust,* published first in English in 1879, appears in a new English version, published in Paris within the last fifteen years, it has a new title and new characters and has gone through the following additional metamorphoses. This new English translation was made from a French translation published at around the turn of the century, which had in turn been translated from a German rendering, which was itself a translation from an earlier French translation of the original and now as good as unrecognizable English. There was also a steady trickle of new works of fiction, the demand for new material being essentially constant and stable in what is always a seller's market. Periodical publications of different degrees of openness and addressed to differing sexual preferences and different social classes were also to be had, some with illustrations and some without. In 1832 Louis Daguerre announced the discovery of his process to the French Academy of Science; shortly thereafter a lively business in photographs of a sexual nature got under way.[8] Pornography supplied an invention of its own; in 1828 a machine "to flog gentlemen upon" was manufactured for Mrs. Theresa Berkeley, a prostitute who specialized in flagellation and who was, according to Ashbee, "the queen of her profession." Ashbee reproduces an engraving of this contraption; it resembles a large football blocking-dummy and may be thought of as perversity's contribution to the Industrial Revolution. The single modern convenience of which the Victorians were deprived was moving pictures. We find then that in this area of culture, as in so many others, the Victorian period is essentially continuous with our own.

Among the chief adornments of this subculture were the booksellers John Camden Hotten and William Dugdale. Both of them appear to have been personally known to Ashbee, and he supplies us with a good deal of information about the way they ran their operations. Hotten seems to have been, so to say, the Maurice Girodias of Victorian England; he was, as Ashbee observes, "almost the only respectable English publisher of tabooed literature," a circumstance in which "he took great delight." As is well known, Hotten published Swinburne's *Poems and Ballads,* agreeing to take over the volume after Moxon's had withdrawn it from circulation because of the violent reception it had met with in the press. He also seems to have had a hand in the publication and popularization of American writers in England. Hotten's life was short—he was born in 1832 and died in 1873—but very active. Ashbee writes that "his

[8] Ashbee tells us of an English photographer named Henry Hayler, "whose photographic studies from life enjoy an European reputation." In 1874 the police descended on two London houses in which Hayler conducted his operations, and "no less than 130,248 obscene photographs, and 5,000 slides were seized and destroyed. Hayler himself absconded, and thereby escaped punishment; he went to Berlin, but has not been heard of publicly since." Ashbee goes on to quote a newspaper report which stated that "in the more offensive pictures were discernible the portraits of the owner of the house, his wife, and two sons." To this it may be added that by the end of the century a new convention had become part of the stock-in-trade of pornographic fiction; novels now occasionally contained within them a scene describing some part of the workings of the pornographic industry itself. And by today several pornographic novels whose excuse for a subject is the pornography business—that is to say, pornographic novels about pornography—have been published.

private library of erotic literature was extensive, and was, at his death, purchased *en bloc* by a London amateur." That amateur, there is reason to believe, was Ashbee himself, since in his small essay on Hotten he reprints some of Hotten's scribblings toward an autobiographical narrative, and adds that these are from "a MS still existing in his own handwriting."

Hotten was born in London and, according to his own account, "showed a great passion for books" at an early age. At the age of fifteen, he prevailed upon one Petheram, "the author of an Anglo-Saxon Grammar, and other kindred works" and owner of a book shop, to allow him to spend a few hours each day in the shop. Thomas Babington Macaulay, Hotten's account proceeds, "used to make daily visits to Mr. Petheram's shop for the purpose of securing any old books and tracts which might suit his collections. I used to lay aside anything which I thought might interest the historian, and would often submit to him memoranda of books I had seen elsewhere. These little attentions made me a favorite with Macaulay, who however, on one occasion when in an irritable mood, threatened me with chastisement for not speedily obtaining change for a £5.-Note, and in the heat of the moment actually did topple upon me a large quarto volume which he held in his hand at the time." It is difficult to determine to what extent young Hotten's brains were scrambled by the trauma of this event, but it is certain that something went wrong. Soon after this, the narrative continues, Hotten departed for the West Indies, accompanying an elder brother on "a Robinson Crusoe scheme of adventure," whatever that may mean. Eventually the brothers wound up in New Orleans, where they separated, the elder going off to Minnesota, and Hotten himself accepting "the offer of a gentleman to accompany him to"—of all places—Galena, Illinois. One knows what has to come next, and it does: "The Tannery of Mr. Grant, now President Grant, lay just below my rooms. . . . I knew him very well, and certainly never supposed from his quiet manner that he would reach his present position." In 1854 Hotten made his way back to England—the autobiographical fragment ends here—and in 1855, Ashbee tells us, he began business "in a very small shop, No. 151b Piccadilly, directly opposite the larger establishment which acquired a world wide renown under his rule." He soon became successful, and at the time of his death in 1873 had placed himself, according to the obituary tribute of a friend, "at the very summit of his calling." "A modest tombstone," in Highgate Cemetery, Ashbee writes, "was erected to his memory by the London booksellers."

Hotten's character is sufficiently revealed to us by his memorializing friend. "During the last eight years he occupied a position as publisher second to none in the trade. His acuteness in feeling the pulse of the bookmarket, in gauging the public taste, and supplying it with exactly the sort of literary pabulum it required, was truly extraordinary." Whether or not we agree with the idea that pornography is a species of breakfast cereal, there is no doubt that Hotten pursued his occupation with energy and vigor. Indeed, concludes his friend: "His fertile brain seemed never to be at rest. He overtasked it, and it has at last given way under the strain." This may be the first recorded instance of death caused by brain fever brought on by pornography.

Out of a number of examples I have chosen three to illustrate Hotten's dealings. In 1865 Hotten reprinted Richard Payne Knight's famous *A Discourse on the Worship of Priapus*. First published in 1786, this work is antiquarian in kind, and may be thought of as proto-archeology or proto-anthropology. Although the first printing of this book could not have been large, Knight came in for a certain amount of strong criticism for writing publicly on such a subject and seems to have made an effort to suppress or recall as many volumes as he could. Ashbee himself appears not to have owned a copy of it, since he notes that a copy of the original edition is to be found "in the reserved library of the British Museum," the same institution to which Knight, on his death in 1824, bequeathed that "collection of antiquities, which became the pride of his life," and which his large personal fortune had enabled him to amass—there is a tradition for these things. Hotten's reprinting has added to it another essay, longer than Knight's, and entitled *An Essay on the Worship of the Generative Powers During the Middle Ages of Western Europe*. This work, Ashbee informs us, is "from the pen of Mr. Thomas Wright, assisted by Sir James Emerson Tennent, and Mr. George Witt." Wright was also an antiquary; he took his degree at Cambridge in 1834, and was one of the founders of the Camden Society, and of the British Archeological Society. His essay seems to have been written at about the time of Hotten's reprinting, and since it exists at exactly the same stage of intellectual development as Knight's work, which preceded it by some eighty years, it strikes one as being less justified.

Hotten's issue of this printing was in 125 copies only, Ashbee specifies, "of which 6 on large paper, price, to subscribers (only), small paper £4. 10s, large paper £10. 10s; Roxburg binding." If this notation is correct, we get an idea of the part of the market at which Hotten was aiming: it was very small and very rich. There is, however, some ambiguity in that parenthetical "only": it may mean that this volume was sold only by subscription, or even by subscription in advance, Hotten circularizing his customers and raising enough money to pay for the printing beforehand, as certain European printing houses do today; or it may possibly mean, since the specification is written by Ashbee, that this was the price paid only by those who subscribed, and that a customer walking in off the street might get it at a knocked-down figure, or that Hotten would sell it for whatever he could get—a practice common enough in bookselling of this kind. Hotten did write a circular for this issue, which Ashbee happily reproduces, and it gives us a chance of examining that great man's prose. "This is a very extraordinary volume," its simple eloquence runs, "upon a subject that is now attracting the almost universal attention of the learned and curious in Europe." One of the distinctive attributes of publishers of pornography, we shall often see, is their peculiar sense of time. There follows a short ramble through the subject of the volume, and the circular closes with this paragraph: "As *only one hundred and twenty-five* copies have been privately printed, and the great libraries of Europe have absorbed many of these, the volume will soon become one of the RAREST OF MODERN BOOKS. *Five* or *six* copies, it is understood, have been printed on LARGE PAPER." This is of course the usual come-on, and in the bit about the great libraries of Europe contains the familiar, pleasant fantasy of megalomania. I say fantasy of megalomania because it is hard to imagine anyone believing this nonsense—not Hotten or his customers. But it is all part of the ritual, as is the last sentence, which serves to thicken the atmosphere of the arcane. In it Hotten is acting as a front or agent for himself, and by this slight removal of himself from the scene of the crime seems to imply that the real pornographer is the printer's boy.

In the course of his summary of the contents of this volume, Hotten offers his customers a few examples of Priapus worship; one of these, he states, is "the horse-shoe placed over a stable or other door, or nailed to the orchard-gate," which represents "nothing more or less than a bent priapus—the twisted and perverted emblem of an ancient creed, that numbered, probably, more devout followers than any other humanly-devised system of worship." This seems like a charming, if distinctly odd, pseudo-fact until one consults the passage in Wright's essay to which it refers. "Thus the figure of the female organ," Wright states, "easily assumed the rude form of a horseshoe, and as the original meaning was forgotten, would be readily taken for that object, and a real horseshoe nailed up for the same purpose. In this way originated . . . the vulgar practice of nailing a horseshoe upon buildings to protect them and all they contain against the power of witchcraft." One need not from this conclude that confusion of mind is always accompanied by confusion of sex. This little slip in the life of a busy pornographer does, however, help to reveal the typical care with which Hotten took his subject to himself and dramatizes the motto of his business—anything goes.

The second example concerns a work which Hotten intended as another sequel to Payne Knight's treatise. This book was written by John Davenport, a semilearned pornographic hack whom Ashbee regards with a certain amount of sympathy and respect. The book is called *Aphrodisiacs and Anti-Aphrodisiacs,* and Ashbee speaks of it as "an able and erudite work, well written, and fairly exhaustive of the subjects it treats of." It is none of these, unless one equates learning with the ability to copy out one's notes or repeat stories; in this sense gossip is a form of erudition. At the bottom of the title page is printed, "London: Privately Printed. 1869." The work was in fact printed in 1873—Hotten died before it came out of the press. But the custom of back-dating a new text is as common in this business as the practice of up-dating an old one; and one may add that in about half the cases of this practice no conceivable function is served. Except perhaps a psychological one— namely, that in the pornography business one should try as a rule never to tell the truth about anything; one should in fact lie on principle and transform petty fraud into a way of life. Hotten also wrote a circular in advertisement of this work, whose first paragraph reads: "Beautifully printed on toned paper, and only ONE HUNDRED COPIES, for private distribution. . . . £2. 10s." In reality, Ashbee lets us know, two hundred and fifty copies were printed; about half of these were sold in Europe, and the remainder went *"en bloc"* to J. W. Bouton of New York, a bookseller with whom Hotten had previous dealings. This illustrates the almost universal custom of misrepresenting the number of copies of a privately printed and "limited" edition. Most of the time the direction taken by this misrepresentation is to announce fewer copies than are actually printed; occasionally, however, one finds an inexplicable instance of the reverse.

The third illustration is my personal favorite, one of Hotten's wilder aberrations, and a kind of masterpiece of senseless obfuscation. In 1872 he reprinted seven works on flagellation, adding to them the date 1777, which is of course false. He also entitled the whole series as *Library Illustrative of Social Progress. From the Original Editions collected by the late Henry Thomas Buckle, Author of "A History of Civilization in England."* In a fly-sheet that Hotten distributed among his private customers, he expanded on these circumstances. "It is well known," he wrote, "that the late Henry Thomas Buckle . . . collected a large library of curious books. Amongst the many topics that engaged his attention was the subject of CHASTISEMENT, viz., discipline with a Birch or other implement. By rare good fortune, he collected an almost complete set of the astounding books issued by George Peacock, in the last century, and as no other examples of some of these rarities are known to exist, it is proposed to privately print a few copies as 'Curiosities of Literature.' Apart from their extreme rarity, the works are remarkable for the light they throw upon the state of society in the last century, and the mania that possessed all classes for chastising and being chastised." He goes on to describe the volumes and their price and lists their titles. Having reprinted this circular, Ashbee then rises up in what for him (Rome always in the exception) is the closest he ever comes to wrath—he was ever the mildest of debunkers. "Now in all this," he writes, "there is not a word of truth; the original tracts did not come from the library of Buckle, nor had he, in all probability, ever seen them. All seven had been for many years, and are still, in the possession of a well known London collector [guess who?] . . . . The fact is the present possessor of the volume in question lent it to Hotten, who had it surreptitiously reprinted, without the owner's permission or knowledge." One need not conjecture a reconstruction of the event, which must in any case have been simple enough. The striking thing about it is its aimlessness: one can't even determine whether Hotten meant it as a joke. Its floating and incoherent irrelevance, however, is representative of a genre whose only secret sometimes seems to be its ability to persuade the reader that psychosis is merely a heightened form of normality.

John Camden Hotten managed to keep a toehold in the respectable world. Nothing of the kind can be said of William Dugdale, who in the back-alley society of the pornography trade was, like T. S. Eliot's Macavity cat, "the Napoleon of crime." Born in 1800, this regular out-and-outer was, in Ashbee's words, "one of the most prolific publishers of filthy books." He carried on his business in a variety of locations in the vicinity of Drury Lane, Wych Street, and Holywell Street, and worked under the cover of such names as Turner, Smith, Young, and Brown. He spent a good deal of time in prison, and died in 1868 in the House of Correction. There is nothing he would not try, and some of his shifts are of a desperate ingenuity. He was a master of the racket of reprinting. He would, for example, take a work that was some fifty years old, alter but not entirely change the text and title—adding something in the way of further spice to both—and then reprint it as a new work, at two guineas a throw. He would then take this volume, divide it in half, add a few pages of new matter to each half, and publish it as another new work in two volumes, this time for three guineas. He published anything he could lay his hands on— from bawdy songsters at 6d. or 1/ to the gaudiest volumes for as much as he could wheedle. He reprinted the pornography of other pornographic publishers, sometimes changing the title, sometimes not bothering to; and he reprinted his own in as many sizes, shapes, and forms as he could invent—a true pirate, he even tried to steal from himself. He would not only reprint old works and fob them off as new; he would also do the reverse. *The New Epicurean; or, The Delights of Sex, Facetiously and Philosophically Considered, in Graphic Letters Addressed to Young Ladies of Quality* was one of his productions; at the bottom of the title page ran the legend "A New Edition. London: 1740. [Reprinted 1865.]" This was in fact no reprint but an original work, and 1865 was the date of its first publication.

Another one of his stratagems for swindling was to take sections or chapters from novels, give them a new title and print them as complete works. His printing and illustrations, as Ashbee observes, were almost uniformly of "villainous execution."

He printed books purporting to be translations from the French but that were actually English or American in origin. Frequently it is impossible to know what language his publications were written in originally, since most of the time, as Ashbee neatly puts it, his publications only indicate that "a careless printer had added his blunders to those of an illiterate author." He sometimes printed works that had teasing titles, such as *Intrigues and Confessions of a Ballet Girl,* which was followed by a racy and suggestive subtitle, but which was in content altogether innocent. He strikes one as a person who had a mania for print combined with a mania for concealment; and in a pinch he sometimes wrote his own pornography, *The Convent School, or Early Experiences of A Young Flagellant, by* "Rosa Belinda Coote," coming from his own free pen. He wrote his own descriptive and advertising copy, and as a sample of his prose, here is part of his blurb for *La Rose d'Amour,* an American pornographic novelette which he palmed off as a translation from the French. "One of the most remarkable works of the present day. Possessed of unbounded wealth, and of frame and of stamina of body apparently inexhaustible . . . this hero ravishes, seduces, and ruins all the females that come within his reach—rich and poor, gentle and simple, rough and refined, all fall down before his sceptre of flesh, his noble truncheon, his weapon of war. His great passion is for maidenheads, for young and unfledged virgins. . . . He travels the seas for new victims of his raging lust; he buys maidenheads by the score, he initiates them in all the mysteries of Venus, and finally, retires to his chateau with a seraglio of beauties. . . . Every page is a picture of sensual delight, and the book is illustrated with Sixteen Coloured Designs equal to the text. It is in two vols, and the price is Three guineas." One has to be possessed of a special kind of talent to be able to achieve such absolute anonymity, such level deadness of style; and it is not anticipating too much to say that in the writers and publishers of pornography, and in pornography itself, a certain kind of mechanical excitement of emotions through mechanical means, which has since spread itself throughout modern culture in general, is met with here in an early and primitive form.

Dugdale was the publisher of the famous "Don Leon" poems, supposedly by and about Byron. He himself apparently believed that they were genuine, and before he committed the manuscript to print approached a friend of Ashbee's and asked this man "to advise him as to how he could best approach Lady Byron, from whom he expected to get a large sum to suppress the publication." This attempt at extortion came to nothing, and Dugdale went back to his plain and fancy buccaneering. He was also one of the chief publishers during the Victorian period of pornographic periodicals. One of the writers who both translated stories for his magazines and supplied him with original material was James Campbell. And Campbell, we know, was a close associate of Ashbee's. The organic filaments that bind this little world or subculture together come into sight once again, and we see that the Olympian Ashbee and the subterranean Dugdale are connected by something more than a casual common interest. Yet it is Ashbee himself who has helped us to see even this far.

Chapter 3: THE SECRET LIFE—I

I

ASHBEE's singular merit was his ability to withhold comment on books he had seen or read. We now come to a work which, as far as I have been able to ascertain, has been written about exclusively by those who have not read it. By way of introduction, I should like to review some of this printed commentary. This procedure will, I believe, provide the reader with a fuller notion of what ordinarily passes for scholarship in the subculture we are examining.

The work in question is *My Secret Life,* and the single fact upon which all are agreed is its extreme rarity. The first comment I should like to reproduce is taken from Ralph Ginzburg's *An Unhurried View of Erotica,* a work of immaculate ignorance.[1] The comment occurs with typical inappropriateness in a chapter on "Reference Works." After acknowledging the book's great scarcity, Ginzburg goes on to describe it as

> an eleven volume encyclopedia of sexual knowledge of which only one copy is known to exist in the United States. It is titled *My Secret Life* and runs to 4,000 pages. Compiled by an anonymous but exceedingly wealthy Englishman, and printed in 1888 in an edition of just six copies, it describes every known form of sexual perversion, from lesbianism, pederasty and flagellomania to sodomy, incest and bestiality. The extensiveness of the work is indicated by the 223 sub-headings under "Copulation" to be found in its index.
>
> When the one known American copy of this work changed

[1] One notes with a mixture of sadness and dismay that the Introduction to this scandalously bad book was written by Theodor Reik, who called it "a courageous book that presents a valuable piece of conscientious research." *Quis custodiet ipsos custodes?*

hands some twenty-six years ago, the price was said to have been
$7,000.00. The compiler of the encyclopedia claimed to have per-
sonally tested all sexual aberrations described therein, which may
help to explain why the work reads much more like a series of
hastily jotted notations than does, for example, the *Encyclopaedia
Britannica.*

There is about as little truth in this description as is compatible
with the laws of probability. The proximate source of Ginzburg's misinformation, I believe, is a book entitled *Sex Life in
England Illustrated,* which was published in 1934 by a fly-by-
night outfit, the Falstaff Press. This work purports to be a translation of Iwan Bloch's *Das Geschlechtsleben in England,* a performance in three volumes, first published in 1901—but it is
nothing of the kind. Bloch's work was itself a sloppy and con-
scienceless piece of second-hand retailing. He seems to have
been befriended by Ashbee and allowed free-run in the latter's
library; but large portions of *Das Geschlechtsleben in England*
are made up of outright and unacknowledged cribbing from
Ashbee's three-volume bibliography. The 1934 English-
language version of Bloch's work is so mangled as to be virtually indescribable: it was something of a translation, something
of an abridgment, and something of an altogether new creation. The perpetrator of this farrago gave himself as one Richard Deniston, and by 1936, it seems, things had gotten into
such a state of confusion that an "Explanatory Foreword" of
some twelve pages was printed in the form of a folder to be
tipped into the earlier version. This foreword is intended to be
an "analytical comparison of the original German edition with
the completed, modernized, illustrated, checked and corrected"
compound of fraud and theft that Deniston had put out in
1934. Pages 209–210 of that work consist of a description of *My
Secret Life;* they are, apparently, Deniston's handiwork and
were not in Bloch's original three volumes. They are also the
chief source of Ginzburg's passage—the figure of $7,000, how-
ever, occurs in the latterly added "Explanatory Foreword."

But Deniston himself had not read *My Secret Life,* and his

two pages on it are literally pirated from something called *For-bidden Books,* which was an elaborate catalogue put out in 1902 by Charles Carrington, a publisher of pornography whose headquarters were in Paris. Carrington had an undetermined but small number of sets of this work in his possession and was trying to get rid of them for sums ranging from £60 to £75 "according to the condition." [2] The story that Carrington tells is as follows:

> About the year 1888, a well-known bookseller and publisher of Amsterdam, whose specialty was literature of an incandescent kind, was summoned to London by one of his customers, a rich old Englishman, who desired to have privately printed for his own enjoyment an enormous MSS.; containing in the fullest detail all the secret venereal thoughts of his existence. He defrayed all costs of printing, on condition that no more than six copies should be struck off. A few years afterwards, this eccentric amateur shuffled off the mortal coil; and a few copies of the extraordinary work made a timid appearance on the market. . . . It is evident that many more than the half-dozen copies stipulated must have been printed—let us say about twenty-five or so—as I have unfrequently seen a complete series, and I should say that at the time I am writing the book may be obtained by careful searching. . . .

Carrington then proceeds to make his pitch. He further notes that in 1894 the original publisher or printer of the work had issued as a prospectus, "evidently to whet the curiosity of collectors," a volume containing the introduction and prefaces to Volume I, the index to the chapters of all the volumes, and the alphabetical index from the eleventh volume. (And in 1901 Carrington himself had published, in part as a prospectus, the first six chapters of Volume I under the title *The Dawn of Sensuality.*) Carrington makes some additional descriptive remarks about the work, which are largely erroneous, and then concludes his notice with an excerpt from the alphabetical

---

[2] Somewhat earlier than this, Carrington printed a circular advertising three sets of this work for sale at £100 each and implying that a fourth had already been sold. This circular is contained in *Bibliotheca Carringtoniensis,* a unique collection of Carrington's advertising handbills, prospectuses, and catalogues bound together. It is in the possession of the Institute for Sex Research.

index of Volume XI and a lengthy sample quotation. The excerpted part of the index reprints the more than 200 items (on principle I have refused to count them exactly) which in the original are listed under the head of "Fucking," but for which Carrington coyly substitutes "Copulating." The long quotation is made up of two chapters run together—they are the last chapter of Volume VI and the first of Volume VII—and consists of an account, told to the author of *My Secret Life* by a woman with whom he was having an affair, of how on the eve of the Battle of Solferino she and her sister were raped by a number of Austrian soldiers. These passages in the *Forbidden Books* of 1902, therefore, seem to be the ultimate source of almost all the subsequently published information and misinformation about *My Secret Life*.

Carrington was a thoroughgoing rogue, and there is no reason to believe anything he said or wrote, except under one condition. Like most publishers, he was chiefly interested in making money, and it is impossible to believe that he would go to such lengths in advertising if he had not had possession of at least a few of the sets. And the errors of description which occur in his discussion of the book are of a kind with John Camden Hotten's mistaking of a horseshoe for a bent priapus. They are errors made by a man whose brains are addled in the first place and whose defective powers of concentration are the conditions of his interest in this subject—the refinement of nullity involved in the idea of writing advertising copy for pornography is almost beyond contemplation. But they are not the kind of errors made by someone who is unfamiliar with the work. (Of course I do not by this mean to say that Carrington had "read" the work in any reasonable understanding of the word.) In addition, one remark in the text of *My Secret Life* tends to confirm Carrington's account. Toward the end of Volume XI, the author pauses a last time to look back over his work. Most of it is already in print, and he makes a final, italicized description of it as *"eleven volumes, of which six copies only have been struck off and the type then broken up."* Carrington's first advertising circular goes along with this story, but his second notice, the one printed in *Forbidden Books,* clearly implies that the author was tricked or cheated by the printer-publisher, who struck off a good many more copies than had been contracted for. In the light of what little evidence there is, I am inclined to accept Carrington's second account, though I should put the number of sets at a somewhat lower figure than the twenty-five that Carrington breezily specifies.

The other few items in the printing history of this work are easily summarized. In 1923 two volumes entitled *Ma Vie Secrète* were published; these consist of about 350 pages translated from Volumes I and II, and are themselves only a selection from those volumes. In 1930 these were reprinted in three volumes, and illustrations were added. In the early 1930's the first three volumes of the original English were reprinted in New York. Police intervention in the shape of the New York Society for the Suppression of Vice stopped the project at that point, but it seems that someone was able to bribe a policeman to smuggle out Volume V, and in 1934 this volume, with about thirty pages of the original omitted, was published under the title *Marital Frolics.* These are all the relevant external facts or circumstances about *My Secret Life* that I have been able to gather.[3]

---

[3] There is one more: at the present time three copies of this work are known definitely to exist.

The sources of bibliographical information about *My Secret Life* are: Rolf S. Reade (pseud. of Alfred Rose), *Registrum Librorum Eroticorum* (London, 1936), II, 233, 352; Louis Perceau, *Bibliographie du Roman Erotique au XIXe Siècle,* II, 151–155; and unlisted material housed in the Institute for Sex Research. Within the last few years, G. Legman published a bibliographical introduction to a reprinting of Ashbee's three volumes, in which much of this material is rehearsed. (This introduction has been republished in *The Horn Book; Studies in Erotic Folklore and Bibliography* [New Hyde Park, 1964].) In this essay, Legman makes the shrewd and ingenious guess that Ashbee is also the author of *My Secret Life.* There are a number of facts which Legman marshals in support of this bold stab in the dark, and it is possible that he may be right. There are, however, many more facts that seem to me to controvert this argument. In addition, Legman's essay is marred by a number of careless errors in scholarship and above all by the fact that he writes about *My Secret Life* without, apparently, having read more than three or four volumes.

II

My Secret Life consists of eleven uniform volumes, the whole coming to some 4,200 pages. It is in small crown octavo and is printed on handmade ribbed paper. The title page of each volume bears the imprint, "Amsterdam. Not for publication." There is no date, but we can be reasonably certain that it was printed over a period of time in which 1890 can stand as a midpoint. It is printed rather poorly; errors in spelling, syntax, and punctuation occur very frequently and are of a sort to make it almost certain that the compositor or typesetter possessed French—not Dutch—as his native language. The volumes were not proofread, either at the printing house or by the author. The manuscript seems to have been presented in large-sized batches to the printer, who would then run them up, hand over the printed volumes to the author, and receive in turn additional manuscript. At the beginning of Volume III, for example, the author states that the first two volumes are already in print, that he has read them over and noticed the errors in typography and spelling.[4] The work took at least several years to get into print (in his first advertising notice Carrington says seven), and the author, who was by then in his middle sixties, was clearly impatient to get it all done and anxious not to "prolong the time of completion."

The author of *My Secret Life* was genuinely, though not entirely, concerned to maintain his identity in secret. To this end he suppresses dates, changes names, alters places, and resorts to other devices; but he does this so haphazardly and with such lack of consistency and thoroughness that it is no problem at all to discover whatever is necessary for dating or placing the incidents he describes. (We can assume as a self-evident fact that, if

---

[4] In the interests of clarity and ease of reading, I have not hesitated to correct errors in spelling and typography and normalize the text's punctuation. In places where the original punctuation is a source of ambiguity, however, I have preserved the printed version.

he really wanted to keep everything secret, he would not have printed this work or, for that matter, even written the manuscript.) In the short Introduction to Volume I, he tries to hide himself behind himself. He states in that place that he is really only the editor of this manuscript, that the "huge parcel carefully tied up and sealed" was entrusted to him by a friend who was then ill and who instructed him to burn the manuscript if the illness proved fatal. It did, he forgot about the packet for some years, and only rediscovered it by accident. He read it, pondered over it and his friend's instructions for some further years, and finally "feeling that it would be sinful to destroy such a history, I copied the manuscript and destroyed the original," suppressing names, dates, and so forth, and has now decided to give it to the world. This device is transparent and is meant to convince no one—not even the author, since he makes absolutely no further use of it. It reminds one, however, in a sad and feeble little way of the Introduction to *Waverley* and of the frame of *Sartor Resartus,* and is a kind of witless parody of them, just as its serial printing unintentionally parodies the nineteenth-century novel.

The eleven volumes of *My Secret Life* are a unique document. They are the sexual memoirs of a Victorian gentleman who began to memorialize himself at a very early age and who continued to do so for more than forty years. According to the author's own account—which appears as marginalia scattered throughout the eleven volumes—he had, like many other Englishmen of his time, "kept a diary of some sort," which he began in his youth. Some time between his twenty-third and twenty-fifth years, however, he began to write memoirs, extended records or accounts of his sexual adventures or experiences. He pursued this writing for a number of years, then "tired of it and ceased." At about the age of thirty-five, he met a woman with whose aid, and the aid of those to whom she introduced him, he "did, said, saw, and heard, well nigh everything a man and a woman could do with their genitals." Under the impact of this experience, he "began to narrate those events, when quite fresh in my memory, a great variety of incidents extending over four years." He subsequently parted with this woman, and shortly thereafter "set to work to describe the events of the intervening years of my youth and early middle age."

At about this time he was stricken by the first of two illnesses, to which he responded in a double or ambivalent way. He was obliged to stay at home, and during this period, he writes, "I amused myself by reading, sorting and arranging these memoirs. I referred to them by dates in my diary, and made them in their order pretty complete. I used to lock myself in my room for the entire day, and said among other things that I was writing a book." At the same time, the illness evidently frightened him enough to make him "think seriously of burning the whole." He could not bring himself to do so and laid the manuscript "aside again for a couple of years." The second illness then struck him, and during the "long uninterrupted leisure" that convalescence required, he turned once again to the manuscript, reread it, "and filled in some occurrences which I had forgotten, but which my diary enabled me to place in their proper order." It was at this time that the thought first occurred to him that "I would print my work that had been commenced more than twenty years before." He hesitated before this idea, however. He was now about forty-five years old, and had, he interestingly says, "entered upon my maturity, and on to the most lascivious portion of my life." This period was to extend for almost twenty further years; the events in it "were disjointed and fragmentary," and the author's practice and "amusement was to describe them just after they occurred. Most frequently the next day I wrote all down with much prolixity; since, I have much abbreviated it."

What can be observed, then, is that by about the time the author had reached the midpoint of his career as a memoirist a rough paradigm of a method of composition had emerged and stabilized itself. It emerged out of a complicated and irregular series of interchanges between diary notes, notes in the form of copious memoranda, and fully written out episodes, and may be typified as follows. The author would have a sexual experience and would make a diary notation of it. Shortly thereafter, most usually within a couple of days, he would sit down and write out the episode in as much detail as he could. Over a period of time, quantities of manuscript would accumulate, and at uncertain though increasingly frequent intervals the author would reread, rearrange, sort, order, revise, abbreviate, edit, and add comment to portions of the ever enlarging mass. When the author arrived at the decision to commit himself to print, a final further rereading and revision of the manuscript was undertaken. It was at this moment that he began to change names and suppress dates and places; he also decided to change and unify the tense of the narrative throughout—replacing the present tense, in which a good deal of the original manuscript was written, with the past. In the course of his rereadings, he would often add passages of critical or ideological reflection on the episode described, on his own attitudes, on changes that had since occurred in him; and during the final rereading and editing, he sometimes added comments to the comments. On some occasions he would insert these comments in square brackets; on others he would recast an entire passage. Here is a typical passage taken from volume VI:

> During this time I travelled alone, and had no one to interrupt me, or to make demands upon my time for companionship, and so I could arrange my erotic intentions beforehand and surely carry them out. In the intervals of my enjoyment of female society, I amused myself by making notes, or writing the narratives fully. [This I find now by rough perusal of manuscript not yet touched, has a freshness which is not in some of that revised, and which I think I have already said elsewhere, was written out from memoranda (memoranda very copious it is true) many years after.] And I had at the end of two years a very large mass of manuscript, mostly relating to my frolics with the professed Paphians. This I largely abbreviated soon after, and shall do so still more now. This following paragraph I leave exactly as I then wrote it.

Four or five stages of composition can be made out here. The body of the paragraph itself was written at the time of the author's first revision of the section of manuscript to which it refers. The part within brackets was inserted during the final reading and editing (and perhaps transcribing) of the manuscript before it was given to the printer. Behind these are at least two other stages. The first occurred at the time of the sexual experiences, and consisted of notes and full narratives intermixed. The second took place after two years and was an abridgment of what had in that interval been written. And between this and the first final stage of editorial revision there may have occurred another recasting of some of the memoranda into the form of connected narrative.

Here is a slightly different one. "I told Amelia that I saw no objection to women amusing each other sexually if they liked, but she affected dislike—or really felt it. Did she? These thoughts only occur to me as I think over matters, and write this narrative [and still more as I revise them after many years]." In this sample, three phases are clearly present: the final bracketed comment; the reflection set down when the narrative was being written; and the memorandum from which the narrative was copied or composed.

In certain ways, therefore, the text of *My Secret Life* has something of the quality of a palimpsest—particularly since the author was not always concerned to indicate his revisions. But it should in addition be emphasized that the author in no way followed this procedure with any kind of regularity, tenacity of purpose, or organizing conception. He did not hesitate to print unrevised passages, dislocated jottings, repetitive episodes or adventures. He had little interest in formal or internal consistency, and no interest in formal structure. Like Ashbee's bibliography, *My Secret Life* is not to be thought of as primarily a triumph of intellect—of insight shaped by discipline and method—over tabooed and refractory material. But it is something equally interesting, for it reveals to us the workings and broodings of a mind that had for an entire lifetime been possessed by a single subject or interest. It further reveals to us how that interest had shaped the mind and person which it possessed; how the mind which was possessed attempted in turn to cope with the forces which possessed it; and how, during the Victorian period, a man who tried directly to deal with the demons of sexuality lived and felt and thought. That in itself, we shall see, is triumph enough.

The external life history of this man who devoted so much of his time to what he calls his "inner" or "secret," that is, sexual, life is easy enough to outline, his efforts at obscurity and obfuscation being so incomplete and often perfunctory. He seems to have been born some time between 1820 and 1825. When he is about twenty-one years old, he tells us, he meets with a French prostitute, and he goes on to say that there were few French whores in the London of that day because the railway to Paris had not yet opened, and implies that the railway was just about to open. The line between Paris and Rouen was opened in 1843, and so it seems that the author may have been born about 1822. Certain other details of internal evidence allow us to fix his dates with relative certainty. In early adolescence, for example, he remarks of a departed maidservant, " 'Perhaps she has gone with a bobby,' " and adds, "it was a current joke then, policemen not having been long invented." Bobbies were of course invented by the Metropolitan Police Act of 1828, and although there is no record of the literary use of this term before 1851, it was in currency long before that.[5] If we choose a midpoint between those two dates as a possible approximate time of his remark, we arrive again at some date during the period 1820–1825 as the time of his birth. As for a date of termination, we already know something from the printing history of *My Secret Life*. To this it may be added that halfway through Volume X, the author uses the expression "Tommy Atkins," which indicates

[5] See John S. Farmer and W. E. Henley, *Slang and Its Analogues* (London, 1890–1904), I, 270; and Eric Partridge, *A Dictionary of Slang and Unconventional English* (London, 1949), p. 73.

that he was still actively engaged in writing the narrative after 1882, the year of the campaign in Egypt which brought forth that term.

There is, however, an interesting kind of confusion that attaches to the precise dating of *My Secret Life*. In Volume IV, we read the following sentence: "Now in the year 18—, a year of national importance, and one in which strangers came from all parts of the world to London, I was to have a French woman again." This can only be 1851, the year of the Great Exhibition, when the author should be, according to the foregoing calculations, between twenty-five and thirty. Other internal evidence, however, makes it seem likely that he is several years older. Two volumes later, he is recounting an event that took place "two years after the battle of Solferino," and remarks that he "was then entering into middle age." This locates the episode in 1861, and again pleasantly confirms our idea of the author's date of birth, if one assumes that the author regards the age of thirty-five as the entry to middle age. But there is considerable evidence—including the fact that he dates his "maturity" from about the age of forty-five—which leads one to believe that he is at least five years older. Such gaps or discrepancies are not primarily evidence of systematic deception on the part of the author; nor are they essentially proofs of weakness of memory. They are largely a result of the fact that the author measures time by other and more flexible intervals than those marked on the calendar—he lives by sexual time and is, as far as I know, the first person who has ever recorded himself as having done so. He indicates a period in his youth, for instance, by remarking: "How long after this the following took place, I can't say, but my cock was bigger. I have that impression very distinctly." He similarly dates his entrance upon maturity by an increase in the complexity or elaborateness of his sexual life; and his passage into old age begins when he notices a gradual but steady decline in his ability to achieve repeated orgasm. And as the passage I have quoted about 1851 reveals, the really important thing about that year was that while the author was making sexual acquaintance with his second French woman the Great Exhibition happened to take place.

Nevertheless, what we learn of the external circumstances of the author's life is of surpassing interest, not only because it is that aspect of his life which he most wishes to suppress, but also because it creates the indispensable context in which his "inner" or "secret" life was led. He was born into a wealthy upper-middle-class family, and was, he tells us, one of a number of children—he records the death of two brothers and one sister, and the survival, along with himself, of two other sisters and a third brother. Until the age of twelve, he "never went to school; there was a governess in the house who instructed me and the other children; my father was nearly always at home." There were a considerable number of maidservants by whom the children were surrounded, and the author remarks that he "was carefully kept from the grooms and other men servants," who lived in a separate and distant part of the domestic establishment.

Since the author was from childhood "intended for the Army," it seems doubtful that he could have been the eldest son, and it is difficult to decide whether the death of two brothers made him heir. In any event, some short time after the author was sent to school, his father "got into difficulties, we moved into a smaller house, I was sent to another school," and his father went abroad for a year "to look after some plantations." After a year's absence, "my father came home broken hearted, I have heard, and ill. Soon after we only kept two female servants, a man outside the house, and a gardener." His father was ordered to the seaside to rest; "my mother went with him, taking the children and one servant," and the young son "remained at home so as to go to school." This was a public school, and the author was, he says, "a day scholar only," a circumstance in which he took some small amount of comfort since he was a "shy and reserved" boy; and although he "greedily listened to all the lewd talk" of the other boys, he was relieved at being exempt from a forced intimacy. His father's illness seems to have extended for two or three years and was ended by his death, upon which event it was discovered that he was "nearly bankrupt."

The author was about sixteen years old at this time, and he tells us that "after father's death, our circumstances were further reduced . . . we had come to a small house nearer London; one sister went to boarding-school, an aunt (I had many) took another, I went to a neighbouring great school or college, as it was termed," and a younger brother remained at home. Such a reduction was obviously neither very drastic nor permanent, since shortly after the death of his father, he relates, his godfather, who had looked after him in the absence of his father and, later, in the absence of both parents when they were at the seaside, died "and left me a fortune." The author continued to prepare for the Army, and for a while seems to have taken up some obscure employment. When he was of age, however, and "came into my property," he made a decision that caused "great horror" to his mother and his family. He gave up "my post . . . and my intended career, and determined to live and enjoy myself. I had been all but posted to a regiment; that commission I resigned, though all my youth desiring it. I lost much money by doing so." And so at the age of twenty-one, determined to live and enjoy himself in a style befitting his idea of himself, he "went regularly on the town." (In terms of the memoirs, this occurs toward the end of the first volume.)

The next interval of time in the author's life occupies some five years. During that period, he had numerous adventures, many of them occurring in the country, where various branches of his large family lived. "Most of my relatives lived in the provinces," he writes, "and were wealthy." Many of these adventures were undertaken in the company of a particularly wild and profligate cousin of about the same age as the author. From the very start, it seems, the author came in for the severe disapproval of his family; his one "remaining guardian and my mother . . . [were] always at me with advice, which I entirely disregarded, and flung away money in all directions. Had I

spent it only on women it would have lasted years longer."
Within several years, the money he had inherited from his godfather was gone, and he became "almost dependent again on
my mother, who did nothing but upbraid me; my hopes cen-
tered in my old relative, who had promised to make me his
heir. He was not so gracious to me as he used to be; he murmured at my extravagance, and supposed that any money I had
would go down the same sink, by which he meant women. He
died suddenly, just as he was in greatest wrath with me, and
left me nothing." Deprived of this expectation, the author
found consolation in women and in "an aunt in London, child-
less and rich," who gave him certain sums of money and after-
ward left him more.

The author spent about a year in "needy and discontented"
circumstances, and then in his twenty-sixth year he "committed
a more fatal error than spending a fortune in jollity." He married, unquestionably for money, and thereupon became "utterly
wretched." His life, he now writes, was "utterly changed; I
was quite needy, with a yearly income (and that not my own)
not more than I used to spend in a month, sometimes in a fortnight. Every shilling I had to look at, walked miles where I
used to ride . . . amusements were beyond me, my food was
the simplest. . . . I tried to make the best of my life and could
when by myself be cheerful, even in the recollection of the past
fun; but there was that about me now which brought sorrow
over me. The instant I saw her, she checked my smile, sneered
at my past, moaned over my future, was a nightmare to me, a
very spectre." He then goes on to make the following confession, the first of the numerous remarkable statements in *My
Secret Life* that I have occasion to quote.

> I tried to like, to love her. It was impossible. Hateful in day, she
> was loathesome to me in bed. Long I strove to do my duty, and be
> faithful, yet to such a pitch did my disgust at length go, that
> laying by her side, I had wet dreams nightly, sooner than relieve
> myself in her. I have frigged myself in the streets before entering
> my house, sooner than fuck her. I loving women . . . ready to be

kind and loving to her, was driven to avoid her as I would a corpse. I have followed a woman for miles with my prick stiff, yet went to my wretched home pure, because I had vowed to be chaste. My heart was burning to have an affectionate kiss, a voluptuous sigh from some woman, yet I avoided obtaining it. My health began to give way; sleepless nights, weary days made me contemplate suicide.

This is one of the rare passages of self-pity in all the eleven volumes, and the violence and directness of the emotion in it almost redeem the self-pity. It reminds one, furthermore, of a Pre-Raphaelite painting with the missing details, for once, added. In the end, of course, he did not commit suicide or remain chaste, but resumed his career of whoring, whereupon his emotions were again stabilized.

He sums up this period of his "narrowest means" by stating that "in that time I must have seen the privates of fifty women, and copulated with nearly that number. Had it not been for their pleasures, coarse as they were, I think I should have made away with myself, so miserable was I." And he adds that he would have broken down "had it not been for the whores. Cunt came to my rescue, and alone gave me forgetfulness, a relief far better than gambling or drinking, the only other alternatives I could have had recourse to." If one accepts the legitimacy of his terms of choice, I do not see how it is possible to disagree with him. This epoch of extreme constraint comes to an end when "a remnant of my former fortune which had been in litigation was settled in my favour, and I had a little ready money. Immediately I left off frequenting the poor doxies . . . and went to a higher class, in a better neighbourhood. My money was soon gone, for I had debts among other things to settle out of it." Nevertheless, one of the inestimable advantages of being an English gentleman and enjoying the benefits of the English system of inheritance once again makes itself shown, for after a brief interval, he inherits yet again, coming "into a better income through the death of a relative. It was small, but made a difference to me of great importance. I spent it all on myself, that is to say on cunt. . . ." The reader will have already noted that one of the great corollary themes of this work—indeed organically inseparable from its interest in sex—is money.

Meanwhile, he remains married. In reply to a woman acquaintance's question, "why did I not separate from my wife," he candidly answers, "I shall be all but a pauper without her money." "What of that," she returns, "if you are unhappy?" And he reflects to himself, "But I was always hoping for happier days, hoping,—hoping,—hoping"—hoping in fact for his wife's death and his inheritance of her fortune. Moreover, at this stage of his life, his miserable marriage offers him a further means of rationalizing his behavior and making his compulsive promiscuity acceptable to himself. One evening, a typical episode occurs. Returning home late through darkened streets, he becomes embroiled in a three-sided escapade with a street whore and a drunken sailor. A few minutes later, he lets himself into his house.

> Then a dread came over me, I had fucked a common street nymph, and in the sperm of a common sailor; both might have the pox—what more probable. I could feel the sperm wet and sticky around my prick, and on my balls. I had then taken to sleep in my dressing-room. My wife, I thought, must have been according to habit an hour abed. On entering my room there sat she reading, which was a very unusual thing. I sat down wishing she would leave the room, for I wanted to wash; and wondered what she would say if she saw me washing my prick at that time of night, or heard me splashing.

He retires to the water closet to wash and then returns to his room.

> Fear of the pox kept me awake some time. Then the scene I had passed through excited me so violently, that my prick stood like steel. I could not dismiss it from my mind. I was violently in rut. I thought of frigging, but an irrepressible desire for cunt, cunt, and nothing but it made me forget my fear, my dislike to my wife, our quarrel, and everything else—and jumping out of bed I went into her room.
>
> "I shan't let you,—what do you wake me for, and come to me in

such a hurry after you have not been near me for a couple of months,—I shan't,—you shan't,—I dare say you know where to go."

But I jumped into bed, and forcing her on to her back, drove my prick up her. It must have been stiff, and I violent, for she cried out that I hurt her. "Don't do it so hard,—what are you about!" But I felt that I could murder her with my prick, and drove, and drove, and spent up her cursing. While I fucked her I hated her,—she was my spunk-emptier. "Get off, you've done it,— and your language is most revolting." Off I went into my bedroom for the night.

However one wishes to judge this man, his representation of this scene has an unmistakable ring of authenticity. On this occasion, fantasy or "ideality" is not blurring or distorting his powers of observation; and there is none of the self-inflation and self-aggrandizement that make most sexual memoirs so distasteful and untrustworthy—for example, the autobiography of Frank Harris. In addition, as we shall see, the relation of such scenes to Victorian literature is of considerable interest.

His marriage continues for several years, as do his extramarital activities. Luckily for him, and in a surprisingly un-Victorian fashion, he seems never to have had a child by his wife, although he does report a number of instances in which he impregnated women of various kinds—servants, respectable women with whom he had affairs, courtesans whom he briefly kept. A few of these had children, the largest number procured abortion, which seems to have been fairly easy to arrange in the England of the time (he does not report on this in detail). His family is dispersed, his mother dies, "one sister was married, and was not much comfort to me; the other was far off, my brother nowhere." Just then, as in countless Victorian novels, another inheritance falls upon him and changes the course of his life; "a distant relative left me a largish sum of money" is his characteristic way of representing it.[6] Our author, however,

---

[6] Whether such an event is fact or fantasy is not, in this context, decisive. If it is fact, then we have to assimilate this fact—of repeated inheritance—to our knowledge of Victorian life and literature. If it is fantasy, then it is significant that, out of all the possible ways of being liberated that could be imagined, he chooses this one repeatedly, this stock in trade, this hoary convention of the Victorian novelistic imagination.

is not the hero of the Victorian novel, and his manner of dealing with his good fortune is to keep it a secret.

> . . . it was scarcely known to any one of my friends, quite un-
> known at home, and to none until I had spent a good deal of it. I
> kept the fact to myself till I had put matters in such train that I
> could get a couple of thousand pounds on account, then quietly
> fitted myself out with clothes. One day I sent home new portman-
> teaus, and packed up my clothes the same day. "I am going
> abroad," I said. "When?" "Tonight." "Where to?" "I don't know,
> —that is my business." "When do you come back?" "Perhaps in a
> week,—perhaps a year"—nor did I for a long time. I never wrote
> to England during that time, excepting to my solicitors and
> bankers who necessarily knew where I had been at times.

He then enters a new phase in his sexual career. He goes to
Europe and undertakes an Erotic Grand Tour of the Continent. He travels to the great cities and the watering places, and
he writes of his adventures with English, American, and European travelers, with servants, and of course with prostitutes. He
seeks out the brothels wherever he finds himself and writes of
his experiences in them. In short, he represents Europe as seen
through the eye of a penis. We are now in Volume IV, and
throughout the balance of the work he regularly interrupts his
pursuits in England with travels abroad.

He continues to accumulate experiences. By the time we get
to Volume VI he is about thirty-five years old and is on one of
his tours of the Continent when "a special messenger overtook
me and brought me news. I had missed letters at the *poste
restante*. Death had done its work. Hurrah! I was free at last. I
travelled home night and day, hurriedly arranged affairs, gave
carte blanche to solicitors and agents, and with lighter heart
than I had had for years went abroad again." He is now a
wealthy man, lives and travels "under changed social conditions . . . was free from care . . . and altogether it was a
happy time. I raced about Europe for two or three months, and
had constant change of scene." His new opulence gives him the
opportunity to elaborate his sexual activities still further, to act
out his fantasy life, and in the brothels of Europe (mostly
Paris) and in the company of the high-priced courtesans of

London he extends his experiences in the only direction they can go—toward the sexual life as it is represented in pornographic fiction.

After about four or five years, another change occurs. He falls in love, apparently remarries, and for fifteen months leads a "chaste," that is, faithful, life. It is agony. He prints memoranda written at the time.

> It is a full quarter of a century since my prick first entered a woman's cunt. A great change has now taken place in my social condition, and full fifteen months passed away during which I have been chaste. I do not find a single note or memorandum about illicit amours as they are called. Indeed can swear that I never had any, and that all my sexual worship was given to one woman. Never before or since have I been so faithful, but *she* is worthy of it. Then a change ensued. How well I recollect when I lapsed into my former habits of sensuality, spite of my struggles with myself to avoid doing so.

> For fifteen months, I have been contented with one woman. I love her devotedly. I would die to make her happy. Yet such is my sensuous temperament, such my love of women, that much as I strive against it, I find it impossible to keep faithful to her, to keep to her alone.
>
> I have wept over this weakness, have punished myself in fines, giving heavily to charities the money which would have paid for other women. I have frigged myself to avoid having a woman whose beauty has tempted my lust. I have when on the point of accosting a lovely frail one jumped into a cab and frigged myself right off, though unavoidably thinking of the charms I had not seen. I have avoided Argyle and Cremorne, and any other place to which whores resort, for fear of being tempted. I have fucked at home with fury and repetition, so that no sperm should be left to rise my prick to stiffness when away from home; fucked indeed till advised by my doctor that it was as bad for her as for me.
>
> All is useless. The desire for change seems invincible. . . . I sicken with desire, pine for unseen, unknown cunts. My life is almost unbearable from unsatisfied lust. It is constantly on me, depresses me, and I must yield.

And in a bracketed passage of reflection written at some later date he remarks: "I loved deeply, truly, shall love to my dying hour, and in spite of my infidelity, would at any time have slain any one of my paramours rather than have given her pain. Why with this feeling I sought the Cyprians, demireps, sluts, and strumpets, which I have done, I cannot explain, nor the frame of mind which led me into lascivious vagaries and aberrations, fancies and caprices yet to be told of." He tells us nothing about this woman, barely mentions her again. And just as there is a note of authenticity in his stating that he gave money to charities in an effort to avoid infidelity, so also does it seem authentic that the one woman whom he loves and "respects" should not be part of his "secret life."

Having broken down again in his attempt to be faithful, he resumes his former activities, and from here until the end of the work he leads a life of stable promiscuity. His appetite for an endless variety of women never abates; at the same time he intermixes his casual adventures with a number of long-lasting liaisons with several London courtesans. His sexual tastes continue to evolve, and his experiments in perversity continue as well. As his years advance his sexual powers gradually and concomitantly decline. When he finishes Volume XI he is somewhere in his sixties.

III

Since *My Secret Life* is the most important document of its kind about Victorian England, we might use it to test the thesis which holds that writings of a sexual nature are of a unique value or importance as social history. In other words, what in the way of social history do we learn from such a work? Does it contain matters of general importance that have been suppressed, overlooked, or forgotten by historians?[7] In the first place, a work of more than 4,000 pages which concentrates re-

---

[7] I am aware that in Chapter 2 I argued against the value of this notion and that this may seem a contradiction of that argument. I trust that the reader will see that I am not following the line of reasoning pursued by Ashbee—and others—and that my arguments tend in an altogether different direction. Furthermore, *My Secret Life* is the only work from the period that I know of which can even pretend to offer this kind of material for analysis.

morselessly on one image, the human body—its organs, functions, and operations—is bound to provide a host of details
about how that image, or body, is managed, how its biology is
dealt with. *My Secret Life* tells us a good deal about the excre-
mental functions, and about the conduct of personal hygiene in
Victorian England. For example, we learn that, before the
middle of the century, in such places of public resort as Hamp-
ton Court Park there were no toilets. Men and women, including gentlemen and ladies, would go off into the bushes, to
"some vacant place on which dead leaves and sweepings were
shot down," and relieve themselves. Women would wipe themselves by tucking their shifts between their legs. We learn as
well that during the early part of the period women, "even
ladies," wore no drawers. Some time after the turn of the middle of the century, women began to wear undergarments, and
this change in fashion is not welcomed by our author. "More
and more this fashion of wearing drawers seems to be spreading," he complains in Volume IX. "Formerly no woman wore
them, but now whether lady, servant, or whore, they all wear
them. I find they hinder those comfortable chance feels of bum
and cunt, of which I have had so many." Similarly, we learn
that until fairly late in the century the London streets were a
veritable barnyard.

> The angle of the street named as leading out of the Strand was
> dark of a night and a favorite place for doxies to go to relieve their
> bladders. The police took no notice of such trifles, provided it was
> not done in the greater thoroughfare (although I have seen at
> night women do it openly in the gutters in the Strand); in the
> particular street I have seen them pissing almost in rows; yet they
> mostly went in twos to do that job, for a woman likes a screen,
> one usually standing up till the other has finished, and then tak-
> ing her turn. Indeed the pissing in all bye-streets of the Strand
> was continuous, for although the population of London was only
> half of what it now is, the number of gay ladies seemed double
> there.

Such typical details are thickly scattered throughout the pages
of *My Secret Life* and act, I suppose, as a useful reminder of the
adage that civilizations are built on middens.

Since the author describes literally hundreds of his experiences with prostitutes, *My Secret Life* provides us with a good deal of information about how part of sexual life in Victorian England was organized or institutionalized.[8] As we read his accounts of the London streets and parks at night, we are reminded that in one respect at least the London of 1850 still bore considerable resemblance to the city of Boswell's London Journal. If one wanted to take a prostitute—or any woman—to some place indoors, "accommodation houses" of various degrees of costliness were to be found in every part of London. Here is one to which the author resorted when he was still a youth: "It was a gentleman's house, although the room cost but five shillings: red curtains, looking-glasses, wax lights, clean linen, a huge chair, a large bed, and a cheval-glass, large enough for the biggest couple to be reflected in, were all there." In the sixties and seventies "any coffee house with the word 'beds' on the windows" was also available for sexual use. The author is extremely knowledgeable about the economics of sexuality in the England of his time and is as precise—and as interested—in his notations of costs as he is in his descriptions of physiology. At one point, he strikes up an acquaintance with the manageress of one accommodation house and helps her cast up her accounts, discovering by accident that she cannot write.

> The takings were put on slips of paper by the servants, and by some process of her own which she could not explain, she got a rough sort of check on the servants to prevent them robbing her. She had to account to the real owner of the house—and how she did it she alone knows. This is certain (she once admitted it), that from the takings she put a pound a day into her own pocket. Whether she robbed the owner to that extent, or whether it was her admitted share, I never knew. She was well dressed, had excellent food, allowed her Guardsman money, her sister's husband money, and others too, I rather think. But after she had taken her

---

[8] One of the author's counterparts by analogy was William Ewart Gladstone. He too regularly walked the London streets at night, accosted prostitutes, and then tried to help them—to offer them aid or even take them home to tea. One fancifully imagines a meeting between these two Victorians—what an abyss would have opened between these two representatives of a single culture. See Philip Magnus, *Gladstone: A Biography* (New York, 1954), *passim*.

three or four hundred pounds a year, there was a splendid income handed over to some one. This house had but eight rooms, and two mere closets, to let out for fucking; they often took twenty pounds a day, and sometimes much more.

In such a passage the author is at his best; his tone is exactly right. It inevitably recalls Mayhew, but the writer of *My Secret Life* is even more of an expert and possesses a larger measure of disinterested sympathy than Mayhew and the early descriptive sociologists. To a simple, direct, and morally unshocked human interest he adds a kind of humorous astonishment that a business enterprise should be conducted in such an unrationalized manner. The proper Victorian gentleman, with his respect for order, account books, profits, and method, naturally expects that these virtues should apply as well to the world of sex. He himself always notes precisely how much he pays women, and tots up the costs of each of his more extensive adventures. He also estimates the earnings of the different classes of prostitutes and describes their styles of life. One fancy courtesan, Mrs. Eliza F**m**g [Fleming?], whom he picks up at the Argyll Rooms and with whom he has a short affair, is kept by Lord E**t*r [Exeter?]. The author soon learns "how very heavy her expenses were. She had several servants, and a brougham to keep. . . . I found that she made from fifty to seventy pounds a week by the exercise of her profession." This woman confesses to a liking for the author, and expresses the wish that he should keep her; she then candidly adds, "but I should only get you in debt, for somehow I never can make any money I have do." This seems to be the common result with most of the prostitutes in all of the social classes.

In addition to presenting such facts, *My Secret Life* shows us that amid and underneath the world of Victorian England as we know it—and as it tended to represent itself to itself—a real, secret social life was being conducted, the secret life of sexuality. Every day, everywhere, people were meeting, encountering one another, coming together, and moving on. And although it is true that the Victorians could not help but know of this, almost no one was reporting on it; the social history of their own sexual experiences was not part of the Victorians' official consciousness of themselves or of their society. An example will serve to represent the author's sense of this point.[9]

One day while he is in his twenties he goes to visit his mother, who is living in a country village. He wanders along the lanes and comes to a

huge church-yard, half of it mere field; at one end the rich were buried, and there were rows of tombs and monuments; the rest was only partially filled with tombstones of all sizes. As I entered it two women passed me; they were tall, stout, and dusty, had very short petticoats, and thick hob-nailed boots, dark blue dresses hung over big haunches, little black shawls no larger than handkerchiefs over their backs. They had big black bonnets cocked right upon the tops of their heads, and seemed women who worked out of doors, agricultural laborers perhaps, or perhaps the wives of bargemen, for there was a canal through the village. They had the strong steady walk and the body balanced from the hips that you see in women engaged in out-door occupations; perhaps they carried strawberries to the London markets in large baskets on their heads, and they walked as firmly as soldiers.

They went past me towards the monuments, both looked at me, and they quickened their pace as they went off. I was dying with want of a fuck. "They are going to piss," I thought. I knew the spot. We when boys, and when youths years later, had laid in wait to see nursemaids and their little charges turn up among the tombs to ease themselves; so I stopped and looked after them.

Employing the privilege of his rank, he accosts the two women; they answer back, and a good deal of rather convincing banter is exchanged. The two women know at once what he is after, and soon he is offering them money. After further prolonged discussion, one of them accepts, and he takes her around a corner.

I stripped off my coat, made it into a bundle, and placed it for her head. "There—there," I said, and pulled her down. She made no

[9] The reader will note that the one or two examples given as illustrative of any single idea are always representative and always chosen from a multitude of possible instances. The discussion of *My Secret Life* is truly an embarrassment of riches.

resistance. I saw white thighs and belly, black hair on her cunt; and the next minute I was spending up her.

"Shove on," said she, "I was just coming"; and she was wriggling and heaving, "go on." I could always go on pushing after a spend in those days; my prick would not lose its stiffness for minutes afterwards; so I pushed till I thought of doing her a second time; but her pleasure came on, her cunt contracted, and with the usual wriggle and sigh she was over, and there were we laying in copulation, with the dead all around us; another living creature might that moment have been begotten, in its turn to eat, drink, fuck, die, be buried, and rot.

The author's Sweeneyesque comment accords perfectly well with his blank amazement, his animal dismay, at the whole situation. Shortly after this, he also has the second woman, pays them both, exchanges some further words with them, and then they part.

I watched them going along with their steady step; who could have known from their look and manner, that both had just been fucked! Who can tell the state of any woman's cunt, whom you may meet anywhere! . . .

What were the women?—certainly not gay. Did they fuck with me for fun, for letch, or for money? I often have thought of it, and came to the conclusion that both were lewd, that my bawdy suggestions made them worse, my prick upset them, and the money finished it; but that wanting a fuck was the main cause; that one whose old man had been away three months, how she looked at me and at my doodle after I had fucked the first one!

It is all rather like "The Solitary Reaper" written in a sewer. And the author is aware that his "explanation" of this event is really not adequate, that its meaning, if it has one, escapes him. In a later volume, after a similar episode, he writes: "The oddest incidents, I am convinced, are taking place daily everywhere, between men and women, who are, or who are going to, or have been fucking on the sly, but of which the world can know nothing. I suppose such risks really add to our enjoyment. Such are my conclusions after the experience of nearly a quarter of a century of intriguing and fucking women, including all classes, from a marchioness to well nigh a beggar." The author of *My Secret Life* is the social historian of this world. He records its "facts" and his fantasies about them, but he is not concerned to gather them into any general significance. Nor, had he desired to, would he have been able, since neither an adequate terminology nor instruments of interpretation were then available. As simple social history, then, the facts and details of *My Secret Life* are interesting and useful, and there can be no question that we should know them. They add to and thicken our sense of the Victorian reality, and they move it further ahead in the direction toward which much modern historical research has already tended. Taken by themselves, however, the details and revelations of *My Secret Life* do not immediately or automatically fall into new patterns of generalization. Something must be done to them before their meanings can emerge.

In this connection, *My Secret Life* is perhaps most interesting if we consider it in relation to the Victorian novel. Its material bears directly on both the concerns or interests of the great Victorian novelists and on their ways of representing those interests. A few examples will demonstrate the character of this relation.

At one point the author takes an outing in the company of a friend to one of the London docks.

> As we walked outside, I saw a number of stout, vulgar looking, flamingly dressed women without bonnets, some in twos—some alone—some with sailors—talking bawdily and openly in the public streets. It was to me quite a new phase of London life. . . .
> My friend knew sailors' necessities, and their habits, and those of their female acquaintances ashore, for he was a large ship owner. . . . To amuse me and satisfy my curiosity, we dined together a few days afterwards, and after our dinner, visited several of the public houses. To avoid remark and possibly offensive behavior towards us, we dressed in the shabbiest possible manner, and with caps bought just opposite the docks, and such as were worn largely by the working people in the neighbourhood, we flattered ourselves that we looked as common a couple of men as ever rolled barrows along the street.

Thus costumed, we spent the evening at public houses, among sailors, whores, and working men—in an atmosphere thick and foul with tobacco smoke, sweat, and gas. We ordered liquors which we threw under the table or spilt when not observed; we treated some gay women, but in a very modest way, and altogether had a very entertaining evening. It was difficult to act up to our disguise. At one time I had a whore on my knee, and my friend another. We asked the women to bet which of us had the biggest prick, and the girls felt us outside quite openly. There was, however, nothing likely to shock people there. Of lewd talk there was plenty, though no gross indecency was practised. The barmen, or potboys, or the master were always there and checked it.—"Now you Sally, none of that; or out you go."—"Now hook it smart, you bitch," were phrases we heard with others, used by the master or servants when things got too hot. At one house, they turned a woman and a sailor out by force, who were too noisy and rather drunk. "Let's go and fuck, Tom," said the woman, who was readier to leave than the man.

Such a scene brings at once to mind Miss Abbey Potterson's Six Jolly Fellowship-Porters in *Our Mutual Friend*. The differences and similarities between the two representations are instructive. The most important thing about both places is the absolute authority exercised by the owners over their customers. "Miss Potterson, sole proprietor and manager of the Fellowship-Porters, reigned supreme on her throne, the Bar, and a man must have drunk himself mad drunk indeed if he thought he could contest a point with her," Dickens writes, and then calls her "Abbey the supreme" and likens her to a schoolmistress and her waterside characters to pupils. She tells them when they must leave and go home, and they obey: " 'It has been hard work to establish order here,' " she says, " 'and make the Fellowships what it is, and it is daily and nightly hard work to keep it so. The Fellowships must not have a taint upon it that may give it a bad name.' " What Dickens does, of course, is to suppress any references to prostitutes and to censor his report on the language of the dockside. The first thing we learn, then, from such scenes (and there are hundreds of them in *My Secret Life*) is what did *not* get into the Victorian novel, what was by common consent and convention left out or suppressed. But this suppression does not merely have a distorting and negative effect; in Dickens's imaginative abstraction from and reconstruction of such an establishment, certain positive values, already inherent in it, are brought into view and focused upon. And as one reads through the thousands of pages of *My Secret Life,* with scene after scene of this kind, one achieves a renewed sense of how immensely humane a project the Victorian novel was, how it broadened out the circle of humanity, and how it represented the effort of Victorian England at its best.

One sees this relation most vividly in the author's accounts of his many dealings with poor girls, cheap whores, and domestic servants. One of these adventures is particularly revealing. At some point when he is in his twenties, the author's "erotic fancies took the desire for a young lass. . . . I was not versed in the walks and ways of little ones, and looking about at night saw none. Talking about it at my Club, I heard they were to be seen mostly in the daytime, so I looked out in the Strand for what I wanted, and during day-light." At length he finds two young girls; "they were not got up in any showy way, but looked like the children of decent mechanics." He approaches them, offers to buy them some sweets, then says directly, "Come with me, and I'll give you money," offering them three and six pence each. The girls confer, disagree, quarrel, and one of them decides to go with him. He takes her to a bawdy house, the usual takes place, and after it is over he has a long chat with this girl, about whom "there was a frankness, openness, and freshness . . . which delighted me." She is just fifteen, she says, and then he goes on, characteristically, to question her further.

"How long have you been gay?" "I ain't gay," said she, astonished. "Yes you are." "No I ain't." "You let men fuck you, don't you?" "Yes, but I ain't gay." "What do you call gay?" "Why the gals who come out regular of a night, dressed up, and gets their livings by it." I was amused.

"Don't you?" "No. Mother keeps me." "What is your father?" "Got none; he's dead three months back,—mother works and keeps us. She is a charwoman, and goes out on odd jobs." "Don't you work?" "Not now," said she in a confused way; "mother does not want me to; I takes care of the others." "What others?" "The young ones." "How many?" "Two,—one's a boy, and one's a gal." "How old?" "Sister's about six, and brother's nearly eight,—but what do you ask me all this for?" "Only for amusement,—then you are in mourning for your father?" "Yes, it's shabby, ain't it? I wish I could have nice clothes. I've got nice boots,—ain't they?"— cocking up one leg—"a lady gived em me when father died,—they are my best."

"Are you often in the Strand?" "When I gets out I likes walk- ing in it, and looking at the shops,—I do if mother's out for the day." "Does she know you are out?" The girl, who had been lying on her back with her head full towards me, turned on her side and, giggling, said in a sort of confidential way, "Bless you, no,— she'd beat me if she knew,—when she be out I locks them up, and takes the key, and then I goes back to them,—I've got the key in my pocket, and shall be home before mother,—she is out for the whole day." . . .

"They may set fire to themselves," said I. "There ain't no fire; after we have had breakfast, I puts it out, and lights it at night if mother wants hot water."

"What do you do with yourself all day?" "I washes both of them; I gives them food if we've got any, then washes the floor and everything, and then washes myself; then I looks out of the winder." "Wash yourself?" "Yes, I washes from head to foot, allus." "Have you a tub?" "No, we've only got a pail and a bowl, but I'm beautiful clean,—mother tells everyone I'm the beautiful- lest clean gal a mother ever had,—I wash everything; mother's too tired. Sometimes we all go out and walk, but that's at night; sometime I lays abed nearly all day."

The author is quite genuinely taken by this girl's charm and directness—as well as by her sexuality—and for a time he sees her regularly. "I questioned her many a time," he remarks, "and put together here consecutively what she said. She was as much pleased to gossip about it as I was." Moreover, he states, she "was delighted to tell me all, it seemed quite a relief to her to do so. She had never spoken to any one else about it. To a man? she should think not,—it was not likely. And though I asked her often and often about it at times, she never varied the account. I believed it implicitly, and that is why I narrate it here." The narrative takes up sixty pages of text and includes both an account of the author's sexual activities with this girl, whose name is Kitty, and Kitty's account of her own life and sexual history. At one point, this passage occurs. It concerns her reasons for prostituting herself.

> She said, "I buy things to eat; I can't eat what mother gives us. She is poor, and works very hard; she'd give us more, but she can't; so I buy foods, and gives the others what mother gives me; they don't know better,—if mother's there, I eat some; sometimes we have only gruel and salt; if we have a fire we toast the bread, but I can't eat it if I am not dreadful hungry." "What do you like?" "Pies and sausage-rolls," said the girl, smacking her lips and laughing. "Oh! my eye, ain't they prime,—oh!" "That's what you went gay for?" "I'm not gay," said she sulkily. "Well, what you let men fuck you for?" "Yes." "Sausage-rolls?" "Yes, meat-pies and pastry too."

In the first place, the style of such passages should be considered. It is, of course, superb in its observingness and authenticity, but it is also a style which strikes a familiar note. It is a period style, and is in fact a dead ringer for the style of interview one meets with in the blue books, those imperishable documents of the humane spirit. Such a style did not exist—and could not have existed, since the interests which actuated it did not yet effectively exist—before the middle of the nineteenth century. It seems to me an excellent example of how a culture operates—one of the chief means of its operations always being registered in style—and of how pervasive its influences are that a work like *My Secret Life,* written from the very underbelly of the Victorian world and out of very different impulses from those that supplied the motives for the blue books, should as it were bear the unmistakable impress of one of the age's great achievements.

But the passages I have quoted also have an immediately relevant novelistic counterpart. It occurs in Chapter XV of *Bleak House*. Esther Summerson, Mr. Jarndyce, and others go seeking the orphaned children of Neckett, the sheriff's officer with whom they have had some contact. They find them, and the elements of the scene are almost identical with those in *My Secret Life*. The two younger children are locked up alone during the day by their older sister; there is no fire in the room; the poverty is extreme; the one available activity is washing, which the older sister resorts to. The chief difference between the two episodes is that Charley, the older sister in *Bleak House,* has made a different choice than Kitty in *My Secret Life*. She has chosen to care for and feed her younger brother and sister by going out and doing washing, while Kitty has chosen prostitution as a means of getting food. (Later on, Kitty becomes a full-fledged prostitute and in addition supports "her mother who had been disabled by rheumatic fever.") There can be no doubt that both choices were made all the time in Victorian England, and in the pages of *My Secret Life* Kitty exists for us in a fully human way—her reality is not to be denied. But her humanity is of a different kind than that of Charley in *Bleak House,* and this difference is itself the result of the difference in consciousness between Dickens and the author of *My Secret Life*. In Dickens, Mr. Jarndyce looks at the three children and their surroundings, and whispers, "Is it possible . . . that this child works for the rest? Look at this! For God's sake look at this!" And Esther then remarks, "It was a thing to look at. The three children close together and two of them relying on the third, and the third so young and yet with an air of age and steadiness that sat so strangely on the childish figure." The scene continues for a considerable length and is intensely moving. It is moving not only because it represents incomparably the fullness of effort made by these children to establish and retain their humanity; it is moving also because it dramatizes Dickens's consciousness—and his readers' as well—that these children are members of ourselves, that their humanity belongs to ours, that we are their society. Dickens, the supreme novelist, the conscience and consciousness of his age, is outraged that in our world anyone should have to endure such agony to remain human—yet he is at the same time aware that through such agony, and its effort, is humanity in part created. The author of

My Secret Life, another representative consciousness, regards Kitty with interest, amusement, and pleasure. He thinks of her choice as a common and legitimate one, and is rather glad that she is there at his disposal. He regards her as human, but her humanity is of a lesser order than his own. He sees nothing degrading or dehumanizing in her selling herself. In this he is wrong. Yet it adds considerably to our understanding of the Victorian novel if we read it against such scenes as those represented in *My Secret Life,* if we understand that the Victorian novelists were aware of such scenes, and that their great project, taken as a whole, was directed dialectically against what such scenes meant.

There is no doubt that the Victorian conventions of censorship had a severely limiting effect on the range of the novel. Having accepted censorship on explicit sexual statements, however, the Victorian novelists had to find less direct means of communicating the sexual component in the situations they described; and any one at all familiar with the fiction of the period knows that these means were very much in use. One example demonstrates this circumstance clearly. One of the members of the club to which the author belongs is an impecunious and dissolute old Major. "Ask him to dinner in a quiet way by himself, give him unlimited wine, and he would in an hour or two begin his confidential advice in the amatory line, and in a wonderful manner tell of his own adventures. . . ." The author then reproduces a sample of the Major's speech.

> "If you want to get over a girl," he would say, "never flurry her till her belly's full of meat and wine; let the grub work. As long as she is worth fucking, it's sure to make a woman randy at some time. If she is not twenty-five she'll be randy directly her belly is filled,—then go at her. If she's thirty, give her half an hour. If she's thirty-five, let her digest an hour; she won't feel the warmth of the dinner in her cunt till then. Then she'll want to piss, and directly after that she'll be ready for you without her knowing it. But don't flurry your young un,—talk a little quiet smut whilst feeding, just to make her laugh and think of bawdy things; then when she has left table, go at her. But it's well," the Major would

say, "to leave a woman alone in a room for a few minutes after she has dined; perhaps then she will let slip a fart or two; perhaps she'll piss,—she'll be all the better for the wind and water being out. A woman's cunt doesn't get piss-proud like a man's prick, you know; they're differently made from us, my boy,—but show any one of them your prick as soon as you can; it's a great persuader. Once they have seen it they can't forget it; it will keep in their minds. And a bawdy book, they won't ever look at till you've fucked them?—oh! won't they!—they would at church if you left them alone with it." And so the Major instructed us.

Who is this Major except Major Bagstock in *Dombey and Son?* It is astonishing to see how Dickens achieves the equivalent results—and more—without having recourse to open sexual language. Both Majors share in common their age, loquacity, and coarseness (which they think of as manly directness, no nonsense), their inflamed aggressiveness, which they also connect with food, or feeding, and both act as sexual advisers to their juniors—Bagstock in fact playing the pimp or bawd in company with Mrs. Skewton. Dickens uses a variety of means to communicate to the reader the intense, disturbed, and corrupted sexuality of the Major; from his very name, which conceals a sexual pun, to the descriptions of him swilling hot spiced drinks and then swelling apoplectically and turning red and blue, to his frequent reference to the old "Bagstock breed," there is no doubt what Dickens has in mind. In this instance, we can conclude, very little was lost through the limitation of the novelist's diction; it is even possible that the constraint acted to stimulate his imaginative and metaphoric powers. Such was not usually the case, however; and if one reads some of the episodes in *My Secret Life* which describe the author's adventures in the English countryside and on farms and compares them with, say, *Adam Bede* or Hardy's novels, one gets a fuller sense of both the boundaries within which the nineteenth-century novelists worked and of what they were trying to do with their fiction. The first use to which *My Secret Life* can be put, therefore, is as an additional context for the study of Victorian literature. To which we must add the proviso that *My Secret Life* is itself a piece of literature. Like a novel, it is the product of the mind of a single man, and whatever authority we wish to ascribe to it must be exercised within the framework of that definition.

I V

Another way of putting the matter is to say that a work such as *My Secret Life* falls within the scope of G. M. Young's statement that "the real, central theme of History is not what happened, but what people felt about it when it was happening." That is to say, *My Secret Life* is important by virtue of its authenticity. It is the authentic record of what one man perceived, felt, saw, believed, and wanted to believe. Regarding it within the context of social history, we understand it as being informed at all points by a consciousness which is subjective and historical; everything that is in it, everything that it is, comes to us through this universal and universally distorting filter. But then there is no other way for anything to come to us.

It is in the first place authentic in the ignorance about certain sexual matters that it shares with its time. Having been raised in a typical Victorian household, the author reaches early adolescence in a state of bewilderment; he has received no official or formal instruction about sexual matters, yet has by this time had considerable experience of sex and considerable exposure to sexual scenes.

> It seemed to me scarcely possible that the sweet, well-dressed, smooth-spoken ladies who came to our house could let men put the spunk up their cunts. Then came the wonder if, and how, women spent; what pleasure they had in fucking, and so on; in all ways I was wondering about copulation, the oddity of the gruelly, close-smelling sperm being ejected into the hole between a woman's thighs so astonished me. I often thought the whole business must be a dream of mine. . . .

The authenticity of such a passage is not to be questioned; but its authenticity is also trans-historical—one has the strong suspicion that adolescents today are still overwhelmed by the up-heaval. The author takes to masturbating at the usual age, goes through a certain amount of communal experience at school, and then comes to this conclusion:

> My two intimate school-friends left off frigging, the elder brother, who had a very long red nose, having come to the conclusion with me that frigging made people mad and, worse, prevented them afterwards from fucking and having a family. Fred, my favorite cousin, arrived at the same conclusion—by what mental process we all arrived at it, I don't know.

Such a statement is interesting on several grounds. First, it indi-cates, for what must be the thousandth time, how really univer-sal these beliefs about masturbation were—and in some way probably still are. Second, it demonstrates how the process of repression works in the service of culture, for the author has already provided considerable evidence to show that from an early age he was regularly warned against the harmful effects of masturbation; nevertheless, at this moment he and his com-panions choose to believe that they have arrived at their decision spontaneously. By internalizing this restraint and repressing the memory of its original source, one both strengthens and legiti-mizes its inhibiting force. Furthermore, although he never in the course of a long career modifies this belief, he never ceases to masturbate intermittently either. He does not go mad, but he does report that he suffered from depression, guilt, fatigue, and general feelings of debilitation after masturbation (he is afflicted with the same group of symptoms whenever he has a nocturnal emission). He feels none of these after sexual inter-course; even after a prolonged bout of activities he generally feels nothing more than a pleasant fatigue. That he does not question himself about this disparity, that it was not within the bounds of possibility for this question to occur to him, indicates to us again the point of intellectual development to which thinking about sex had attained in his culture.

Another typical conviction that he authentically holds has to do with the magical properties of semen—"sperm is the only true source of copulative power," he characteristically remarks. In this connection, a further belief comes into play. He believes that women ejaculate. This is one of the most widely cherished of male fantasies, and its function is self-evident. How the author acquired this belief we do not learn; but he has it as a young man, and when at the end of this work, after he has had sexual intercourse with well over a thousand women, we learn that he still believes it, we are justified in calling into question not only the character of his experience but the character of experience itself, seeing how deeply preconditioned it can be by our needs, by what we want it to be. For not only does he believe in female ejaculation, he also experiences it, and on countless occasions routinely describes to himself and us what it is like to experience, to feel, the seminal discharge of a woman while she is having an orgasm. There is still a further step of complication, for in addition to his—and other men's—belief, the women themselves also believed that they ejaculated, experienced this "fact," and described it to and discussed it with him. This raises a number of interesting matters. It shows us to what a remarkable extent men's conceptions of women's anatomy and sexuality are formed and controlled by unconscious defensive formations. It also shows us, as anthropologists have recently done, that women's idea of their own sexuality (at least in a large majority of cultures) is historically a response to what men want and demand that sexuality to be, and that in general women are content to accept whatever model of their own sexuality men offer to and demand of them. *Mutatis mutandis*, a little reflection will yield the insight that the same thing is happening today.[10]

To what degree, then, is the credibility of the author's account impaired by such distortions, by these fantasies and falsehoods? The answer to this question is altogether evident. Its credibility is not impaired in the least; indeed it is, if anything,

[10] See George Devereux, "The Significance of the External Female Genitalia and of Female Orgasm for the Male," *Journal of the American Psychoanalytic Association*, VI (1958), 278–286.

enhanced by them. They are an important part of its authenticity, an authenticity which is subjective, historical, and profoundly conditioned, and which is considerably more complex, interesting, and problematical than an authenticity which confines itself to "fact" alone. These fantasies, we should remember, are also facts. And even if it were to be proved that the whole eleven volumes of *My Secret Life* were nothing but fantasy, such a discovery could not, in this context, radically alter the circumstances or our attitude toward them. In either case, they would be coming to us through the filter of the same consciousness imposed upon them. Moreover, since it has been demonstrated that, when it comes to matters of reporting about sexual experience, there is always an intermixture of fact and fantasy, that the fantasies are at least equally important as the "facts," and that they have as much if not more meaning to them, we must in our examination of these documents pay as much respect to their errors and falsifications as we do to those parts of the account which seem, in the usual sense of the expression, to have actually happened.

The authenticity of the author's ignorance serves as an introduction to larger problems. It raises certain theoretical questions which always pertain to the use and analysis of historical documents and helps us to establish at the outset the groundwork of our discussion. *My Secret Life,* however, is authentic in many more important ways. It is authentic in its presentation of sexual attitudes, responses, and scenes. It also has, in other words, the authenticity of fact. This note of truth can be sensed, I believe, in some of the passages already adduced, but it is there throughout. It is there, in the first place, in the author's representation of himself and his own attitudes. For example, he candidly describes his anxiety about the size of his penis. At one point, when he is about to get into bed with a prostitute, he looks at himself in a mirror.

> Then I had a sudden fear that she would think my prick small; what put it into my head I never could exactly say. I used when at school to fancy mine was smaller than that of other boys, and

some remark of a gay woman about its size made me most sensitive on the topic. I was constantly asking the women if my prick was not smaller than other men's. When they said it was a very good size—as big as most—I did not believe them, and I used when I pulled it out to say in an apologetic tone, "Let's put it up, there's not much of it." "Oh! it's quite big enough," one would say. "I've seen plenty smaller," would say another. But still the idea clung to me that it was not a prick to be in any way proud of,—which was a great error. But I have told of this weakness more than once before, I think.

He has told of it before, and he recurs to it on a number of occasions later on. This interest is as universal among men as their anxiety about castration, and it is not to be allayed by experience. He knows from experience that most women are quite indifferent to the size of a man's penis and that their perception of this organ is very often indistinct and imprecise (whether this common failure of perception arises from indifference or from some specific inhibition is not clear). He also knows from a long accumulation of the evidence of his own senses that his penis is of average goodly proportions and that therefore he can take pride in it; but this too makes little difference. However, the inclusion of such passages in this work demonstrates that it is something more than a pornographic fantasy and something other than a long sexual self-glorification, which most of the better-known sexual autobiographies tend to be. To be sure, *My Secret Life* was written out of sexual impulses and with sexual purposes, but other purposes are at work in it as well. It is important to observe that the author can accommodate himself to such purposes, that he can include such passages, that he is not so entirely at the mercy of his fantasies that he must censor or deny them. Passages such as this—and there are many of them—are authentic in themselves; but they serve as well to authenticate the passages around them, passages which would, in a setting of unblemished and inhuman sexual triumphs, be wholly unconvincing.

In a similar way, the author reports on his periodic though infrequent experiences of impotence. One of these is of classic

interest. It occurs shortly after the author's first marriage. He
has some desultory kind of employment but spends most of his
time at home being miserable, sitting "for hours by myself reading, brooding, fretting, and even crying bitter tears." One after-
noon he tries to make the hours pass by reading, but cannot and
so sits down "on a chair by the dining-room table, laid my head
on my hands upon it, and thought of my unhappy home till I
cried bitterly." He then feels a hand on his shoulder, and a
voice says, "Don't you take on so, Master,—don't you know,—
she's not worth it,—cheer up,—don't you take on so." It is
Mary, a handsome but quiet young domestic servant employed
by his wife; until that moment, the author says, he has hardly
noticed her. He starts up, astonished. "'I beg your pardon,' said
she looking uncomfortable, 'I couldn't bear to see you so unhappy.'" The author then states that "Her interest in me struck
me to the heart; without premeditation I threw my arms
around her, pressed her mouth to mine, it unresistingly met it."
He kisses her, the tears still running down his face, until he
recovers his senses, and then says to her, "Mary, you *are* kind,—
you are a dear, good girl,—a good, affectionate, loving creature,
—I am unhappy, miserable, but how do you know that?" She
replies in kind (and the author's recording of her speech is
charming), he kisses her again, and they sit and "talked of my
miseries; yet as far as I recollect not the slightest desire to have
her had then come into my head; all was delight at my trouble
being shared, at a kind, soft, pretty woman commiserating me."
He also says that "morally she affected me." Things proceed in
this way until the author suddenly becomes "conscious of what
I was driving on to unpremeditatingly." He now drives on with
premeditation, and it is clear that Mary is willing to give herself
to him, though she puts up a token resistance. He quickly gets
to the point.

> Gently pressing her back on the sofa, she raised her limbs, I lifted
> her clothes, and tearing open my trousers threw myself on her.
> My fingers for an instant touched her cunt, a rapid probe, and
> then my prick! My God! it was not standing, not a bit of swell or

stiffness was in it; it was as a sucked gooseberry, a mere bit of dwindling, flexible, skinny gristle.

I had been occasionally but rarely suddenly unequal to love's duty, as already told, had gone home with gay women, my prick standing as I entered their houses; then suddenly it had shrunk, something about them having upset me. Occasionally it was a sudden fear of the ladies' fever, or something looked less inviting when their petticoats were off than I had imagined when drapery hid their charms, or else the fear that my prick would be thought small. At other times I could not account for it at all. I told my doctor of it. He said that it was nervousness, but the knowledge that I had once been so affected, affected me often afterwards when I went indoors with girls. "Shall I be able to fuck?" I used to think, I who had already fucked two hundred women. But so it was, a fear of inability brought on the inability. The power often returned to me a few minutes afterwards, yet sometimes not for hours.

There was nothing to account for it now. I had more or less abstained for weeks; there lay one of the choicest female forms ever presented to man's eyes. . . . And I liked the woman, felt mad for her; yet as my belly touched hers, and my prick rubbed against her pleasure-pit, it became useless. I got up, looked at her as she lay motionless with thighs extended, stood almost frantic, frigged my prick, probed her, and again threw myself on her as I stiffened; but no sooner had my prick touched her beautiful cunt, then as if bewitched it shrunk from entering it; I could not even thumb it up.

I broke into a sweat. "My God, what will she think of me?" I dreaded to get off and look her in the face, feeling so ashamed. . . . So time wore on, she never moving excepting to push her clothes down as I rose and exposed her, not opening her eyes, nor uttering a word. "My God, what is the matter with me; I don't know but I can't," I said at last. Then she put quite down her clothes, and sitting up on the sofa gave me a kiss, said, "I must go and see about laying the things for dinner," and off she went.

Our man, however, is not one to accept defeat lightly. It goes on like this for pages, as he pursues Mary about the house in a sweat of importunity. He does not succeed that day but does on the next and achieves what they both want. "I've fucked you,— I'm a man you see," he cries at the moment of his triumph. He goes on to have a considerable affair with her, which he describes in detail, including within it the story of Mary's own life until that time.

The authenticity of this description does not consist alone in the open—and undismayed—admission of impotence. It consists as well in the fullness of representation which the author gives to his emotions, and in the coherence of those emotions with the experience of impotence. Mary catches the author in an unguarded and uncharacteristic moment; his feelings of misery and self-pity have broken him down, and he is at the mercy of his weakness. She responds to him spontaneously, with sympathy and pity, and in a direct and simple human way. She is the first woman, according to the account of *My Secret Life,* who has ever really done so, who regards the author with open and uninflected tenderness. And the author responds with tenderness of his own, his emotions corresponding to hers. It is virtually the first time in his account that he has done so as well. The fact that he kisses her without being aware of sexual desire and that he feels morally affected by her are part of this response. When his sexual drive or desire then makes itself felt, as it always does with him, the necessary quantity of aggression is suddenly not available to him, since that aggression tends always to exist in isolation from the emotions of tenderness—in him the isolation is extreme—and as a result he is impotent. The situation was analyzed definitively in Freud's great essay "The Most Prevalent Form of Degradation in Erotic Life." The author of *My Secret Life* had of course no way of knowing why he should have responded in the way he did, but the authenticity of such a passage largely depends on the fact that he was capable of faithfully recording his emotions —of being faithful to his unconscious, really—even though he could not understand them, and that we at this much later date can see that they are truly coherent and do indeed have a meaning. The quality of such descriptions is considerably closer to the Joyce of Leopold Bloom than it is to the traditional literature of sex.

The author often remarks that he is chiefly interested in himself and in writing about himself rather than about the women with whom he has had his adventures. He naturally cannot adhere to this policy in any consistent sense, and, as we have seen, his interest is sometimes so engaged by certain women that he sets down long descriptions of their persons and behavior and recounts the stories of their lives as he gathered them from their conversation. It is nevertheless true that the largest majority of the women in *My Secret Life* tend to be anonymous. This is not surprising when we consider that the author was really interested in the anonymous parts of them. Despite such a curtailment, one of the most authentic sides of this work is to be found in its representations of women and of female attitudes. In this connection, however, one must be careful to distinguish what we can accept as an accurate or authentic description of how women behave from a male fantasy of that behavior or from the now familiar projection of a male sexual response onto a female object. For instance, we can as a general rule regard the author's statements about women's orgasms with skepticism—this is a subject on which no man is a good witness. He himself is intermittently aware of this, and sometimes issues to himself a warning to be cautious. "Some women new at the amorous play and quite young," he writes at an appropriate moment, "spend so quietly that unless their cunts tighten much (and some cunts don't), it is difficult to know if they have spent or not." On another occasion he writes:

> Both sisters spent with me, I'm sure I make no mistake?—So many gay women have done the same and have offered me a second poke, unasked by me, that I sometimes doubt whether they spent, or whether they shammed, as an inducement to get me to visit them again. Do they spend so with chance friends; don't they reserve their pleasure and their spending for men they especially like? . . . [He then reports the conversation of one woman whom he describes as] a whore to the backbone. "I spend when I want fucking," said she, "and if I like the man, though he be a stranger, I ask him to fuck again if he pleases me; why shouldn't we?"

> Later experience teaches me that whores generally follow their instincts and their lusts with men, and spend whenever they feel the want of it.

In this instance, one can see how his doubts finally boil down to a generalization which is virtually without content. Despite such occasional efforts of wariness, his accounts of female responsiveness are extremely difficult to accept. In general, the ease, rapidity, and capacity for continuous repetition in achieving orgasm that he ascribes to the vast majority of all classes of women with whom he has had experiences would, if we were to accept his account, force us to revise our whole conception not only of Victorian England but of modern culture itself. Although he does not fail to put down certain occasions on which women did not come to orgasm with him, the idea of frigidity is as good as unknown to him, and he cannot be said ever to have had a frigid woman. His version of female sexuality is the exact opposite of the official version, the version we met with in Acton. And if there can be no doubt of the incorrectness of the official version, there is something equally incorrect about this one. The weight of all the evidence that we can gather, both from the period itself and from our own time, contradicts such a portrait of uniformity. In *My Secret Life,* three circumstances can be made out as contributing to the error: the blurred perceptions of an observer who was also a participant; the unquestionable presence of fantasy and wish-fulfillment in his descriptions; and the projection onto women of the male conception of sexuality and the resulting disposition to regard women's responsiveness as identical with men's.

Putting this one aspect of his representation into the discard, we can say that the balance of his descriptions of women, their dress, talk, ideas, attitudes, general and specifically sexual behavior are authentic in the extreme. One additional example will have to serve as representative of what I hope is already clear, and of what the author devotes some four thousand pages to achieving. In Volume VIII he tells of his experiences with two young prostitutes named "Nelly L**l*e and Sophy S***h."

By this time, his methods of writing have become more sophisticated, and he tells us that we are reading an edited version of
the story. "My libidinous amusements with them were all of the
ordinary kind. . . . They were as usual described by me at
length in my original manuscript, but the repetition of salacious tricks seem tedious now, so I have carefully weeded out,
arranged in some order, condensed, abbreviated this part of my
narrative to about one fifth of its original length; leaving only
certain episodes worth retaining for their variety, which I shall
put in their chronological order nearly." Going along Leicester
Square one evening, he accosts two young women of about seventeen or eighteen years of age. Nelly and Sophy are two country girls who have just come to London and are making their
debut as prostitutes under the tutelage of a German-Jewish
dressmaker who "let her upper floors to quiet gay women."
The author goes home with both of them, has them together,
sees them regularly for a few weeks, and learns their history.
They had left their village, he remarks, because "both had been
caught fucking without a license." Both had gotten pregnant,
procured abortion through the aid of a "local dressmaker,"
who subsequently put them onto the dressmaker in London.
The girls felt "uncomfortable at their village," and so "off they
ran." "They knew they were going to be gay, though it was not
said so." He then makes the ineffable remark that "both afterwards liked gay life, but neither rose to eminence."

Nelly is a nice, quiet girl, but Sophy is something of a character, and it is in the author's descriptions of her that the authenticity is turned to a notable account.

> She was exquisitely made, had the loveliest breasts, and from the
> nape of her neck to the sole of her feet was as white as snow. Her
> features were good, her eyes blue, and yet she looked like a fool,
> and when she laughed was like an idiot. Her laugh was a vulgar,
> idiotic, coarse, offensive chuckle; she opened her mouth quite
> wide (it was large with splendid teeth), and she rolled her head
> from side to side. Her hands were coarse. . . .
>   Of all the women I ever had, none had so soft, so voluptuous a
> cunt. . . . Sophy shivered, quivered, but not noisily, and heaved

gently; her cunt went clip, clip, suck, suck, in a wonderful way towards her crisis, and then with a gentle heave of her belly and arse, she seemed as if she wished to get my whole body up her, and with an "Ahaa—my dear man—aha, aha," she subsided. She was full of juice, would often spend twice to my once. . . . Before the first week of our acquaintance was out, she gave way to her passions with me. She liked me and used to patter out in her ugly, hoarse, coarse, vulgar voice, bawdy words, and coarse but loving expressions. Nelly, watching us, used then to say, "Sophy—what are you at?" but it did not stop her. Never have I had more completely voluptuous fucking as far as mere cunt was concerned, but that was all; I was sick of the sight of her directly our bodies unjoined.

I saw both girls daily for nearly a fortnight, and Sophy had my seminal libations more frequently than Nelly—but I could not talk to her; her language was indescribably common and coarse, and whether eating, drinking, speaking, washing or even pissing, her vulgarity and idiotcy were intolerable. She was . . . a magnificent bit of fucking flesh but nothing more.

For a year or two, the author then writes, he sees these girls on infrequent occasions. Then Sophy quarrels with Nelly, goes off to live by herself, and for a few years disappears from the author's life, though he continues to see Nelly. One day Nelly tells him that Sophy "had married an artisan, who was then dying, had two children by him, that they'd lived respectably and she quietly, but that now having pawned everything to keep them, she was going onto the streets again to live. They literally had nothing in their room but a bed, chair, table and piss pot, and would have starved if Nelly had not sent them food for some time." Characteristically, the author is aroused by this tale and has Sophy sent for. When she arrives "she had nothing on but a cloak and a gown; I pulled up her clothes to see." He has her wash herself, sends out for some gin, has her tell him her troubles while he is getting her drunk, and then proceeds to his work.

Never did a woman enjoy a poking more. "Oh! I ain't had a fuck for three months—not one damned fuck; frigging ain't fucking my dear—is it?—Shove harder—I'm coming." She'd lost of course all modesty, if she ever had any, but she must have been reared like a pig.—The first fortnight after she came to town, Nell used to say, "Do it, put it in,—up my thing," and so on. Sophy would say "fuck—cunt—prick" to express herself within a few days of her coming to London. When we were all three together, she would sit looking at the fire quietly, and suddenly say to herself aloud, as if thinking, "fuck."—I recollect her brushing her hair at the glass when Nell and I were sitting down, and when in her vulgar way and harsh, croaking voice she broke out singing, "Fuck, fuck, fucky, oh fuck, fuck, fuck—fuck her and fuck him, and fuck, fuck, fuck." "Shut up you beast," said Nelly, throwing her slipper at her.—She only laughed and, turning round, 'I shan't,—I like saying it—what does it matter—fuckee and fucking, and fuck, fuck, fuck."

As for the rest, Sophy's husband dies, as do her two children. She then becomes "a fearful drunkard, the lowest of the low." The author sees her a couple of more times, and then, as he does with all other women, causes her to disappear from his life.

These passages contain an interesting mixture of elements. It is possible on principle to doubt his statements about Sophy's responsiveness, though one ought to note that doubting on principle is itself doubtable. It is not possible, I believe, to doubt his rendering of Sophy's speech, particularly the last part of it. It rings absolutely true to the ear, and all of one's experience of life and literature combine to support its authenticity. No one who has ever spent much time in the army or who has lived in certain districts of a modern large city can be unacquainted with the obsessive frequency or the lunatic virtuosity with which the word "fuck" is used. (In his testimony at the *Lady Chatterley's Lover* trial, Richard Hoggart reports a similar experience.) In addition, if one were to persist in doubt over the authenticity of this kind of passage, the only alternative conclusion would be to say that we are confronted in this book with a remarkable novelistic talent. In any event, we are confronted by something very formidable. Passages such as this come like bolts out of the blue; and, as I have said, *My Secret Life* is full of them. Each one of them jolts the reader's whole sensibility; this is Victorian

England, one keeps reminding himself, that one is reading about. Every student of the period knows, in some sense, that such things were going on, but no one else has ever written about them in this way, and therefore no one else has ever made us really "know" about them. The effect of such a work, as we assimilate to it to our more inclusive sense of what literature and life were like in the nineteenth century, is bound to be considerable.

Another side of the authenticity of these scenes has to do with the author's attitude toward Sophy, which is fairly complex. He is drawn toward her, disgusted by her, and amused by her. The one thing that he does not feel for this poor, witless creature is sympathy. He does not identify with her, and he regards her from a vast remoteness. Yet it is possible to suggest that it is just this pitilessness, this distance he maintains, which in part permits him to regard her with such clarity and to create this startling, and shocking, portrait. This is by no means the immense feeling for common humanity which served Dickens when he created a very similar character, say Maggy, the idiot in *Little Dorrit*. Indeed the "objectivity" of the author of *My Secret Life* springs from sources opposite to those which Dickens draws upon. In this instance extremes meet, and the aggressive, unblinking eye of the author makes a contribution to our understanding of humanity that can, for once, be compared to the great novelist's comprehensive and, for the most part, unwavering gaze at the human condition.

There is still a further way in which *My Secret Life* is authentic, and that is in its representation of certain perverse sexual practices. The use to which we can put these accounts is as a check on the way such practices are represented in pure fantasy and its literature, pornography. One example illustrates this circumstance particularly well. Fairly late in his life, the author becomes involved in a long-standing affair with a young courtesan whom he calls Helen Marwood. She is an energetic, bold, and apparently hyper-responsive woman whose interests run to the perverse and experimental. This suits the author, whose own temperament has in the course of years evolved in the same directions. They act out various fantasies, and at one point enlist the services of a young prostitute who is in the steady employ of the owner of a flagellation parlor. This owner, traditionally called "the abbess," was herself "an expert in flagellation," and the author learns that "swells both old and young came under her experienced hand." The couple then pay a visit to the establishment, and the abbess rather proudly shows them around, points out the various items of equipment, and explains to them how the place is run.

Both H. and I desired to see the operation, and heard that some men liked to be seen by other men when being flogged. If we would come on a certain day, there would be then a gentleman who had a taste for being made a spectacle, and she would arrange for us to see—for pay of course.

We went on the day, but the man did not appear. . . .

At our next visit the flagellation came off. As H., who'd only her chemise on, and I, my shirt and wearing a mask, entered the room, there was a man kneeling on a large chair at the foot of the bed, over which he was bending. Over the seat and back of the chair was a large towel to receive his spendings. He had a woman's dress on tucked up to his waist, showing his naked rump and thighs, with his feet in male socks and boots. On his head was a woman's cap tied carefully round his face to hide whiskers—if he had any—and he wore a half mask which left his mouth free. At his back, standing, was one youngish girl holding a birch and dressed as a ballet dancer, with petticoats far up above her knees, and showing naked thighs. Her breasts were naked, hanging over her stays and showing dark-haired armpits. Another tall, well formed though thinnish female, naked all but boots and stockings, with hair died a bright yellow, whilst her cunt and armpit fringes were dark brown, stood also at his back—a bold, insolent looking bitch. . . .

What he had done with the women before we entered, we were told afterwards by yellow head, was very simple. He'd stripped both women naked, and saw the one dress herself as ballet girl, nothing more. Neither had touched his prick nor he their cunts. When the door was closed after we entered, he whispered to the abbess that he wanted to see my prick. Determined to go through the whole performance, I lifted my shirt and shewed it big but not

stiff. He wanted to feel it, but that I refused. "Be a good boy or
Miss Yellow (as I shall call her) will whip you hard," said the
abbess. "Oh—no—no—pray don't," he whispered in reply. He
spoke always in whispers. . . . He never turned round during
this but remained kneeling. Then after childish talk between him
and the abbess (he always in whispers), "Now she shall whip
you, you naughty boy," said the abbess—and "swish," the rod descended heavily upon his rump.

"Oho—Ho—Ho," he whispered as he felt the twinge. I moved
round to the other side of him where I could see his prick more
plainly. It was longish, pendant. . . . Swish, swish went the
birch, and again he cried in whispers, "Ho, Ho." . . . Yellow
head from behind him felt his prick.—The abbess winked at me.
—Then he laid his head on the bedstead frame and grasped it
with both hands, whilst very leisurely the birch fell on him and he
cried, "Ho—Ho." His rump got red, and then he cried *aloud,—*
"Oh, I can't,"—then sunk his voice to a whisper in finishing his
sentence.—Yellow head again felt his prick, which was stiffer, and
he sideways felt *her* cunt, but still not looking around.

There was a rest and a little talk, he still speaking in whispers.
The abbess treated him like a child. . . . Yellow head then took
up the birch, and H. and I moved to the other side of the bed.
Both of us were excited. . . .

I moved round him again, looking curiously at his prick which
was not stiff.—"Let *him* feel it," he whispered more loudly than
usual. I felt and frigged it for a second. Whilst I did so, swish
swish, fell the rod on his rump, which writhed. . . . Yellow head
laid hold of his prick, gave it two or three gentle frigs, and out
spurted a shower of semen. Then he was quiet . . . he was life-
less. . . .

Neither of us had seen such a sight before; never had either of
us even seen anyone flogged, and we talked about it till the abbess
came up. . . . [Later on] we heard more about the rich victim
. . . who was between fifty and sixty.

On another occasion, they witness another gentleman being
beaten. The situation is very much the same, as is the author's
account of it.

This description will be of use to us in our examination of the
literature of flagellation. At this point, it is enough to say that
this passage from *My Secret Life* simply puts the literature of
flagellation out of the running. It does so by showing how that

literature is a completely distorted and idealized version of what actually happens, and how all the elements which are synthesized into the impossibilities of that literature appear in their actual separated state. First, there is the clear distinction of class; in England this sexual practice seemed almost universally to be confined to the gentlemanly ranks, a fact which is made explicit in the quoted passage—including the masks—and in the literature itself. Then there is the confusion of sexual identity, which is demonstrated in this scene by the mixed clothing of the man being beaten; in the literature of flagellation this confused identity is also always present, but it is concealed and unacknowledged. Connected with this is the unmistakable pregenital character of this activity, along with a pronounced fear of the genitals and severe disturbances of potency; these too can be made out in the literature, though naturally only through analyzing its latent tendencies and meanings. In addition, the ritualistic quality of such behavior comes through palpably in the author's descriptions, as does the fact that the principal character in such scenes seems to be rehearsing some twisted recollection from early childhood; and the whole atmosphere of some kind of play, of roles and role playing, of a little domestic drama comes through as well. All of these are standard conventions of the literature of flagellation too. But the representation in *My Secret Life* does something which the pornography naturally cannot. It demonstrates how truly and literally childish such behavior is; it shows us, as nothing else that I know does, the pathos of perversity, how deeply sad, how cheerless a condemnation it really is. It is more than a condemnation; it is—or was—an imprisonment for life. For if it is bad enough that we are all imprisoned within our own sexuality, how much worse, how much sadder must it be to be still further confined within this foreshortened, abridged, and parodically grotesque version of it. All the details of the scene impress this sense on us; from the girl standing idly by in her ballet costume to the woman's cap tied carefully to hide his whiskers, from his mumbled whispers to his final, ritualized "Oh, I

can't," from the slow, heavy swish of the birch and the mutual
isolation from one another of all the characters to the final relief of his poor, useless penis, it is all a depressing picture. No
wit enlivens it; no excitement energizes it; it is all slow-motion,
like a dream. And the violence, the beating, that too is as unlike
its representation in pornography as possible. It is slow ("about
a stroke a minute" for the most part, he tells us) and moderate;
it is not the wild, excessive, impossible violence of the written
fantasy.

I have said that the scene is depressing. I should have said
that it is depressing to us, because it does not depress the author.
And this too is part of its authenticity. He is interested in and
amused by the spectacle, and experiencing it in the company of
his mistress along with other women arouses him. Why he
should not be depressed is a subject whose discussion must be
temporarily postponed. At this point, however, two things can
be said. First, depression would be useless; it would serve no
function. Second, in this episode too, it is his remoteness, his
distance, his lack of identification with anyone except himself
which permits him to perceive the scene with such brutal clarity and to experience it without disturbance. The authenticity of
this work is inseparable from the authenticity of the author's
aggressiveness. He is a man deeply seated within himself, a
genuine specimen of the "inner-directed" man—his gyroscope,
however, is running backward. It seems strange that the nineteenth-century paradigm of character should make its presence
felt even here. Strange, but no less convincing.

V

It should be apparent from what has gone before that one of the
central interests of *My Secret Life* is to be found in the way it
embodies and presents certain social attitudes. Chief among
these attitudes are those which make up the nexus of sex, class,
and money. They form an inseparable matrix in the author's

mind and provide, in an external way, the unifying theme of this document. The vast majority of the author's experiences are had with three kinds of women—domestic servants, girls from the working or lower classes, and prostitutes of varying degrees of expensiveness. He describes, to be sure, numbers of adventures with women of different ranks, positions, nationalities, etc., but these do not, in a simple statistical way, make up the bulk of his experience (his descriptions of such experiences, however, are in their attitudes consistent with his attitudes elsewhere). Most of the women whom he knows sexually, therefore, come from a single and fairly homogeneous population, since it is safe to say that both servants and prostitutes were by and large recruited from the same parts of society, the agricultural and urban laboring or working classes.

Having been raised in a wealthy family, the author was from an early age familiar with servants and surrounded by them.[11] In early adolescence, he discovers what most young men of his rank discovered, "that servants were fair game," and sets out on the hunt which has no ending—". . . soon there was not one in the house whom I had not kissed. I had a soft voice and have heard an insinuating way, was timorous, feared repulse, and above all being found out; yet I succeeded. Some of the servants must have liked it, who called me a foolish boy at first; for they would stop with me on a landing, or in a room, when we were alone, and let me kiss them for a minute together." At about this time, his mother issues the conventional warning to him.

> I was then ordered by my mother to cease speaking to the servants, excepting when I wanted anything, though I am sure my mother never suspected my kissing one. I obeyed her hypocritically, and was even at times reprimanded for speaking to them in too imperious a tone. She told me to speak to servants respectfully. For all that I was after them; my curiosity was insatiable; I knew the time each went up to dress, or for other purposes, and if

[11] The reader should note that, until sometime during the mid-Victorian period, the number of domestic servants exceeded the number of industrial workers in England; they seemed to have made up the largest single group in the population until a surprisingly late date.

at home would get into the lobby or near the staircase to see their
legs as they went upstairs. I would listen at their door, trying to
hear them piss, and began for the first time to peep through key-
holes at them.

The account is convincing and full of assumptions: mother
does her duty and then remains in ignorance; she doesn't *want*
to know anything about what is going on. The son accepts the
code and continues undeterred in his pursuit of the "fair
game." The servants themselves accept it and would not dream
of peaching on him; that could only mean the loss of their position, possibly even a loss of their "character."

The loss of his father's fortune and his father's subsequent
death, along with the general decline in the family's circumstances, decrease the number of servants in the household. The
size of the family is also reduced, and he has increased opportunities to be alone with the servants in private. He takes advantage of this and soon is at work on one, who is content to re-
spond. He gets to fondling her, but timidity holds him back.
"She gave me lots of opportunities which my timidity prevented me from availing myself of. One day she said, 'You're
not game for much, although you are so big,' and then kissed
me long and furiously, but I never saw her wants, nor my
chances that I now know of, though I see now plainly enough
that, boy as I was, she wanted me to mount her." The last
clause of this passage seems particularly authentic, not only in
its purity of self-reference but also in the way it tends to minimize, simplify, and brush aside the character of the woman's
response. Unconsciously he has been able to do this all along,
even though he is at the same time frightened of sex in general
and of venereal disease in particular, which he has recently
learned about. He continues his pursuit, and one evening when
the family is out he gets to the point. He goes to the kitchen,
without premeditation, and finds her "sitting at needlework by
candle-light. I talked, kissed, coaxed her, began to pull up her
clothes, and it ended in her running round the kitchen and my
chasing her; both laughing and stopping at intervals, to hear if

my aunt knocked." After taking precautions with doors and gates, they continue.

> I got her onto my knees; I was now a big fellow, and though but a boy, my voice was changing; she chaffed me about that; then my hand went up her petticoats, and she gave me such a violent pinch on my cock (outside the clothes) that I hollowed. Whenever I was getting the better of her in our amatory struggles, she said, "Oh! hush! there is your aunt knocking," and frightened me away, but at last she was sitting on my knees, my hand touching her thighs, she feeling my prick; she felt it all around and under. "You have no hair," she said. That annoyed me, for I had just a little growing.

They then repair to the parlor and a sofa, where for the first time in his life he feels a woman's genitals. He is overwhelmed and thrown into a panic by the experience. The servant, however, is far ahead of him, cannot perceive his state, and urges him on. He is unable to continue, and displaces the fear he has just felt at touching her genitals onto the fear of venereal disease. " 'Go on, go on,' said she, moving her belly up. I could not, said nothing, but sat down by her side. She rose up. 'You're not man enough,' said she, laying hold of my prick. It was not stiff; I put my hand down, and again the great size—as it seemed to me—of her cunt made me wonder." "Wonder" is not quite the right word, but it at least allows him to try again. Again he fails and again she says, "You're not man enough." The returning family puts a stop to the proceedings, and he retires to his room feeling disgraced; "my pride was hurt in a woeful manner." For three days thereafter he avoids the servant, thinks about the occurrences, and washes himself compulsively. "When I sneaked into the kitchen again, I was ashamed to look at her, and left almost directly, but one day I felt her again. Laughing she put her hand outside my trousers, gave my doodle a gentle pinch and kissed me. 'Let's do it!' I said. 'Lor! you ain't man enough,' and again I slunk away." One of the most striking things about such passages is how they reveal to us a number of the assumptions that governed the relations of masters and servants. It is assumed by everyone, including the servants, that the author has a right to be doing what he is doing; if he is caught at it, the consequences will fall almost entirely on her. Her only means of defense are to fend him off as long as she can, but this must be done in secret. On the other side, there is no nonsense about affections, and she need not hide her feelings. There is something raw and savage about these scenes, and in her remarks to him we can make out not merely sexual antagonism and the revenge that the one sex takes upon the other, but class antagonism and revenge at the same time. The anger, the coarseness, the insults and general verbal cruelty are assumed to be as much her prerogatives as the pursuit of her is his.

The author does not succeed with this servant, but shortly thereafter seduces a young servant of about his own age, both of them losing their virginities in this encounter. He then goes on to further domestic conquests, the configuration of these experiences being always essentially the same. The relation of master and servant gives him the opportunity to express that aggression which for him is the principal component in his potency. "That did not stop my tongue," he typically comments on his pursuit of one servant, "for I now got angry and reckless, sang out my wants, bawling out about her cunt. . . ." This free-wheeling aggressiveness is combined with a sexual ideology of class which, he reports, was held by men of his rank. "As to servants and women of the humbler class . . . they all took cock on the quiet and were proud of having a gentleman to cover them. Such was the opinion of men in my class of life and of my age. My experience with my mother's servants corroborated it." However much of fantasy and distortion we wish to attribute to such remarks, it is plain that in this instance certain class assumptions are being used to support and confirm sexual fantasies, and vice versa. This fusion is one of the keys to the author's behavior.

At one point he undertakes to generalize about servants, and the following passage will serve as an adequate commentary on most of his experiences with them.

Then I had had so many gay women that I wanted a change in the class. I enjoyed their lubricity, their skilled embraces, their passionate fucking when they wanted it themselves, and liked me. . . . Yet I was tired of their lies, tricks, and dissatisfied, money-grabbing, money-begging style. I wanted a change, and began to look out for a nice fresh servant. I have now had many servants in my time, and know no better companions in amorous amusements. They have rarely lost all modesty, a new lover is a treat and a fresh experience to them, even when they have had several, and few have had that. They only get the chance of copulating once a week or so, they are clean, well-fed, full-blooded, and when they come out to meet their friend, or give way with a chance man on the sly, are ready, yielding, hot-arsed, lewd, and lubricious. Their cunts throb at the first touch of a finger, and moisten, and they spend freely and copiously. . . . No one will take more spunk out of a man and give more herself than a lass who says, "I couldn't get out before,—I'm sorry you had to wait,— I must really get back by ten." How they kiss in silence . . . what pleasure they quietly show,—how they love you, and die as your hot spunk spurts, and their cunt liquidizes. So I longed for a servant, and soon found my chance. I suppose all men do if they set their mind upon a woman, for there are thousands of cunts waiting to be fed, and ready to open to opportunity and male importunity.

This passage contains a paradoxical combination of attitudes. On the one hand, he appreciates certain human qualities in these women: they are not mercenary, are to some extent sincere and open in their responses, and give of themselves with appealing generosity. On the other, the language he uses to describe them is that of a horse-fancier or stableman: "a nice fresh servant" is "clean, well-fed, full-blooded," has not been used, ridden, or raced for a week, and is ready for service. One need only be aggressive, importunate, masterful enough, and the animal is yours. Once again we can see how—to use Marx's terms —the "objectification" of human relations which the circumstances of social class help to bring about combines with those sexual and pornographic fantasies in which all other human beings are only objects whose sole function is to satisfy our needs. The prepotency of class goes hand in hand with the om-

nipotence of thought, and permits fantasy to be translated into
behavior. The structure of social relations co-operates with the
structure of the unconscious mind; the analogy is a real one,
and beneath the combined force of the two, these women are
transformed into something less than human beings.

The author approves of and takes pleasure in the relatively
free sexuality of these servants; he approves of it morally and
makes use of it personally. It cannot occur to him, however, to
object to the convention under which these women were punished if their activities happened to be discovered. On one occasion, his wife discovers that a servant has had a sexual history
before entering their employ. The girl is sacked at the end of a
week, and the author comments, "I could not of course inter-
fere without injuring the poor woman and implicating myself,
—no good to either of us." On another, a servant has been discovered in some minor sexual irregularity. "One or two days
later I was told the woman had been dismissed. That I quite
expected, for it was the Mistress' custom to coax out the facts
from poor devils in a kind way, and then to kick them out
mercilessly; any suspicion of unchastity was enough for that.
Middle-age married women are always hard upon the young in
matters of copulation." Although these remarks reveal a certain
sympathy for the objects of such punishment, the sympathy is
of a passive kind, and reveals to us the author's sense of his own
possibilities for action. Another, more complex situation arises
when he discovers in his own household that two servants have
been having sexual relations. Lucy, a parlor maid, has been
caught in a severe indiscretion.

> It passed through my mind that she would be an exquisite sweet-
> heart, but I resisted incipient desire, avoiding by prudence and
> custom all intrigues with my own household.
> Suddenly this girl was dismissed, and I was requested to dismiss
> my man, who had . . . been in my service nearly two years. He
> was the best man I ever had, and was moreover a fine, handsome
> fellow, five feet ten high, and pleasant to look upon. He had been
> caught in loving familiarities with Lucy, who it was said also was
> with child by him; the poor girl had let this out to the cook or

someone else, and the cook split upon her. James was impudent and denied it all, but I think the case was proved. It would not have done to have passed over open fornication. Had I done so, the habit would have spread throughout the household; so I reluctantly gave him notice. The poor girl went off very quietly in tears. I never felt so sorry for a woman, especially as, whilst denying that she had let him have her, she said that he had promised her marriage, which James, when I told him, said was a lie. But this statement of hers confirmed me in the belief that he had tailed her.

These comments demonstrate several things. In the first place, the author is not quite consistent or has omitted either to tell the truth or to recollect it. He has not avoided all intrigues within his own household; but it seems useful to him at this point (both for his story and in his own self-interest) to say that he has. Second, for him it is the "open fornication" that cannot be condoned; he evidently believes that the spreading of open sexuality throughout the household would be demoralizing—and no doubt he is correct. What is most interesting about these statements, however, is the difficulty they present to us in determining the degree of moral reservation he feels about the whole business. They further demonstrate how he can maneuver within and make tactical use of a moral system or convention; even more, they show us how subtle and fluid even the most rigid conventional moral situation can be when it is seen from the inside.

What follows is a yet more striking demonstration. Lucy, the author tells us, "could not get a situation, for her uncharitable brute of a mistress, always after giving her a good character, somehow let out about this *faux pas.*" The author decides to intervene, in his own inimitable style. He goes to visit Lucy, seduces her in short order, and has his pleasure of this next-to-helpless girl. He then procures an abortion for her, cajoles and coerces James into marrying her, arranges with his solicitors to have £50 handed over to them after the marriage, and sets them both up in a new way of service in a distant village. Whether this entire episode is fact or fantasy cannot immediately be said to count; what matters is the characteristic way in which the events are represented. It is a striking example of class benevolence, and the author appears here in a new role— he is the Mr. Pickwick of the bedroom department. Indeed there would be something comic about this episode were it not for the fact that the author lacks any self-consciousness, any critical awareness, of what he is doing. For him the absolute reality of class, its "naturalness," is as self-evident, inevitable, and unquestionable as his own sexual drives.[12] The two are inextricably joined, and he experiences his own sexuality, as well as the sexuality of women, in class terms. It is this confluence that helps to explain how, in his dealings with Lucy (and there are others that illustrate the same operations), brutality and benevolence can consort without the author's ever coming to awareness of contradiction. It also helps to remind us of what we have all at one time learned—the depths of being to which social reality can penetrate, and the way it seems able sometimes to imbed itself in what is virtually our biology.

The author's accounts of his experiences with servants are only special instances of a general case. The nexus formed by his attitudes toward sex, class, and money constitutes the very tissue of his sensibility and is actively present in almost every story he tells. These attitudes are, naturally, overwhelmingly present in his descriptions of his relations with women from the lower social orders. At one point, when the author is still quite a young man, for example, he pays a visit to a large farm owned by some members of his family. One of the sons of this family is his cousin Fred, a bold and rakish person of about the same age as the author. They walk in the fields of a morning, and inspect the women working there. The author says, " 'There are half-a-dozen girls in the field I would not mind sleeping with.' 'Why don't you have them?' said Fred. 'I don't

---

[12] The attitude is omnipresent in him and in the language he uses. He speaks, for example, of his "class in life." What this conventional phrase implies is that social class was thought of as a fact of nature and that society and nature were in all ways congruent, not to say identical.

want to lose my character here.' 'That be damned; you can always have a field-girl; nobody cares,—I have had a dozen or two.'" In this comment of his cousin, it is worth noting that "nobody cares" evidently includes the field girls themselves—they are nobody, and neither do they care. They cannot be said to possess a distant human identity. Following his cousin's advice, the author picks out a fifteen- or sixteen-year-old girl, follows her at the right time, gets her alone, engages her in talk, and then proceeds to make further advances. To his surprise, she resists and continues to resist, which only serves to add to his arousal. He overpowers her—although she never stops fighting—and commits what must be called rape. The scene is described with uncompromising and brutal realism, and ends in this way.

> Her tears ran down. If I had not committed a rape, it looked uncommonly like one. . . .
>
> I got off her, saw for an instant her legs wide open, cunt and thighs wet and bloody, she crying, sobbing, rubbing her eyes. I was now in a complete funk; I had heard field-women so lightly spoken of that I expected only to go up a road that had often been travelled. This resistance and crying upset me, the more so when at length rising she said, "I'll tell my sister, and go to the magistrate, and tell how you have served me out."
>
> I really had violated her, saw that it would bear that complexion before a magistrate, so would not let her go, but retained her, coaxed, begged, and promised her money. I would love her, longed for her again, would take her from the fields, and every other sort of nonsense a man would utter under the circumstances. She ceased crying, and stood in sullen mood as I held her, asking me to let her go. I took out my purse and offered her money, which she would not take, but eyed wishfully as I kept chinking the gold in my hand. What a temptation bright sovereigns must have been to a girl who earned ninepence a day, and often was without work at all.

He continues to talk to her, and eventually up comes old Smith, the foreman of the farm, who in his day had exercised what amounted to seigneurial rights over the women laborers. The girl appeals to him, but he pooh-poohs her protestations. The author then breaks in again.

> "Take the sovereign" (she had refused it before), "I'll give you more another day; it will help to keep you a while,—hold your tongue and no one will know," said I. She hesitated, pouted, wriggled her shoulders, but at last took the sovereign . . . saying she would tell her sister. Then said the foreman, "None o' that, gal; an I hears more on that, you won't work here any more, nor anywheres else in this parish,—I knows the whole lot on you; I knows who got yer sister's belly up,—she at her age, she ought to be ashamed on herself; and I knows summut about you too,— now take care gal." "I've nothing to be ashamed on," said the girl; "you're a hard man to the women, they all say. . . ." "Well, there," said he, dropping his bullying tone, "the squire won't harm you; I think you be in luck if he loikes you,—say you nought;—that be my advice." The girl muttering went her way.

Having read this, one wants again to make some kind of wholesale reference to the Victorian novel. *This* is the kind of thing, one wants to say, that it was all about; *this* is the kind of thing that the Victorian novelists could not but be aware of —even though their explicit dealings with it were very circumspect—that their work as a whole was directed against. If we read the Victorian novel against the context of such scenes, we get a renewed and increased sense of how humanizing a work that genre was. Such scenes have of course taken place since time immemorial; they help constitute the very stuff of what we sometimes like to call traditional civilization. And such scenes continued without question to occur in Victorian England. What had changed was the consciousness with which these happenings were regarded; the Victorian novel was among the chief agents of that new and altered consciousness. For the first time in history it could be asserted, before what almost amounted to a mass audience, and in a public way, that persons of the lower social orders were not be treated in this way. Such treatment was now understood as an intolerable violation of that human nature which—again, effectively, for the first time in history—members of the lower social classes shared fully with their betters—that is, "ourselves." It was an alienation from them of rights that are inalienable from the condition of being human. The author of *My Secret Life* does not share this consciousness or the values which inhere in it, but he has none the less been affected by both. We see this in his very description of the scene, particularly in the way he records the conflict taking place within the girl whom he has brutalized. Two possibilities, or roles, are at war in her. On the one side, she wants to assert her existence as a human being with absolute rights over her own person. On the other, money, brute force, a *fait accompli,* and the cumulative power of a whole social system press her toward resignation to her role as a field girl. The latter inevitably win, but the author, who is the system's representative, has in his very rendering of the event also shown us the shape of things to come.

At a slightly later date he has a more protracted affair with another woman who works on the farm. This woman is of mature age, has made an unhappy marriage to an older man, is warm-hearted, kind, and even intelligent, and falls in love with the young gentleman. Here is the summary of his report on one of their last meetings.

> She loved me, begged me to take her away, where, how, she cared not, so long as she knew that I alone could have her; she would live alone if only I came to see her once a month, she said.
> I was sorry for this. What had been pastime to me was going to be misery to her. I had to show her the impossibility of my keeping her; then she said she would drown herself. Altogether it was not a very comfortable meeting apart from the fucking, which was as good as usual, I dare say, though I don't recollect much about that.

Here we can see how the lines of class and the condition of emotional deadness interact and sustain each other—an insight that Dickens was the first to elaborate in *Dombey and Son* and that other Victorian novelists would subsequently make much of. That such women should have feelings is clearly an inconvenience, both in terms of the author's personal needs and of his social position. The language in which the author expresses his sense of inconvenience is altogether familiar. With proper modifications, that last sentence could come right out of Trollope; it is precisely the kind of thing he puts into the mouth of a character like Dolly Longestaffe. For most of his career Trollope was amused and entertained by this kind of hard, aggressive indifference; he even was in favor of it since it was so clearly one of the norms of gentlemanly behavior. But when, toward the end of his career, he took a look around him and undertook that remarkable reversal which *The Way We Live Now* realizes, one of the things he saw was that a whole class of Englishmen were walking about like zombies. And like zombies they didn't even know they were dead. From here it is but a short step to modern literature, to Eliot, Kafka, et al. It may be useful to note, however, that this grand, universal theme of modern literature should find one of its earliest articulations through circumstances that have to do with social class; rather, we can say that in this early instance the circumstances of class are serving both to mask and give positive sanction to the emotional anesthesia.

One further episode reveals still greater depths of complexity in this subject. It occurs much later on in the author's life and is typical of his casual adventures in London. One evening he is going along the streets of a suburb of London.

> It was in a dull though widish road, where the houses lay back from the roads in gardens. A slight fog came on. On the opposite side of the way, I saw through the mist two young girls, singing, laughing, and talking loudly whilst walking on. A man carrying a basket on his back passed them, and I heard him say, "I should like to tickle up both of your legs a bit."—"Tickle us up then," said one in a loud cheeky tone, and then both ran across the road and down a turning close by me. I heard them laughing loudly when just out of sight in the mist, as if they enjoyed the bawdy suggestion.

He follows them, approaches them, and asks for a direction. "I began to talk and said they were both pretty girls. 'Give me a

kiss, and I will give each of you six pence.' They laughed, said
no, but in a minute I gave each a kiss and six pence. As I kissed
the biggest, I whispered to her, 'I'll give you a shilling if you
will do something for me and get your companion away.'—
'What?' said she boldly.—'Send her away.'—'No. She'll tell, but
at **** Street she goes another way.'—'You come back then.' "
As he says, "I know how to deal with young lasses well, having
had experience now." He reassures her that there is no danger,
and she does come back. He then engages her in talk, immediately introducing his sole concern. She laughs, is embarrassed,
and

began to walk away. "Never mind, here is your shilling." She
turned round and took it. "How foolish to go away; you might
get more money, and no one but you and I know anything about
—and directly I ask you a question, off you go."—"You talk improper," said she. . . .

"What are you doing about here?" said I, turning the conversation. "Going home from work."—"What do you work at?"—
"Folding up seeds at **** nursery," and she told me where.
"What do you get a day?"—"Nine pence. We both work there"—
(meaning the other girl). "You can get half a crown if you'll do
what I wish."—"I can't do anything."—"Yes, you can feel me."—
"Feel you, what's that?"—I rattled the money. "Here are two and
six pence; none will see us." We were by a long wall, and the fog
was not thickish. "Here is the money—give me your hand."

She looks down at him and says, "You old beast, let me go,"
but having broken off, she does not go far away.

She came back saying, "I must go, or I'll catch it." At the corner I
gave her a half a crown and said, "Every night you feel my cock I
will give you a shilling, and I'll give you half a crown if you let
me feel your bum."—"You old beast," said she again, as the
money dropped into her hand. Then she bolted off like lightning.

I went to the spot at the same time next night, but she did not
appear. On the third night, I saw her, and she was alone. . . . She
recognized me. "Go away, or I'll run," said she.—"I'm not going
to hurt you; give me a kiss, and I'll give you a shilling." I induced
her to turn up the same place, and there gave her both. Then she
felt my cock again and had another shilling. She was not in a
hurry to take away her hand from my cock as on the first night. I

fancied she liked feeling it. "Meet me every night" (it just suited
me then). "I can't, cause *she* comes home with me"—meaning the
other girl. How cunning young sluts are. . . .

Another night I caught her alone. I was that night in a frenzy
of randiness, put her hand round my prick and my own hand
outside hers, and so frigging, I spent copiously. "What is the
matter, sir," said she, looking up in my face, for I dare say I was
sighing and giving evidence of sexual emotion.

He then misses her, temporarily forgets about her, but about
two weeks later

by mere chance passing by there, I saw the little devil loitering
near the turning where she had first felt me. Crossing the road, I
said in passing, "Come on," and in two minutes she stood by my
side.

She had been ill; her mother said it was fever. But with a
chuckle, "I know what it was—I eat too much of them sweets and
fruit.—Mother said it was the smell from the privy and told the
doctor so. He asked me what I had been eating, and I said nothing." Then I found that she spent her money in fruit, sugar candy
and bull's eyes, and in riding in omnibuses. When she felt sick,
she got some brandy, and she only gave her companion a little bit
of sweet, "because she'd wonder where I got the money and
would tell." This much amused me. . . . A girl of fifteen riding
in an omnibus by herself for pleasure, and gorging herself with
sweets, out of the money got by feeling a man's prick in a street,
seems an amusing fact.

She missed the money, evidently, and *her* want was *my* opportunity. Said I, "I can only give you money if you let me feel your
bum."—"Oh no, not that." . . . She struggled, though quietly,
and escaped me, but as before stopped till I went to her to give the
money; then she went off. I felt sure that she had come out to
meet me that night.

He continues his advances on another night and then, appre-
hensive about being seen with her in the streets, hails a cab, tells
the driver to drive about in a park, and makes further advances.
"She got frightened and wanted to get out. I pacified her,
promised her five shillings instead of the smaller sum I usually
gave." He proceeds to fondle her more intimately, and she resists; "thrusting away my hand, she again sat on the opposite

seat, holding her clothes down; but I soon got her by my side again. The bawdiness I know pleased her." After some further masturbatory activities, he reports,

> she got anxious to go home, so telling the cabman to drive to a convenient spot, I let her out.
>
> The affair fascinated me. I went again to that quarter of the town at the time the girl left work, but never saw her for a fort-night. She, I believed, had avoided me till she had spent all her money. Then she only felt my cock, got her shilling and went off. She resisted everything else.

Perplexed, frustrated, and feeling in addition certain compunc-tions, he consults with a prostitute friend of long standing, who gives him this typical piece of advice: "Sarah said I had better leave it alone, but that someone would do it to that girl before long, for she evidently knew more than she should. One of the lads at the nursery would have her. She was more likely to let a lad have her than to let me. Perhaps she'd been fucked already, spite of her resistance. 'Those little bitches are so damned cun-ning that it would surprise you; she'll be gay, whether *you* do it to her or not.' That gave me comfort, and again I thought I'd try to get the girl." Again he sees her, again they enter a cab. "Familiarity had, I found, removed her fears," he remarks, and he continues to pursue his advances. At one point in the pro-ceedings, he stops, looks at her, and then:— " 'Do you know what fucking is,' I said. To which she made reply, 'I only knows what you tells me.' " He does not see fit to make any comment on this staggerer but continues at his labors. The whole arrangement, he remarks,

> was inconvenient, but the lewdness pleased me.—The cab kept slowly jogging on.
>
> My pleasure increased, and with it the desire to fuck. "Oh! I will give you half a sovereign if you'll do what I want,"—and I left off frigging. "Ten shillings?"—"Yes, ten shillings." She seemed reflecting. My desire grew stronger. "I'll give you a sover-eign if you'll let me put my prick between your legs—not in your cunt, but only between your thighs, and you shall hold it there."
>
> "Oh, no,—none of that," said she hastily. "I ain't going to let

you do that. I want to get out of the cab; let me go; oh do." She was taking fright and beginning to struggle.

I let her talk on. Opening my purse, I took out a sovereign. "Here's a golden sovereign," shewing it to her as we passed one of the few gas lamps. "You shall have it if you let me; you can wrap it up in a piece of paper, then make the paper muddy, and tell your mother you found it." I once taught another girl this.

The girl was silent long, looking me in the face (as it seemed) in the dark. Then, "No—oh no," disappointment in her manner and tone. I saw she would yield. She'd laid hold of my prick again unasked, and I replaced it and my hands before.

"If you won't, I shan't see you again. I can get fifty girls to feel my prick for a shilling."—"Has any other girl done it? You didn't tell me so."—"A dozen have."—"Lor," and she seemed to be reflecting on the information.

Things approach the crisis, and he tries to force her. She fights back and cries out, "Oho—don't—oh you beast—I'll scream.— Cabman, cabman—Let me out." She continues to struggle, as does he, and finally he ejaculates without succeeding in entering her. The adventure comes to an end in this way.

The driver, if he heard, took no notice, but she got so vociferous that I stopped the cab. She got out, ran off, not waiting for her gift, and in a second was lost in the darkness. . . . I never saw the girl afterwards, for the scene of my amatory doings was not near my home. I was going to visit a friend when I got this piece of luck, and first met this little stupid, who might have had the pleasure of a fuck, and profit as well.—As it is, I dare say some dirty young boy will open her cunt, and give her a black eye if she upbraids him if her belly swells. That is the course of events in her class.—It is not the gentlemen who get the virginities of these poor little bitches, but the street boys of their own class.

His final comment is that all this experience had "at a cost of a pound or two amused me, as all chance adventures do. They break the monotony of matter of fact hard fucking.— Yet that I should have taken all that trouble for a dirty little work girl, whose face I never saw excepting by the light of a street lamp, astonishes me often when I think of it." It astonishes the modern reader too, though in radically different senses. First of all there is the simple anguish of the girl's economic condition: for a couple of minutes of harmless activity she can earn five times as much as she does in an entire day of pointless drudgery. Who would not be tempted by such a possibility? Conversely we must try to imagine what an order of self-restraint must have been required for a sustained refusal. To this there is the added pathos of what she does with the few odd shillings he gives her. She cannot bring it home or spend it on anything visible or permanent since she would automatically come under suspicion (such a fact helps us to recollect how naked, unadorned, and destitute of privacy the life of certain classes once was). And the suspicion would be correct—she could have come by the money only in one way. So she spends her money on fruits and sweets, and the image we get of her chewing dreamily away and riding endlessly back and forth on omnibuses until her money is consumed and she is sick to her stomach stuns our senses and sensibilities. The author, however, is not stunned but is "amused" by this revelation of the grotesquely narrow range of possibilities open to her. It would be incorrect, I think, to attribute this response of his to simple or unmodified personal brutality alone. It is as much the emotional distance which the traditional situation of class tended to create that is being expressed here. The author is altogether unable to put himself in her place or to imagine what must be going on in her; and this restriction serves to remind us how the actualities of class could affect not merely one's moral view of the world but one's perception of reality itself. The workings of class here can be seen as penetrating virtually to one's organs of sense and as conditioning fundamental mental structures. It even seems possible, in the light of such passages, that one might construct different epistemological models following the lines of these distinctions.[13]

As one reads this episode, one's sympathies are enlisted on the side of the young girl (that is one of the differences between this work and pornography; in pornography, one never feels

[13] Something of this kind was suggested in Karl Mannheim's theory of "the sociology of knowledge." See especially his *Ideology and Utopia.*

sympathy for any sexual object, and whenever women are represented as resisting, the function of such representations is to
stimulate aggressive and sadistic fantasies). The reader wants
the girl not to give in; he wants her to get away and is pleased
when she does. Her escape represents a triumph, however temporary it may have been, of certain values which are alien and
antagonistic to the author and his purposes. And the entire episode—again it is a typical one—leads one to reconsider certain
general questions which seem almost to have come to be taken
for granted. Everyone knows what the eighteenth-century London "mob" was like; and it is hardly to be questioned that
much of its character persisted, though in modified forms,
among the urban lower classes until well into the nineteenth
century. That life was degraded and often bestial; drink, violence, early and promiscuous sexuality, and disease were the
counterparts of poverty, endless labor, and a life whose vision of
futurity was at best cheerless. In such a context, the typical Victorian values, and indeed Victorianism itself, take on new
meaning. It is not usual nowadays to regard such values as
chastity, propriety, modesty, even rigid prudery as positive
moral values, but it is difficult to doubt that in the situation of
the urban lower social classes they operated with positive force.
The discipline and self-restraint which the exercise of such virtues required could not but be a giant step toward the humani-
zation of a class of persons who had been traditionally regarded
as almost of another species. Indeed, the whole question of "respectability" stands revealed in a new light when we consider it
from this point of view. One of the chief components of respectability is self-respect, and when we see this young girl resisting
all that money, class, privilege, and power, we understand how
vital an importance the moral idea of respectability could have
for persons in her circumstances.[14]

[14] In 1883, in the midst of his prolonged engagement to and separation from
Martha Bernays, the young Freud wrote to his future wife that "it is neither
pleasant nor edifying to watch the masses amusing themselves; we at least
don't have much taste for it. . . . I remember something that occurred to me
while watching a performance of *Carmen*: the mob gives vent to its appetites,

Even more, a work like *My Secret Life* leads one to understand how the deflection of one's sexuality, how even frigidity itself, could have an important social function or purpose. This is a very complex matter, and I can only touch upon certain points here. I have said that the author's account of the responsiveness of most of the women he has known is not to be trusted in detail; the evidences of fantasy are too strong. One general impression, however, we may provisionally accept as accurate—that these women recruited from the lowest ranks of society were genuinely responsive in a direct sexual way, and had not in their childhood or youth been reared within that elaborate system of arrangements which is required to create what we know as the modern middle-class character.[15] We may assume that numbers of persons of the laboring classes were unhappy with the kind of lives they had inherited and saw being led all around them, and that they as-

---

and we deprive ourselves. We deprive ourselves in order to maintain our integrity, we economize in our health, our capacity for enjoyment, our emotions; we save ourselves for something, not knowing for what. And this constant suppression of natural instincts gives us the quality of refinement. . . . Why don't we get drunk? . . . Why don't we fall in love with a different person every month? . . . Thus we strive more toward avoiding pain than seeking pleasure. And the extreme case are people like ourselves who chain themselves together for life and death, who deprive themselves and pine for years so as to remain faithful, and who probably wouldn't survive a catastrophe that robbed them of their beloved. . . . Our whole conduct of life presupposes that we are protected from the direst poverty and that the possibility exists of being able to free ourselves increasingly from social ills. The poor people, the masses, could not survive without their thick skins and their easygoing ways. Why should they take their relationships seriously when all the misfortune nature and society have in store threatens those they love? Why should they scorn the pleasures of the moment when no other awaits them? The poor are too helpless, too exposed, to behave like us. When I see the people indulging themselves, disregarding all sense of moderation, I invariably think that this is their compensation for being a helpless target for all the taxes, epidemics, sicknesses, and evils of social institutions."

[15] See Sigmund Freud, *A General Introduction to Psychoanalysis*, Chap. 22. In his parable of the caretaker's daughter and the gentleman's daughter, Freud proposes that the different responses of both girls to childhood sexual experiences are a result of the differences in their homes and educations and that these in turn lead to very different kinds of sexual responsiveness in maturity. See also Robert Waelder, *Basic Theory of Psychoanalysis* (New York, 1960), pp. 41–44.

pired to something other; we may further assume that the values and style of life to which they aspired were generally those of the middle classes—there was indeed no other model available to them. The preparations for such an effort of change usually involve first a change in certain fundamental habits of behavior and an emulation of the styles or habits of the class to which one wishes to ascend. In this particular instance, what was required was an immense effort of self-discipline and self-denial, the ability to learn how to defer gratification indefinitely and to persist in the deferral, and a concomitant labor of rationalizing and systematizing all of one's daily activities and almost all of one's impulses. It seems to me impossible to deny that one's sexuality would be affected by these sustained efforts of will—in particular, I believe, the sexuality of women had to be affected. I am not suggesting simply that repression of sexuality took place, although repression was certainly part of a more complex process. What happened was that a general restructuring of the personality occurred, and what emerged at the end was a character which was more armored and more rigidified, a character capable of sustained executive action, yet a character also less spontaneous, less openly sexual—and probably sexually thwarted. This is the character which the modern middle class has inherited and that everyone is miserable about; and it is not open to doubt that a loss of tragic magnitude was entailed in the change. That is the price which is invariably exacted by social advances of any significance. Yet if, with the aid of documents such as *My Secret Life,* we gain a clearer and fuller understanding of what the life of the urban poor was like, how they were regarded by their superiors, and how they tended to regard themselves, we will not be so quick or certain in our judgment that it was all a mistake and that the loss totally outweighs what was gained. If we take this episode from *My Secret Life* as exemplary in character, we can conclude that in the degree to which that young girl succeeded in denying her sexuality to the author, and to other men, and in the degree to which she even made her own sexuality inaccessible to herself, in that degree might she have the chance of extending her humanity in other directions.[16]

At the end of the episode the author takes a last farewell of "the little stupid" and pronounces on her fate. It will be, he says, a class fate and a wretched one. Despite the savageness of language in which he makes this utterance, it must be allowed that he was overwhelmingly likely to be right. In this connection, there is something important for us to observe about the author's development. Although he is never what one could possibly think of as an inhibited person, he does start out in life with certain fears, anxieties, and reluctances about sexual behavior, and with certain beliefs as well. Until he is about thirty years old, he states, "my habits with women in my lust were for the most part simple, commonplace, and unintellectual." At about that time, however, he became gradually aware of a change going on in him.

> I was evidently no longer displeased with that which in years previously would have shocked me. My prejudices have now pretty well vanished with the approach of middle age. I have conquered antipathies and reaped the reward, in seeing before me a great variety of frolics, suitable to my maturity, but which I am glad I did not have prematurely in my youth, when I did not need them and should not have appreciated them as I do now. . . . No blame attaches to woman for liking or for submitting to such frolics, abnormal whims and fancies, which fools call obscene, but

---

[16] In this section I have tried to add a further dimension to Weber's great work on the relation between modern forms of economic and social organization and the kind of character that was necessary to create those forms and to perpetuate them—namely, I have tried to demonstrate that the theory should include an account of how sexual energies were enlisted in and affected by the change. A classic example of what I have been describing is represented in the relation of Mr. and Mrs. Morel in *Sons and Lovers*. Much work has been done on the effect of the religious revival in eighteenth- and nineteenth-century England on this process, and a book such as E. P. Thompson's *The Making of the English Working Class* (London, 1964) provides a gathering place for a great deal of relevant material. See also W. L. Burn, *The Age of Equipoise* (London, 1964) for other useful material.

A similar methodological problem has been handled with considerable expertness by Stanley Elkins in *Slavery: A Problem in American Institutional and Intellectual Life* (Chicago, 1962).

which are natural and proper, and perhaps universally practised, and which concern only those who practise and profit by them. In my experience many women delight equally in them, when their imaginations are once evoked. Nothing can perhaps be justly called unnatural which nature prompts us to do. If others don't like them, they are not natural to *them,* and no one should force them to act them.

This is a later passage of reflection, inserted after an account of one of his adventures. It occurs in Volume V, and this and subsequent volumes of the work are frequently interspersed with similar remarks. At a slightly later date, for example, he begins to read pornography.

This literature amused me much, as did the pictures of fantastic combinations of male and female, in lascivious play and in coition. . . . There is no end of variety in such amusements, and no limits to eccentricities, and no harm in gratifying them, either alone with one woman, or man, or in society to whom it is congenial. A field of lascivious enjoyment new to me seemed opening, and I thought about the out of the way erotic tricks portrayed, and of those I also might play, and that I should like to try them. I began to see that such things are harmless, though the world may say they are naughty, and saw through the absurdity of conventional views and prejudices as to the ways a cock and cunt may be pleasurably employed.

Why for instance, is it permissible for a man and woman to enjoy themselves lasciviously, but improper for two men and two women to do the same things all together in the same room?— Why is it abominable for anyone to look at a man and woman fucking when every man, woman, and child would do so if they had the opportunity? Is copulation an improper thing to do; if not, why is it disgraceful to look at its being done?—Why may a man and woman handle each others' privates, and yet it be wrong for a man to feel another's prick—or a woman to feel another's cunt? Everyone in each sex has at one period of their lives done so, and why should not any society or association of people indulge in these innocent though sensual amusements if they like, in private? What is there in their doing so that is disgraceful? It is the prejudice of education alone which teaches that it is.

Such reflections had crossed my mind for some years; they tended to sweep away prejudices. And though I still have prejudices—yet for the most part I can see no harm in gratifying my lust in the ways which the world would say is highly improper, but which appear to me that men and women are intended by instinct as well as by reflection to gratify. This frame of mind seems to me to have been gradually developing for some time past—and accounts for much that follows.

These passages are in part, of course, rationalizations and justifications for his own behavior, but that does not make them any the less remarkable. Starting by himself, alone, in the high-Victorian period, the author has evolved for himself out of his own experiences, fantasies, and contemplations a point of view which—despite the crudity and coarseness of his terminology—is a significant anticipation of what is generally thought of as the modern, liberal, and liberated conception of sexual morality. It is important to note that one of the foundation stones of this morality is based on the idea of an English gentleman's private right to do whatever he likes with his own person and to let others do the same—and that this idea is in turn connected with notions of *laissez-faire* and property. That is to say, within and beneath official Victorian culture, a subversive and counter-tendency can be made out at work. This tendency, however, appropriated for its erosive work a number of the central conceptions of value of the official culture; and when the explosion of modernity took place, some of the chief weapons used in the attack upon the older moral world were themselves values which that older world had originated and based itself upon. The careers of Sigmund Freud and James Joyce are two of the grand elaborated paradigms of this process. The author of *My Secret Life* comes before either of them, but he too is, to the degree that his abilities and interests extend, involved in similar work.

One might reasonably expect that the evolution of such "advanced" views would have some further results, would tend to cause analogous changes in other areas and attitudes. In some measure, this does appear to occur in him. On one occasion, for example, he exchanges chaff with a servant whom he is trying to seduce.

. . . her eyes twinkled, and she laughed much. I had now broken down the barrier, had brought myself to her level, and she as every other woman would have done, took advantage of it, and began to return my chaffing and banter. Every woman feels instinctively that when a man is chaffing her (be it ever so decently veiled) about fucking, that she may safely return it: both are at once on a common level. A washerwoman would banter a prince if the subject was cunt, without the prince being offended. To talk of fucking with a woman is to remove all social distinctions. . . .

The language that the author uses clearly indicates which end of the telescope he is looking down, and whatever attitudes he may have toward the situation he is here describing, the conclusions are inescapable: sex and democracy are somehow equated. More precisely, perhaps, sexual liberation and a collapse in social distinctions seem, at this stage in historical development, logically to imply one another. And at another point he happily remarks, "Fucking is the great humanizer of the world." This, I take it, is the point of view of Mr. Wayland Young among others. It is a charming sentiment, and most modern people have probably believed in it at one moment or another in their lives. Unfortunately it happens not to be true. It is not true in general, and it is not true about the author of *My Secret Life*. Although there is no reason to doubt the sincerity of such statements, it must also be remarked that they have almost no resonance beyond themselves in either his attitudes or his behavior. His liberation from sexual-moral prejudices is not accompanied by a parallel development in his ideas about class and society. Until the very end of his life, he maintains the belief that distinctions of social class somehow correspond to differences of a quasi-biological sort. Here is a typical description: "She was a well-grown, good looking woman about twenty-three years old, of the costermonger class. She looked like one who sold goods from a barrow, or a very small shop. She was commonly but comfortably clad, not warmly enough perhaps for well-to-do people, but enough so for her class who don't feel cold as we do." The very form in which he makes this statement demonstrates again his absolute and unquestioning acceptance of the reality, the permanence, and the "naturalness" of social and class circumstances. Furthermore, in view of the fact that much of his sexual experience was taken in company with women of these ranks, one wonders what heroic efforts of denial were required in order for him to be able to make such statements without any qualification at all. One wonders how he experienced these women and even whether he experienced them at all—a point to which we shall return. One is even tempted to ask why he doesn't regard them in the same way sexually, why he doesn't say they don't feel sex as we do, with the same implied contempt. He might of course double back and reply that this is exactly the point, that since they endure the wind and weather like beasts of the field, their sexuality is also of a bestial directness, which is what he likes. In other places, however, he denies the inferences that I have just drawn, and asserts that although the sexual manners of women of the middle classes are different from those of the lower classes, their responsiveness cannot be distinguished in a generalized way. At any rate, his conscious attitudes are not coherent enough to bear this pitch of examination. What remains are certain broad beliefs and their accompanying unconscious contradictions.

One more passage will have to serve for all the rest, for it has to be admitted that the author never tires of reiterating himself on this subject.

Much talk with gay women, and my own experiences make me believe . . . that nearly the whole of the girls of the lowest classes begin copulating with boys of about their own age when about fourteen years old.

Few of the tens of thousands of whores in London gave their virginities either to gentlemen, or to young or old men—or to men at all. Their own low class lads had them. The street boys' dirty pricks went up their little cunts first.—This is greatly to be regretted, for street boys cannot appreciate the treasures they destroy. A virginity taken by a street boy of sixteen is a pearl cast to a swine. Any cunt is good enough for such inexperience.—To such an animal, a matron of fifty or sixty would give him as much, if not more pleasure than a virgin.

Although we should not overlook the disclaimer entered in the names of experience and appreciation, the general force of the passage is unmistakable. It is a force that defines one whole area of the document we are discussing and the things it refers to.

What we are confronted with is a situation whose meaning cannot be explained or exhausted by reference to the process of isolation alone, though isolation is doubtless connected with the process. In short, the author of *My Secret Life* underwent a development in his sexual beliefs and attitudes that can be called revolutionary; at the same time, and contrary to what one might expect, these developments seemed to find no corollary or further consequences in other and adjacent areas of social and moral belief and behavior. In this experience, he was anticipating in a significant way the future development of his own and our society. We have in our own time been witness to a sexual revolution which has also been split off from what might have been expected to accompany it—impulses of a social revolutionary kind. The reasons for this occurrence are of the profoundest kind, and have to do with such immense matters as the economic structure and history of our society, with the course of development that the Industrial Revolution pursued in the West, with the development of our forms of parliamentary and social democracy, and even with the confrontation of communist and capitalist systems of society. That is to say, they have to do with everything; in matters such as these, we can no longer, unfortunately, continue shaving with Occam's razor. It is still necessary to note, however, that the structure and history of modern Western society made possible, or legitimized, the revolution in sexual beliefs and behavior through which we are now living; conversely, those same forces have steadily worked to reduce both the possibility and the legitimacy of those impulses that have historically found expression in thought and action of a socially radical nature. There is no reason to doubt the authenticity of the sexual revolution, which is now after all more than sixty years old; it is possible, however, to question part of its larger significance, particularly in view of the fact that the socially radical impulses with which the sexually revolutionary impulses have, historically, been symbiotically connected seem to have been almost systematically thwarted in their search for legitimate means of expression. It would be far too simple to say that the sexual revolution has taken place only because a social revolution did not, or that one is the substitute for the other. It is not to be denied, nevertheless, that connections between the two—both genetically and dynamically—go very deep, and that the relations between them, as mutually informing presences and absences, have much to tell us about the character and the possibilities of modern society. Nor is it, of course, to be denied that social changes of a considerable nature have taken place. What seems to have happened is that in our society sexual beliefs, practices, and institutions were more susceptible to radical alteration than their counterparts in economic and social activity; another way of putting it is to say that in our society the fundamental organizations of economic and social behavior have been more resistant to radical change than have the institutions which govern and express sexual beliefs and behavior. From this point of view, then, sexual moral beliefs and certain forms of sexual practice take on the surprising appearance of a superstructure, to which the more resistant institutions of economic and social organization function as a substructure. The author of *My Secret Life* was living at a time when far different things were happening in the society about him. A representative figure of cultural subversion in his own time, he representatively anticipates what is about to become the conformity of ours.

The third component in the nexus, money, is much easier to understand. Like class, it has become fused with almost all the author's sexual responses. Since most of his experiences are with prostitutes or poor women, money is actively present throughout the work and is in fact one of its principal characters. Money in *My Secret Life* is what money is in the nineteenth-century novel or in *Das Kapital*. It is the universal commodity that has the power of converting all other things into commodities, or that all other things can be converted into. The author is uncommonly careful and precise in his accounts, and never fails to put down how much he did or did not pay or to record the nature of the transaction that went on between himself and a woman. In the course of these descriptions, we learn a good deal of casual social history—which mostly amounts to the conclusion that the price of sex, like the price of most other commodities, underwent a gradual but steady inflation as the century advanced. In his youth, the author tells us, "a sovereign would get any woman, and ten shillings as nice a one as you needed. Two good furnished rooms near the Clubs could be had by women for from fifteen to twenty shillings per week, a handsome silk dress for five or ten pounds, and other things in proportion. So cunt was a more reasonable article than it now is, and I got quite nice girls at from five to ten shillings a poke, and had several in their own rooms, but sometimes paying half-a-crown extra for a room elsewhere." He even offers us a comparative set of prices, saying of one prostitute whom he knew in his early twenties that she "was young, handsome, well made, and in the Haymarket would now get anything from one to five pounds; yet I had her several times for three and four shillings a time." You pay for what you get, and the author is always willing to pay, but sometimes even he is beset by doubts. "As I think of it," he once writes, "there is wonderfully little difference between the woman you have for five shillings and the one you pay five pounds, excepting in the silk, linen, and manners." Exactly: they are both women—and prostitutes.

The author's attitude toward the relation of money to sex is not different from his attitude toward the relation of class to sex. He accepts its existence as part of the order of nature and happily makes use of it. Like many Englishmen of his time, the author on occasion experienced a peculiarly intense desire to deflower a young virgin, the younger the better. The scenes which describe the outcome of these desires are the most brutal and disgusting in the book. Apart from their open sadism—which will be discussed in another context—they chiefly consist of lengthy accounts of the financial maneuverings required to bring them to successful conclusion. Here is his description of the consummation of one of these episodes: "The job was done; months of anticipation, hopes, fears, and desire were over; my prick was in the cunt of a French virgin, at a cost of two hundred pounds. . . . I had a feeling of pleasure and tranquillity, a weight off my mind, a future of voluptuousness before me." Two hundred pounds is an exorbitant amount, but the author was young at the time, "very green," he says. The women who procured these girls and children for him were mostly prostitutes, and his accounts of the proceedings agree in detail with those published in 1885 by W. T. Stead in his exposure in the *Pall Mall Gazette* of the considerable trade in the bodies of children that had been going on for years in London. On a later occasion, after he has violated a ten-year-old girl, he reports this conversation with the woman who sold the girl to him: "We talked afterwards. She was not the mother, nor the aunt, though the child called her so; the child was parentless; she had taken charge of her and prevented her going to the workhouse. She was in difficulties, she must live, the child would be sure to have it done to her some day, why not make a little money by her? Someone else would if she did not. So spoke the fat, middle-aged woman." Indeed, at moments when he tends philosophically to expand, he regards the whole question of chastity and virginity as a matter of money.

In my youth, the smallest and youngest girl . . . called the female she was with "aunt." Another girl, if not two, whose names I just now forget, but of whom I have told, called the mistresses "aunt," and I fancy that many aunts among the humbler classes make a little money out of their nieces' virginities.—They know well that at about fourteen years of age, girls escape their care, will play with boys and youths, and are pretty sure to be broached before they are sixteen. Aunts often think that a gentleman may as well have the broaching of a little cunt, and pay for it, as a coster lad have it for nothing.—Indeed I believe that to be a philosophical way of looking at it, common to a large number of the poor people in all countries. . . . Other girls have got their young female relations for me, and liked doing it, liked the pimping.— The poor, and wisely and right in their simplicity of nature, see no harm in copulation, as those better off profess to do (but whether they really see harm is another question).—A girl is not among nine-tenths of the population morally damaged by a little illicit fucking, as she is among those who look upon a hymen as a prize and guarantee in the woman they seek as a wife.

All said, the female who keeps her cunt hymenized and under seal among the well-to-do classes, only does so that she may get a higher price for it, either in money or position. She sometimes never attains either, and mostly has to wait long for it, wait for years, and frigs herself during her waiting, languishing for want of a prick and spermatic lubrication, which is health-giving to a female.—A poorer girl has earlier the prick up her, and every day, perhaps, has the intense pleasure of fucking. . . . Thus the happinesses of life are pretty evenly distributed.—Perhaps the woman who follows her sexual instincts, and who is thus the most natural, has the best of it. Fucking is the greatest pleasure of life, and the woman who delays getting it for years loses much.

And at another point he sums up his views in this way:

It was a wonder to me that when both sexes feel so much pleasure in looking at each other's genitals—that they should take such extreme pains to hide them, should think it disgraceful to show them without mutual consent, and penal to do so separately or together in public—I came to the conclusion that in the women it is the result of training, with the cunning intention of selling the view of their privates at the highest price—and inducing the man to give them that huge price for it—the marriage ring. Women are all bought in the market—from the whore to the Princess. The price alone is different, and the highest price, in money or rank, obtains the woman.

We can put aside the considerable influx of fantasy in the passages—the immensely oversimplified view of morality, the exaggerated statistics. Two things are of larger interest. First, the author asserts that the connection between sex and money was a normative one, an assumed value, among all classes in Victorian England. This is generally in accord with what we know from Victorian literature and other sources. Second, although the author serenely accepts this norm, his attitude in the passages I have quoted presents an interesting combination of qualities. It is, again, both brutal and humane at once. It is brutal in its unwavering acceptance of such a moral system and in the cynicism that such an acceptance entails. It is humane in its sympathy for the poor and its sense of the difficulties involved in matters of sexual choice. This tone which combines brutality and humaneness is the characteristic tone of the entire document and is, I think, unique to it. It may be suggested that a work such as *My Secret Life* could only have been written by a man in whom this peculiar admixture of qualities was to be found. It may be further suggested that a man in Victorian England (and perhaps still today) who wished to pursue a life of uninhibited promiscuity had to be possessed not merely of courage and aggressiveness, but had to carry both to the point where they were transformed into brutishness and ugliness and dead indifference. And it may be useful to remind ourselves that the struggle for sexual freedom, at least in the lives of individual persons, requires considerable stepping over the bodies of others and that it is not only in political revolutions that crimes are committed in the name of liberty.

The author does not of course consider himself a rebel or revolutionary, and in point of fact he is not. He wholeheartedly accepts the existing situation and thoroughly enjoys going through what he calls "the mercantile business." And at last he brings the whole thing to its logical conclusion. On two occasions, he makes an experiment and fills the vagina of a woman with shilling pieces. I will not report on the capacities he discovers, and refrain from all comment which the scenes tempt one to make. In a larger sense, however, the issue is clear. Money and class operate in relation to sex in similar ways. One of the principal components in male sexuality is the desire for power, the desire to dominate. In modern society, money is one of the two or three most important instruments of personal power, and the association of sex and money through the medium of power is an inevitable one. Money operates in still an-

other way to further the author's sense of power. It interposes
itself between the author and the women whose bodies he is
both paying for and seeking to enter. It creates an even further
distance—in both a social and psychic sense—between the two
partners to this transaction, and turns the women into commodities, objects—to use the classic term once more, a process
of "objectification" occurs. The dehumanization which such an
experience incurs is always evident, on both sides of the transaction. It is only one of the many paradoxes inherent in this relation that a man seeking the most intimate union with another
person should do so by creating the maximum possible distance
between them, or that the fullest expression of his inmost humanity should be achieved only through circumstances which
are bound to depersonalize both himself and his partner. We
begin to unpack the paradox when we realize that the author is
not actually seeking union with another person. He is seeking
to fulfill or act out certain fantasies; and the success of such a
project depends on the degree to which he can dominate or
control his sexual partners, the degree to which he can turn
them into objects. In masturbation and the fantasies which accompany it, such total domination is assured. For a man who
needs a more "realistic" form of sexual drama, the passive co-
operation of women who have chosen to regard their bodies,
and persons, as objects to be manipulated is and always has
been an adequate substitute.

   In order to discover what these fantasies are, we have to shift
our point of view and examine material of a different kind.
Thus far we have discussed, so to speak, the outer part of *My
Secret Life,* the part that refers to society and social existence.
Now we have to move inward and regard this document with
different instruments and different purposes.

Chapter 4: THE SECRET LIFE—II

THE chief conscious or explicit intention of *My Secret Life* is to be honest. The author tells us at the outset that it was his determination "to write my private life freely as to fact, and in the spirit of the lustful acts done by me, or witnessed; it is written therefore with absolute truth, and without any regard for what the world calls decency. Decency and voluptuousness in its fullest acceptance cannot exist together; one would kill the other. . . ." There can be no doubt that the author does make a considerable effort of honesty—in reporting on thoughts and attitudes as well as in recording behavior. He is not ashamed of revealing himself in an unflattering light, and he does not shrink from admitting to puzzlement, frustration, and failure. Late in life, for example, when he has fully developed his notion that in sexual matters everything is permissible, he decides to have an elaborate, multipersoned experience which will include for himself homosexual behavior. He succeeds with considerable difficulty in going through with it and is immediately disgusted with himself and the other man. Reflecting on the episode, he writes: "There can be no indecency or impropriety in women or men amusing themselves any way they like in private—objections arise from prejudice and custom. Yet I was glad to get Eugene out of the room. It annoys me to think that I had him, as I write this—which is absurd. What is the use of my philosophy if it leaves me thus minded?" On other occasions, he makes similar confessions. This ability to admit to the discrepancy between fantasy and reality, between belief or attitude and experience, is, one should suppose, a necessary precondition to any credible account of one's own life.

Part of this honesty is principled in character and is specifically directed against the prevailing moral code. He concludes his description of his first fully consummated affair in this way: "In all respects we were as much like man and wife as circumstances would let us be. We poked and poked, whenever we got a chance; we divided our money; if I had not, she spent her wages; when I had it, I paid for her boots and clothes—a present in the usual sense of the term I never gave her; our sexual pleasures were of the simplest; the old fashioned way was what we followed, and altogether it was a natural, virtuous, wholesome connection, but the world will not agree with me on that point." To make such an affirmation in Victorian England required, in addition to honesty, courage and defiance. One ought to note, however, the tone of the passage, which is characteristic, I believe, of writing of this sort. Although he is asserting the innocence, even the holiness and chastity, of this experience, he is doing so in a tone of sadness and almost resignation; it is as if by now he didn't quite believe in what he was saying, or as if the more clearly he affirmed his convictions, the more confusing things became. We tend to think of honesty as invigorating; we forget that often it can be depressing. The literature of sex, in all its branches, is not a particularly joyful or happy literature. It is on the whole rather grim and sad; even at its most intense moments there is something defeated in it. Something in the nature of its subject, one may reflect, dictates this prevailing tone.

Another side of the author's anti-Victorian effort of honesty has to do with his intention of revealing the extent to which hypocrisy about sexual matters dominated life at his time. This intention provides him, in addition, with a conscious justification of his own work: "whatever society may say, it is but a narrative of human life, perhaps the everyday life of thousands, if the confession could be had." He is also concerned to deny or debunk the cult of "pure love" which then enjoyed much currency; and although his repudiation of this idea is coarse, harsh, and vulgar, there is some point to it, particularly in view of the context in which it was made. Similarly, on one occasion he has a Leopold Bloomish experience—he spends some time spying on women defecating and urinating. He is subsequently distressed and disgusted with himself, and on reading over his account of the incident doubts "if I should not omit the whole." Nevertheless, he concludes, "a secret life should have no omissions. There is nothing to be ashamed of, it was a passing phase, and after all man cannot see too much of human nature." However unguarded in their contradictions such passages may be, however transparently they act as rationalizations for other motives, there is also a glimmer of truth in these assertions. Finally, in its very emphasis on sex, in its obsessive and exclusive concern with it, this work was in its own time subversive. It was subversive of that characteristic Victorian arrangement in which the existence of a whole universe of sexuality and sexual activity was tacitly acknowledged and actively participated in, while at the same time one's consciousness of all this was, as far as possible, kept apart from one's larger, more general, and public consciousness of both self and society.[1] A work like *My Secret Life,* along with the efflorescence during the Victorian period of all kinds of pornographic literature, is directly connected with this peculiar historical separation.

Surrounded by darkness and ignorance, and living amid what he took to be a conspiracy of silence in regard to sexual matters, the author often wonders about his own oddness or singularity. Do all men act as I do, he asks; "does every man kiss, coax, hint smuttily, then talk bawdily, snatch a feel, smell his fingers, assault and win, exactly as I have done?" And he asks similar questions about women. Furthermore, he continues, "have all men had the strange letches which late in life have enraptured me, though in early days the idea of them revolted me? I can never know this; my experience if printed may enable others to compare as I cannot." Once again, although such statements function without doubt as rationaliza-

---

[1] Gladstone, for example, was totally unable to understand any joke that contained a sexual reference.

tions, the rationalizations also refer to something real and cannot be dismissed as mere screens or distortions. And a similar mixture of partial components—requiring a similar differential analysis—is evident throughout the work. For not only does the author write down as accurately as he can what he experienced, but he also makes further efforts to find out "the truth," or at least, as they say, "the facts." To this end he does several things. At some point toward the middle of his career, he prepares what I take to be the first questionnaire on sexual behavior in history. And like the later team of researchers led by Alfred C. Kinsey, he memorized his list of questions, having perhaps some intuition that in matters of this kind a "formal" style of questioning can only increase resistance and inhibition. He reprints his list of questions; there are about one hundred of them and they are the obvious ones. He remarks that they "are leading questions. The replies suggested others." He freely admits that one of his motives in this undertaking was sexual pleasure, the pleasure of seeing and knowing "all that women had hidden of their bodies, to compare and note differences, and ask every one of them questions about their sexual tastes, sensations, and habits." But we should note as well that this sexual curiosity is not to be wholly distinguished from curiosity itself; moreover, the grounding of all other kinds of curiosity in the sexual curiosity of childhood is too well known by now to require further or repeated demonstration. What we have in *My Secret Life* is an unusual documentation of how this process may also work itself out culturally.

During the course of the work, he also finds occasion to write three long separate essays—one on copulation in general and one each on the male and female genitals. The author states that he has "reflected on the secrecy with which human beings envelop their amours—of the shame which they so ridiculously attach to any mention or reference to copulation in plain language, or indeed at all—although it is the prime mover of humanity, and finds expression in every day life in some shape or another, by word or deed; and is a subject which passes through the mind almost daily of men and women who are in a healthy state of body." Although he is not a physician and cannot therefore speak with authority or exactitude about anatomical details, he has undertaken to write "what may be termed essentially a popular description, suitable to the smallest capacities, and fit for both sexes—or, if you please, instructive reading for the young. It is to the young essential knowledge, yet the great aim of adults seems to be to prevent youths from knowing anything about it." And though the essay that follows contains inaccuracies and errors, it is by far the best—the openest, plainest, boldest and most honest—account of sexual activity that I have come across from the period. Certainly it is more to the point than anything in Acton. The author concludes it by affirming again that such an essay "will spare many young but full grown people trouble and loss of time, in searching for knowledge which ought to be known to all, but which owing to a false morality is a subject put aside as improper." And in his essays on the genitals he follows the same course, and includes an almost touching account of his efforts to determine the average shapes and sizes of the various organs and of the average duration, rates of movement, and other mechanical operations of coitus. The impulse to describe and classify represents of course the earliest stage of all empirical research, and the degree of honesty required of it is commensurate with its goals.

Such honesty can take one only so far, and it is by no means incompatible with a disinclination for self-investigation or fear of analysis. In the Preface the author writes that this "secret history, which bears the impress of truth on every page [is] a contribution to psychology." This statement is both true and not true. Whatever "contribution" his work makes is to be found in its presentation of material and not in its attempt at explanation. "I could not now account for my course of action," he typically writes, "nor why I did this, or said that; my conduct seems strange, foolish, absurd, very frequently that of some woman equally so, but I can but state what did occur." At another point, in recounting his relations with a woman considerably older than himself, he remarks that the whole thing seemed "peculiar; I felt as if I was wicked in getting into her, almost as if I was going to poke my mother; but I cannot attempt to analyse motives or sensations; I simply narrate facts." And when anything really out of the way occurs to him, he is almost certain to say that he "cannot explain or reason about it. I am telling facts as they occurred, as far as I recollect them; it is all I can do." All of these statements are ambiguous in both form and content—their vague syntax and uncertain references allow for a number of meanings. On the one hand, there is little doubt that, however puzzled he may often be by his own behavior, he is unwilling to think about it beyond a certain point. It is as if he had somehow correctly surmised that reasoning about himself, inquiring into his motives, pursuing explanations would tend to deprive him of pleasure or endanger his equilibrium. That is to say, the exposure of his behavior and the fantasies embodied in it to the processes of reason would be tantamount either to a questioning of their validity or justification, or to a renunciation. We should also observe that he shares this disinclination for inquiring into reasons and motives with both Acton and Ashbee—and, as I have said before, with almost all the literature of sexuality and with pornography itself—and that we can now conclude that this attitude is characteristic of the last prepsychological epoch of modern culture. Conscious of psychology, and even regarding his own work as a "contribution" to it, he is yet afraid and unable to psychologize.

On the other hand, if we were to suppose that he wanted to discuss and reason about his behavior, how would he have gone about doing it, what instruments or terms were available to him? He could only have resorted to a moralistic and quasi-theological vocabulary to describe his behavior; even the current medical terminology, as we have seen in Acton, was still largely derived from moral and religious conceptions. With these terms to go by, the author of *My Secret Life* could only have judged himself to be some kind of monster or fiend, a depraved creature, probably half-insane, a menace to himself and society. No neutral terms existed with which he could discuss his behavior and his impulses; there was as yet no diction, no way of thinking, which could provide the distance from immediate experience that is necessary if one is to "reason" about it. In such circumstances, what alternative, apart from surrendering to the prevailing modes of judgment, was open to the author? All he could do was to present the "facts" of his experience, as they had occurred, as clearly as he was able and had the courage to do. He himself is acutely aware of the limitations imposed by such conditions. Late in the work, he turns to confront himself once again and writes, "As often before said, fucking is always much the same, the preliminaries alone vary." And he goes on to say, in what seems to me the crowning sentence of the book, that although he has written at endless length about "love's mysteries . . . there is nothing mysterious about it excepting in the psychology." In addition to much insight, there is much merit in such a statement, in the author's being able to make it. Bound within the world of the physiological, the world of organs and actions, and having lived his life as if the mystery existed there and could be discovered there, he is yet able to see that the mystery exists somewhere else. And he enables us to see a further truth about his own writing and about pornography in general, a truth which helps us to understand why it is such a cheerless, frustrated, and defeated kind of literature. Where it seeks mystery, none exists. Where it seeks to discover, nothing is to be discovered. What it looks for cannot be found. The mystery is that there is no mystery.

I I

Whatever mystery exists, therefore, we shall have to discover for ourselves, elsewhere, as it is revealed to us in the "facts" of the author's sexual history. He recounts his history in roughly

chronological form and in great detail. The first one hundred
pages of Volume I are devoted to an account of his sexual experiences in childhood. As far as can be made out, the author's
upbringing seems to have been one that was normal for his
time and family position. His earliest "recollections of things
sexual" date from the time he was about five years old and are
concerned, in the first place, with certain experiences with a
nursemaid. "I recollect that she sometimes held my little prick
when I piddled; was it needful to do so? I don't know. She
attempted to pull my prepuce back, when and how often I
know not. But I am clear at seeing the prick tip show, of feeling
pain, of yelling out, of her soothing me, and of this occurring
more than once." He also describes, rather poetically, a number
of familiar and typical scenes of childhood seduction and masturbation in which this nursemaid occupied the chief role. He
then goes on to recount his early Oedipal terrors, his night fears
and fears of men, and also includes several events which are
pretty clearly edited reconstructions of primal fantasies or
scenes. The one noticeable symptom of his early experience is
his phimosis: "I could not . . . thoroughly uncover my prick
tip without pain till I was sixteen years old. . . . My nursemaid, I expect, thought this curious, and tried to remedy the
error in my make, and hurt me." His parents seem to have
known nothing of his condition, his mother "by her extremely
delicate feeling" choosing to deny its existence, his father making the same choice, though doubtless from other motives. At
school, when he undergoes the mutual exploration of their
bodies that boys make, his defect is disclosed: "we all compared
cocks, and mine was the only one that would not unskin; they
jeered me, I burst into tears, and went away, thinking there was
something wrong with me, and was ashamed to show my cock
again, though I set to work earnestly to try to pull the foreskin
back, but always desisted fearing the pain, for I was very sensitive."

He also recollects his early theories about sex. He recalls as a
child seeing a stallion mount a mare, the stallion entering "in

what appeared to me to be the mare's bottom." Although he remembers seeing women naked during his childhood, he has, he virtually admits, repressed his memories of what he saw, and he speaks of his surprise when he is informed by a cousin about the nature of the female genitals. Moreover, he counteracts or neutralizes this knowledge by speaking of girls' "cocks [as] being flat," admitting and denying their difference at the same time. He speculates obsessively about how girls are made, "how the piddle came out, if they wetted their legs, and if the hole was near the bum hole, or where." At a slightly later date he is shown "a bawdy picture. It was coloured. I wondered at the cunt being a long sort of gash. I had an idea that it was round, like an arse hole." Further inspection of a baby sister leads to the same discovery, yet he and the cousin with whom he made the inspection "clung somehow to the idea of the round hole, and we quarreled about it." Apart from the remarkable acuteness of the author's memory that these passages represent, what is most striking about them is how familiar they seem. In this connection, we should recall that it was only a few years after such passages were written that Freud began to go over the same material with a different—though not altogether different —end in view. What these passages reveal is how the young boy, faced with the anatomical differences between the sexes, tries both to deny and account for those differences. First there is the anal theory of coitus, and probably of birth, a theory which specifically denies any difference at all. Then there is the theory that girls, although they seem castrated, have somewhere and in some way a penis hidden in them.

He enters into adolescence in the usual way and goes on to have the usual experiences and anxieties—with one exception. Along with the characteristic intensity and turbulence of adolescent sexuality, there exists in him from an early date a willingness and an ability to act out his fantasies, to add investigation to speculation, exploration to masturbation. He has coitus for the first time at the age of seventeen or eighteen and from there on has entered upon another stage of his experience.

We can conclude, therefore, that by and large the author's childhood and youth were—as far as he discloses them to us—unexceptionable for their time. Much ignorance, much experience, much anxiety combined to make them what they were. That an active sexual life existed among children and servants, and that servants and contemporaries, rather than parents, were the sources or channels of sexual information are circumstances too well known to require repetition. Several things are worth noting, however, about the author's early recollections. In addition to the castration fears, anxieties, and fantasies that every boy must suffer, he seems to have retained an uncommonly large portion of such experiences as active and conscious memories—that part of his recollections, it may be, was only partly repressed. Furthermore, superadded to the castration anxieties were the feelings and ideas that were connected with his phimosis: these acted both to intensify the anxieties and also perhaps to create a disturbance in what is known as the "body-image," a circumstance to which I shall recur. Finally, the remarkable reservoir of unrepressed sexual impressions and memories was joined to a temperament which from the beginning was notable for its aggressiveness, for its tendency to discharge itself in action rather than in thought.

Having embarked upon his adult career of sexual pursuits, he tells us that until about the age of thirty his tastes and inclinations remained rather "simple": "although I had done most things which were sexually possible once, and almost out of curiosity, or else on sudden impulse (up to this period), yet . . . my habits with women in my lust were for the most part simple, commonplace, and unintellectual . . . I had not sought for out of the way lascivious postures and varied complex delights in copulation or its preliminaries, which a fervid, voluptuous, poetical imagination has since gradually devised for my gratification." After this period, his sexual tastes enlarge, and his experience tends to become, so to speak, more programmatic. He experiments with various attitudes, organs, and other parts of the body; he gives way occasionally to an interest in the excretory functions; he tries out most of the common perversions; he allows his impulses toward voyeurism and sadism to express themselves. In other words, he acts out the universal sexual fantasies of mankind. These fantasies are of course grounded in the sexual life of childhood, but they are not expressed in exactly that way. They are expressed in the secondarily elaborated form they undergo when in adolescence they come under the rule of the genital organization. The end, that is to say, is genital pleasure; and one of the extraordinary things about the author of *My Secret Life* is that, although he freely experiments with the varieties of sexual experience, he never renounces, he never is in danger of renouncing, what in the rather unlovely psychoanalytic terminology is known as "genital primacy." He is no Sade in whom the entire adult sexual organization was dissolved back into the components of infancy.

We cannot, nevertheless, think of the author as an ordinary or "normal" person. If we have avoided the temptation of regarding *My Secret Life* as a kind of rough-and-ready *psychopathia sexualis,* we should nevertheless be aware of certain major tendencies in the author's temperament—whether these are pathological or not is, as Freud repeatedly demonstrated, irrelevant to their critical description.

The first tendency, as I have mentioned before, has to do with his pronounced interest in and concern about the penis— his own in particular and, by an inevitable generalization, all others as well. Behind this unremitting energy of interest we can detect both anxiety about castration and uncertainty about the body-image. He goes to considerable lengths to provide himself with reassurances about his own intactness, and much of his behavior is explicable only if we keep the necessity for such reassurance in mind. For example, one of his unvarying procedures in virtually every seduction or transaction he describes is that at some not very advanced point he exposes himself to the woman he is confronting. He concocts a whole the-

ory to account for this habit, a theory that boils down to the
notion that "the sight of a prick entices a woman." For "entices" one may also read "overwhelms," "excites," "paralyzes"
or any other allied terms, most of which he uses on other occasions. Putting the question of the dubious truth of such a belief
to one side, we can say that the sentence should be read in
reverse, that it is the sight of the penis that acts magically on
him, and that his overestimation of the power of this organ is
in proportion to his doubts and fears.

This impulse to see is extremely pronounced in him and undergoes a process of generalization. From childhood on, he experiences an intense curiosity about the excretory functions, especially as those functions operate in women. He does not
abandon his curiosity in his adult life, and some of the most
unusual episodes in the work—remarkable in both their candor
and in their anticipation of Leopold Bloom—are those in which
he describes his voyeuristic experiences in this regard and his
feelings about them. Another form that this impulse takes is his
desire to see other people copulating; and in his later maturity
he goes to great lengths and considerable expenditure to assure
himself the experience of such sights. His chief visual obsession,
however, is his need to see, look at, inspect, examine, and contemplate the genitals of every woman he is acquainted with.
This, he writes, is "the most important part to me," and he also
states that "some men—and I am one—are insatiable and could
look at a cunt without taking their eyes off for a month." He is
not particularly interested in or attracted by women's faces; it is
their bodies, and this particular zone of their bodies, that draw
all his attention. And it must be said in his favor that the Medusa's head holds no terror for him; he even surpasses Perseus, for
he needs no shield or mirror, but gazes directly at this object of
universal awe. But to commend his courage is not enough, since
we must also account for the fact that he is forced compulsively
to repeat this act—he persists in it to the very end, with no wan-
ing of intensity. The answer is not far to seek, and is to be
found in connection with his compulsive need for variety, for

having many different women all the time. We must conclude that his endlessly repeated need to inspect the female genitals indicates that he is seeking for something that he cannot find. Either he is looking for something (or someone) that he once saw or thought he saw, or he is looking for something that is not there. The two impulses are probably combined, with the latter in stronger prominence. That something which is not there is of course a penis—the author produces a great deal of material, as I have indicated before, which demonstrates his unconscious conviction that women have a penis hidden somewhere about them. Thus, even as he performs a ritual which most palpably reveals to him the difference between the sexes, a ritual through which he can celebrate his masculinity, he is simultaneously denying that difference and has his mind already on the next woman, the next object of his endless quest for what cannot in nature be discovered.

This desire to see "all" or "everything"—that is to say, the desire to see what is not there—is often coupled with another fantasy, the idea of totality, of total pleasure. "I wanted to see her limbs, to feel her breasts," he typically writes; "the desire to see every part of her, that irresistible want to see all, feel all, and satisfy every sense which springs up in the mind of a man when a woman has satisfied his voluptuousness for the first time overcame me." In another place he describes the fantasy as wanting "to fuck, to be frigged, be sucked, all at once—that irresolution as to the act, that desire to have all the sexual pleasures in all ways at once was on me, and intoxicated me with lustful ideas." In this instance, the circularity of form in the author's statement is in accord with the vicious circle that the fantasy in question describes. We may assume that all such desires for totality are manifestations of a corresponding insatiability, that such fantasies are connected with one's earliest experiences in life and are at once an effort to reconstitute that early state and to overcome the anguish and frustration that our inevitable expulsion from that state brings about. In adult life the author strives to recapture the ecstasy of the infant at the breast and the polymorphous pleasures of childhood. In the middle of the nineteenth century, the author of *My Secret Life* undertook to act out in his own life that project which, only a few years ago, Mr. Norman O. Brown suggested was the one hope of salvation for our entire civilization. The reader is left to pass judgment in whichever way he chooses on either of these undertakings.

One of the chief barriers that such a project has to break through is the barrier of homosexuality. In middle age the author seems to pass through an increase in homosexual tendencies; or, to phrase it in another way, as his experimentation and freedom of impulse enlarge, he naturally goes in for certain homosexual experiences. These statements are not incompatible; they in fact mean the same thing. He describes his direct homosexual experiences in detail. One gets the impression from these descriptions that a certain amount of will entered into his decision to try it all out, and he does not report on any great access of pleasure, reporting to the contrary emotions of puzzlement and self-disgust. In addition, his homosexual experiences are not "direct"; he almost always has them in concert with a woman, so that the woman is there to mediate, as it were, between himself and the other man. His major homosexual fantasy and practice, however, develop in middle age and are a reversal of an earlier aversion. He now conceives the desire to have coitus with a woman immediately after another man has had her. Sometimes he desires to see the two in coitus, sometimes he does not. Always, however, he desires to copulate with a woman in another man's semen. This experience, he reports, sends him into a frenzy of pleasure, and he writes long phonographic accounts of his thoughts and words during such episodes. He arranges to have these experiences with prostitutes, and when he is in France enters upon a complicated series of transactions with the owners of a brothel in order to render the fantasy both possible of execution and complete.

The Oedipal components in this homosexual impulse are self-evident. Indeed, his accounts read like re-enactments of an Oedipal fantasy which is very close to the surface of consciousness. One passage in particular exemplifies the condition of his state of consciousness. It describes his experience in a Paris brothel.

> It is singular, seems contradictory, but I write what occurred, that I rarely seemed to have the same excitement, pleasure, or even desire in trailing the women whom I had seen fucked, as I did those who came into me from other rooms.—More often than otherwise I didn't even put my pego up them. Sometimes I only looked at their quims without separating the covers of the vulva, when I did not like the look of the man who'd had them. . . . But I *always desired those who'd been stroked in other parts of the house.*—I always fancied the sperm was that of handsome, very young men, though often it was not so.—I rejected those directly if the suspicion of their having been fucked by seniors occurred to me.

This italicized passage is the author's doing, a rare occurrence. The house is of course the whore house, but it is just as certainly the other house, the house of infancy and childhood, the house that all our other habitations somehow contain. His disinclination for women he has seen in coitus represents both an inhibition—the use of such a word about the author is comical but correct—and a measure designed to prevent interference with the dominant unconscious fantasy. The women coming to him from "other parts of the house" clearly re-enact scenes at bedtime in the nursery. The last part of the passage seems to embody a defense by reversal. Under the guise of a preference for young men, the author rejects those women whom he suspects as having been with older men. Here the inhibition is distinctly operative and functions to permit the principal unconscious fantasy to remain unconscious. The author's state of consciousness, then, is similar to the state of consciousness of the immediate precursors or predecessors of Freud. He is interested and involved in the same material, and produces and contemplates the same material. But he accepts that material at its face value; he does not inquire into its contradictions, though he is aware of them and brings them forward. He does not seek out the meaning, in other terms, and in another realm of discourse, of his behavior. His interest is concentrated on something other than meaning—on the experience itself and on himself within that experience.

This concentration of interest is important for our understanding of the author. Throughout his youth and occasionally in his maturity, he describes himself as suffering what today would be called disturbances in his potency—these largely took the form of premature ejaculations. Yet if his potency was disturbed, he himself was not. Since he was able to perform two or three acts of sexual intercourse in fairly rapid succession, he naturally did not have to think of himself as anything but highly potent (he never boasts of his prowess, by the way). Beneath these circumstances, however, we can make out something else: the precondition of his obsessional state, his hypersexuality,[2] is the fact that his primary object is himself, his own satisfaction. Although he states that in later life the pleasure of the woman increased in importance to him, we cannot take this as literally as he would have us, particularly in view of the fact that most of his partners continue to be drawn from the unvarying source. And although he prefers a genuine response in a woman to a shammed or pretended one, he is not terribly concerned to discriminate between the two—the response he is wholly concerned with is his own.

Such a concern paradoxically expresses itself in the pronounced sadistic tendencies that make themselves felt in his life from an early date. These tendencies are represented most fully in the episodes which describe his defloration of young girls procured for him by prostitutes. Here is a typical statement: "I pushed; a sharp 'oh!'; a harder push; a louder cry; the obstacle was tight indeed; I had never had such difficulty before; my lust grew fierce, her cry of pain gave me inexpressible pleasure; and saying I would not hurt, yet wishing to hurt her and glorying in it, I thrust with all the violence my buttocks could give, till my prick seemed to bend, and pained me." Repeatedly he

---

[2] Hypersexuality implies, of course, a psychic, not a physical, state or condition.

states that "I never had more pleasure in bawdiness than I had in hurting her [whichever young girl it happens to be]. It made my prick stiffen directly she said she was so sore. . . ." Women are objects to him, to be sure; but they are objects to be despoiled and violated. The primary object of pleasure is himself.

It would be mistaken, however, to regard this attitude of his as pure pathology. The scenes of overt sadism are merely the extreme expression of the tendencies which characterize his entire sexual life. This life, we are entitled to say, is in another, an older, style than the one most of us recognize and experience today. The author conceives of his own sexuality, and of male sexuality in general, as almost pure aggression. In this conception, woman is an object who must be dominated; she must be made by the male "to submit to his will in copulation." She should at first resist, and her resistance must be overcome by the impulsive power of the male, by that power itself and by the communication and installation of that lust in herself. The author also experiences his own sexual drive as a kind of direct demonic possession. When he is overtaken by his desires, he says, he is almost deranged, out of control. When a man is in a state of lust, he repeatedly asserts, "he is ready to fuck anything, from his sister to his grandmother, from a ten year old to a woman of sixty." Any object, not a particular one, will do, since the drive itself is impersonal and is experienced as an impersonal, peremptory demand. And he thinks of these states of frenzy as "rutting fits," correctly identifying them with the biological world of their origin. "When I once have my rutting fury on," he writes, "I can think of nothing but cunt, and, even when for the time used up by copulation—*Cunt,—Cunt,—*is all I think of.—Every woman I pass in the street, I wonder what sort of cunt she has, large or small, brown haired or black, much hair or little.—Has it been fucked or is it virgin.—I am mad about cunt—and this lasts usually two or three days till I am completely fucked out."

In attesting to the demonic power of his sexual drives, the author is doing more than making a confession of weakness or depravity. He describes his lust as "strong, unreflecting, unconscious, and unmanageable," and, after rehearsing an episode in which this series of "lewd and sequential impulses" carried him very far indeed, he reflects that the whole thing seems to him now "a psychological phenomenon, and nothing more." This is his way of saying that he doesn't understand what has happened to him or what he did, and we can sympathize with his bewilderment. For he embodies not only a psychological phenomenon but a historical one as well. Though he was born and raised in the nineteenth century, his sexuality—both mentally and in behavior—came somehow to be developed on an archaic model. In a memorable aside in *Three Essays on the Theory of Sexuality,* Freud writes that "the most striking distinction between the erotic life of antiquity and our own no doubt lies in the fact that the ancients laid the stress upon the instinct itself, whereas we emphasize its object. The ancients glorified the instinct and were prepared on its account to honor even an inferior object; while we despise the instinctual activity in itself, and find excuses for it only in the merits of the object." To this profound insight one must only add that large remnants of this older kind of sexuality remained in existence through the eighteenth century. The conflict in a novel such as *Pamela,* after all, is in large measure a conflict over these two competing conceptions of sexuality—a competition that had by this time come to be located in different and opposed social groups or classes. The author of *My Secret Life* embodied this older conception of sexuality: he stresses and glorifies the instinct and on its account honors even inferior objects. In his life and writing—and to a lesser degree in pornography itself—what is being expressed or celebrated is not only a nostalgia for the bliss of infancy, as that bliss is edited and reorganized in the memories of adolescence. What is also being expressed is a recapitulation of part of the infancy of our civilization. Yet because this recapitulation is taking place in the nineteenth century, when our civilization was no longer, as Hegel put it, in the infancy of its consciousness, the form which it takes is bound to be distorted. But this distortion may itself be one of the irreducible contradictions of human sexuality—of sexuality, that is to say, which exists under the conditions and consequences of consciousness, of civilization and its irreversible history.

Another one of the contradictions in which the author is involved has also to do with his aggressive potency. For although it is true that the author is able to abandon himself to his instinctual drives in a demonic and archaic way, it is equally true that he must pay a price for this liberty. This price is exacted in the severe limitation of the emotions that he is able to feel, in the restricted range of his responses to other persons, in his extremely weak capacities for establishing relations with others. His emotional anesthesia is never more apparent than it is immediately after he has successfully seduced a woman. Here, for example, is the conclusion of his long account of an episode which culminated in a success for him. "I was rested, she was fresh, and I sat at breakfast with as much complacency and jollity as a man could; yet beyond fucking, I felt that I did not care one damn about her; and even felt sorry. I cannot explain why I felt that, but recollect it." The admirable honesty should not deter us from noting the emotional deadness that accompanies it. One gets a sense in reading this work that something is missing in the author, that there is a large hole or vacuum somewhere in him, or that his aggressive drives have thwarted the development in him of what we think of as the normal complement of human emotions. This thwarting is in turn connected with confusion about his own feelings and an inability to discriminate clearly between them. He says of one woman with whom he has had a lengthy and important affair, "although I liked her, and more than liked her, I never had a strong affection for her." The point is not that the author is incapable of using the English language correctly—we know that is not true. The point is that such words as "like" and "affection" have no certain, dense, or even actual meaning for him, since he does not experience the reality of other persons along the lines which these words refer to and describe. Such words describe the quality of one's feelings in *relation* to other persons, and it is at precisely this juncture that the author is most clearly defective. He will typically write that he was "glad" when a certain affair "was finished, for there was a tie about it which worried me." The reader will not fail to observe that this antipathy to "ties," this disinclination toward relations, is characteristic not only of the author but of pornographic writing in general as well. But before we criticize this mode of experience for its shallowness and inadequacy, we might suggest that in it is expressed one of the fundamental contradictions of human sexual life. For there can be little doubt that full aggressive potency, demonic genitality is permanently at odds with that elaborately developed life of the emotions which is our civilized heritage—and burden. The clearest demonstration of this tragic division is to be found in the fact that one part of our sexuality has been relegated to the world of fantasy and to the underground of civilization, where, lamely, it continues to persist.

A further contradiction, which goes along with and covers all that has gone before, has to do with the author's compulsion to repeat—his need to repeat everything all the time everywhere.

> What often astonishes me is my desire to do again everything sexual and erotic which I have already done. Yet many things done, I fancied I should never repeat. I have frigged a man. My curiosity satisfied, I said to myself, "I shall never frig a man again." Yet I want to do so. . . .
> I want to do everything over again. All former gratifications which were a little out of the common seem to have faded from my recollection somewhat.—I don't clearly enough recollect my sensations or the quality of the pleasure they gave me. I wish to refresh my memory by repeating the amorous exercises. It is not my lust or powers which wants stimulating by variety; it rather seems as if it were strong animal want which is stimulating my desires and exercising my brain to invent even [more] voluptuous combinations.

And later on, toward the end of the work, he writes: "What is it that after having fucked a thousand cunts, another cunt because unknown, untasted, fresh to me, is irresistible? should destroy resolve, frustrate determination, make me weakly yield to its charm, desire to leave my semen in it, though certain as I look at and feel it that it will give me no more delight by friction, grip and suction than hundreds of the others which my prick has tasted." We arrive here at one of the most complex parts of our subject. In the first place, it should be clear that one important attribute of the author's sexuality—and of the kind of sexuality celebrated in pornographic writing—is expressed in its abstract and quantitative idea of itself. Sexuality in this conception consists of an endless accumulation of experiences. These experiences, like the experiences described in pornography, are both different and the same. The need for variety is itself monotonous, and the mechanical monotonous variety of both compulsive sexuality and pornography is one of their chief common characteristics. If we ask why this should be so, it can be answered that since the grounds of any compulsive repetitive activity are unconscious, and since it is in the nature of the unconscious to be truly unconscious, that is, unknown to us, incapable of being worn away (unlike experiences which are retained in consciousness), and inaccessible to learning, so long as those grounds remain undisturbed so long will the monotonous search for the same variety persist.

But we can go behind this idea, as Freud did, and observe that it is in the nature of instinctual drives to repeat themselves. Instincts are conservative and circular, and exercise their tyranny over us by their recurrence. Their striving for discharge and gratification ends only with the end of the living organism. Yet even as the virtually endless series of repetitions—accumulation of tension, striving for discharge, and gratification—keep occurring can we not make out that something is *not* being gratified as well? We see this combination of circumstances exemplified most clearly in the author of *My Secret Life,* who simultaneously reports deep gratification (there is no reason that I can find for doubting him in this regard) and an endlessly continuing search for what cannot be found, for a gratification that does not exist, or whose existence is incompatible with existence. It was in this borderland between pathology and biology that Freud conducted his later researches and speculations. He was led to it in part precisely by the phenomenon of the repetition compulsion; and what he found there prompted him to postulate a whole new theory of the instincts and to propose a set of instincts whose aim lay beyond the pleasure principle. It is my wholly unsubstantiated opinion that we find in the writings about sex, and in pornography in particular, a peculiarly rich example of this mixture of incompatible drives. I do not know how else we can fully explain the existence of a literature obsessed with pleasure and yet unpleasurable, whose aim is said to be pleasure, although it is a pleasure from which the actuality of gratification is excluded, and whose impulse toward totality is the equivalent of obliteration. It is, I suppose, possible to explain the kind of sexual writings we are discussing strictly according to the pleasure principle, as it undergoes the usual procedures of distortion. I do not think, however, that its distinct unpleasurableness, its violence and aggressiveness, its impulse toward extinction are satisfactorily explained by that principle alone. Something darker seems to be there, something inexorable, from which there is no escape and which cannot be understood as pathology alone. In any case, it is certain that we cannot understand the author of *My Secret Life* solely by his pathology. Psychoanalysis, we should remember, is not a solution for everything, nor is it a way out of everything. For everything there is only one way out.

III

The modern reader will naturally incline to think that one way out of this situation is suggested in the author's other major activity in life, his writing. To this it must first be said that the author did not want a way out; he did not and could not conceive of things in this way, and it never occurs to him to think of himself as anything other than what he is. Nevertheless, it is legitimate for us to ask what function his writing does serve, just as we must keep it always in mind that we are reading a written book. In this connection, one of the first questions that will occur concerns the audience the author has in mind; for whom is he writing? Though the author frequently states that he is writing only for himself and expresses doubts and hesitations about showing his work to anyone and often says that he is tempted to burn his manuscript, it is clear that none of these protestations is to be taken at face value. Had he really meant any of these he would not have had the work printed to begin with, and certainly not in six or more copies. And, as I suggested earlier, had he really wanted to keep his secret life a secret he would not have put pen to paper.[3]

To ask the question for whom did the author write is at the same time to ask the question why did he write. At numerous points the author offers a number of conscious explanations. In the first place, he states, "My secret life was written for my own pleasure, and to be a narrative of what I myself saw and did, and nothing else." And in another place, he writes, "I write for my pleasure alone, and if I print, shall print for my pleasure alone." This is not very helpful, and indeed reveals its inner contradictions in that final clause. A second reason which he occasionally brings forward is that his work is a cry in the dark; aware of his isolation and of his ignorance of the sexual ideas and behavior of others, he desires to learn about them and to communicate something of himself. In a passage I have already quoted, he asks whether all men feel and behave as he does, and concludes, "I can never know this; my experience if printed may enable others to compare as I cannot." We must grant a certain degree of validity to this assertion, reminding ourselves that in the nineteenth century the novel served just such a function. By bringing before readers the lives of groups of people

[3] "The written word gives substance to the evanescent stuff of fantasy, and at the same time is a link to the world of other persons; nothing has ever been written that did not presuppose the existence of a reader, for whom a real language needed to be chosen." Stanley A. Leavey (ed.), *The Freud Journal of Lou Andreas Salomé* (New York, 1964), p. 4.

about whom little was known and much denied—the poor, the outcast, the criminal—and by dramatizing the humanity of these "peripheral" groups, the novelists worked to humanize their middle-class audience. They enabled "others to compare," as does the author.

Sometimes the writing works to help the author confront and understand himself. Going through his growing manuscript periodically, the author will often "add a few observations, which, on reading this, written many years ago, seem now needful to explain even to myself." The observations, in other words, are added so that his behavior will seem coherent and explicable even to himself. In Volume III, he comments on the first two volumes, now in print, which he has just reread. These volumes, like all the subsequent ones, are edited and abbreviated versions of his original immense manuscript. Considerations of space made it necessary to omit certain details, items of conversation, reflections, etc., and the author regrets the omissions. "These details also gave studies of character, and specially of my own character, and as I now read the narratives in print after the lapse of so many years they seem to me to be needed to explain myself, even to myself." Here the poignant confession of incoherence and incapacity of intellect indicates how one of the functions of the writing was, so to speak, to hold the author together, to strengthen what must have often seemed a precarious hold on reality—an expectable circumstance whenever a life consists so largely of fantasies actively dramatized in reality. Sometimes, in addition, the writing worked as a kind of therapeutic discharge or purge. After printing a long account of a particularly distressing experience, he writes: "This episode . . . dwelt so much in my mind that, although I disliked it, yet at the first hotel which I stopped at for a few days afterwards, I wrote this out, and a great deal more. I recollected the face, form, and performances of every woman I had seen." He then says that his obsession and distress passed away.

Finally, however, the writing is part of his sexual experience itself. It is first a kind of dramatized memory, a faculty that for the author is wholly sexualized. "How delightfully the episodes come back to my memory as I read the manuscript," he writes in Volume V. "Incidents fading into forgetfulness come out quite freshly to me, and I almost seem to be living my youthful life over again." He is here speaking as a typical nineteenth-century diarist and is referring to the pleasures of *reading* what he has written and of the accompanying fantasies. But he took equal pleasure in the *writing* of his manuscript: "what pleasure I had in the wordy veracities as I wrote them, childish, fantastic, ludicrous as some of the doings and sayings now seem! How unlike the doing of the couples in erotic books which I since have read, books written with no other object but to stimulate the passions,—no object that of mine in writing this." The first part of that last sentence we can accept as substantially true; to the second part an objection must be entered. It may not be his object to stimulate the passions of others, but it is certainly his object to stimulate his own. He will often interrupt his narrative with a statement such as this: "I now think I feel my sensation up her as I write this, of the rapturous smoothing of her buttocks as I finished." And he justifies his prolixity on the same grounds. "I revelled in the detail as I wrote it, for in doing so I almost had my sexual treats over again. . . . I described them as they had occurred at the time, and the pleasure of doing so was nearly the same, even had I done them twenty times, and described them twenty times." The reader will have already noticed similarities between these procedures and those described by Jean Genet in *Our Lady of the Flowers;* in prison Genet took to writing down his masturbatory fantasies in narrative form. The difference between the highly elaborated structure of Genet's fantasies and the direct "realism" of the author of *My Secret Life* is to be accounted for not only by differences of talent, history, and culture, but by differences in sexual aim and temperament as well.

As time passes, the writing comes to occupy a more and more intimate place in his sexual life. Writing these memoranda, he

states, "seems to have become a habit which I cannot break off."
It would take, I believe, a psychoanalyst to distinguish among
the niceties of the processes that are fused here. On the one
hand, writing, in whatever form, does represent a displacement
of the kind that is referred to as sublimation; and to some degree the principle of reality is being engaged by this activity. On
the other hand, a habit of this kind which cannot be broken off
is distinctly connected with autoerotic activities and their fantasies. Indeed, as he develops, the writing comes to be inseparable
from and as important as the experiences that it rehearses. For
example, in Volume VI, he includes an adventure in which he
seduces an odd and interesting young woman. He takes her to
an accommodation house, and, since she has nowhere to go, he
keeps her there for several days. In the intervals, he talks to her
and she tells him her story. After a day or so, the following
happens:

> I got her a novel to read, a love story—and she devoured it. I got
> writing paper, and amused myself by writing down the incidents
> of this piece of my luck. I noted down what she said—not at that
> moment, but directly after, when she was reading. But my writ-
> ing made her suspicious. Was I writing to her father was her
> anxiety. I told her I was only writing about my affairs. But after a
> while—"You're writing something about me, I'm sure; now do
> tell me."—"What makes you think that?"—"Because you keep
> looking at me so." I suppose I did, but was not conscious of doing
> so. However, I set her mind at rest by some bouncing lies.

It is clear that by this point in his life the impulse to write has
become as urgent as his impulses toward sexual activity and has
been incorporated among those impulses and enlisted in their
service. He is himself aware of this, for shortly after this episode
he says, "writing indeed completed my enjoyment."

The circle is completed later in his life, when he embarks on
his final long affair with the courtesan Helen Marwood.
"Helen soon had great pleasure in talking of her former tricks
—would tell what she'd done or had heard of—reserve was utterly gone between us. She pronounced mine to be a most wonderful amatory career, when she had read a large part of the

manuscript, or I had read it to her whilst in bed and she laid quietly feeling my prick. Sometimes she'd read and I listen, kissing and smelling her lovely alabaster breasts, feeling her cunt, till the spirit moved us both to incorporate our bodies." This, one feels, was the predestined conclusion—the dog has finally caught up with its tail. His accumulated fantasies, written down in the form of recollections of his experiences, now feed back into the reality of the present, heighten that reality, infuse it with further fantasies, and stimulate him to act out everything all over again in a frenzy of reading, feeling, acting, imagining, and going on and on. How much further, one wants to ask, can the omnipotence of thought take one?

More than it liberates him or leads him to insight, then, his writing is consolidated as part of that fantasy–life which his existence dramatizes. It would, however, be both presumptuous and anachronistic to press such ideas much further—the author feels no need of being liberated. This is not to say that he does not feel threatened by the notion of a closer scrutiny of his behavior. When he writes, as he often does, "This is a plain narrative of facts and not a psychological analysis," he is simultaneously expressing his awareness of where the mystery lies and his reluctance to approach it. As he is also doing in the following:

> Why . . . I sought the Cyprians, demireps, sluts, and strumpets, which I have done, I cannot explain, nor the frame of mind which led me into lascivious vagaries and aberrations, fancies and caprices. . . . From time to time, I have already given my views on the sexual relations of man and woman, and of the uses which they may be permitted naturally, if not legitimately, to make of their own bodies.—From those views . . . I might now "in my sere and yellow leaf" form some opinion of my own nature, which seems contradictory enough even to myself. But I make no attempt to theorize on my idiosyncrasy, or to analyse my character. This is a history of my private life which deals with facts alone, and not with conjectures.

If we remark that this is as far as he can go, we must also remark that no one at this time had gone any further. And if we remark that the kind of awareness he has achieved does not

liberate him from the compulsion to repeat, we must also ask
how could he have been liberated, and to what end? For despite the deep unconscious sadness of his work, the author does
not seem unhappy to himself and has successfully adapted to
being what he is (he takes growing old and losing his potency,
for example, with remarkable grace and equanimity). He is
perfectly aware of his demonic compulsion to repeat, yet he is
able to live with this compulsion—he has it built into his ego.
He is equally sensible of "the monotony of the course I have
pursued towards women . . . it has been as similar and repetitive as fucking itself"; yet here too he is untroubled and does
not feel that his compulsion is alien to himself.

Such reflections raise certain other questions. We are now entitled to ask, what has the author learned from experience; and
in the light of his work what does experience itself mean? Toward the end of his career he carefully tots up his score. He
finds that he has "probably fucked now . . . something like
twelve hundred women, and have felt the cunts of certainly
three hundred others of whom I have seen a hundred and fifty
naked." He also tells us that "looking through diaries and
memoranda, I find that I have had women of twenty-seven
different Empires, Kingdoms or Countries, and eighty or more
different nationalities, including every one in Europe except a
Laplander." After having dedicated an entire lifetime to con-
ducting a survey of the sexual United Nations, what has the
author learned from it all? If we recall that, after all this experience, the author still persists in numerous fantasies and delu-
sions—for example, he continues firmly to believe in female
ejaculation—we must conclude that he has learned nothing and
that, when it comes to sexuality, what we mean by experience
usually turns out to be the repeated confirmation of our fantasies, and little more. All his experience has served to confirm his
fantasies, and the unconscious cannot by nature learn. A melancholy conclusion.

Yet what do we mean when we use the phrase "learning
from experience"? We mean in part the acquisition of knowl-

edge, of truth or reality, as we loosely put it. In this sense, the author has learned from his experience, for despite the persistence of many fantasies, he has also acquired knowledge, more knowledge than most men of his time; and he did this in the face of considerable difficulties. But we also tend to mean that learning from experience is somehow the equivalent of changing one's life, and this in turn implies certain repudiations, choices of deprivation, abstinence, and negations—it somehow today implies these much more strongly than it implies corresponding positive choices or values. It further implies that one wants to change and that one is able to change. But the author of *My Secret Life* clearly had no such desire or need, not to speak of ability. And so we must be careful again not to project our own standards and expectations back onto him. In this connection, then, a work like *My Secret Life* serves to remind us that experience is there to be experienced as well, that it is, among other things, an end in itself and not merely a means to something else. The author lived by this assumption, and because he did we may legitimately think of him as an early modern.

I V

In one area, however, the author does change and improve. Throughout the course of the work, he changes and improves as a writer. He has no programmatic intention of doing so, but as his compulsion to write drives him on he improves willy-nilly. His observations are often acute, and he has a good eye for telling detail. And as his facility in writing increases, so does the scope or range of detail in each of the episodes. He has a gift for simple narrative, and he tells each of his stories neatly and relevantly. His style is in general made up of two opposed and imperfectly fused elements or modes. The first of these might be called a plain style, and its attributes should by now be evident to the reader. This style is often quite good, since it is regularly capable of representing directly and without deflection the objects of its interest. It is not what one could call a representative Victorian style; in fact it resembles certain kinds of modern prose more than it does anything from its own period. The reasons for this are not hard to come by. Both the author's interests and a language appropriate to representing them were substantially outlawed in the culture of his time. A language, a diction, a vocabulary suitable for describing the actualities of sexual experience did not form part of the Victorian sensibility. When the author chose to represent his experience in the simplest, plainest, and most direct language he could command, he was choosing in effect to drop out of the world or culture that the official written language of the period encompassed and commanded. He could not naturally drop out altogether, and as we have seen there is much about him that is deeply and typically of his time. Indeed, *My Secret Life* is nothing if it is not a representative Victorian work, yet its representativeness coexists with and helps dialectically to support its uniqueness. This dialectical play is most clearly evident in the contrast between the author's sexual attitudes, and the language he uses to represent them, and his social or class attitudes; but it is evident in other places as well, including his style.

On the whole, that style resembles some modern styles not merely in its freedom of language and plainness and lack of resonance. It is also a rapid style; its phrases are short and almost telegraphic. Above all, it is a style meant to describe action, persons and things in movement. It is attuned to registering changes in the external world of objects, one of those objects being the author himself. For since this style is not designed either to describe or to promote reflection, contemplation, or introspection, it tends to represent the author as an object external to himself (the style of Ernest Hemingway often does the same thing). The defensive intentions of such a style are abundantly clear, as is the confined range of experiences and emotions it is able to transcribe. It can, however, perform a limited number of operations with economy and precision.

The second style I shall with uninventive symmetry call fancy. In this style, the author is acutely conscious of the fact that he is writing, and is even trying to be a writer. He calls it out at moments of climactic excitement or elevation or intensity. Here is a typical passage.

> Then gently backwards and forwards I moved it. We fucked.— That glorious word expresses it all. Slowly, till urged by spermatic wants, that inner sovereignty or force, within my balls, hurrying to ejaculate itself; quicker and quicker went my thrusts, her buttocks responded, her cunt gripped, till with short, sharp thrusts and wriggles, my prick hit against her womb, her cunt constricted and ground, and sucked round my prick from tip to root, moistening both itself and occupant, and my sperm shot out and filled it . . . we were silent, well pleased in each others' arms, our tongues together. Can paradise give any bliss like that, which a man and woman enjoy when loving each other and their prick and cunt perfectly fitting each other, they join their bodies in copulation, till they pour out and mix together the unctuous salt juices, which reproduce their kind.

If we examine this passage certain things become at once clear. To begin with, "that glorious word" does not express it all. It does not in itself, and it does not for the author either, or else he would have no need to go on at such length in other and less glorious words. Furthermore, his language is at odds with itself; an "inner sovereignty" that is yet "within my balls" is hopeless and impossible. Sovereignty is toppled from its throne by being so located—there is nothing majestic about such an urgency. Next, we can make out that in the whole first part of the passage—up to the ellipsis—he is describing not persons, but parts of persons, bits and pieces of them, organs: it is a typical passage of organ grinding.[4] It is the woman's buttocks, not the woman, who is responding; and it is his thrusts that are going quicker, not he who is thrusting more quickly. This combination of abstraction and synecdoche is intended to intensify rather than to elevate the description; one is supposed to get fleeting glimpses of these images in operation. Yet a closer in-

---

[4] I appropriate this apt phrase from Philip Rahv.

spection reveals much distortion and fantasy here, and it is not merely the distortion which necessarily occurs when one describes in written language what happened in action. It is the distortion of fantasy that we meet with here, of an edited and reconstructed account of an event whose aim is to satisfy fantasies. For it is safe to say that no one who is in the almost anonymous condition of consciousness that overtakes one at the point of orgasm—as well as in the intimate condition and position of coitus, a condition and position peculiarly disadvantageous from the point of view of making observations—notes, feels, and observes things with the kind of detached clarity and separateness that the author represents in this passage.

We may also note the disjunction between the parts of the passage before and after the ellipsis. After the ellipsis, man and woman are persons and not merely organs. There may be some justification in this, since, as I have noted, one does lose one's identity in the orgasm. It is to be doubted, however, that the loss of conscious identity is the same thing as becoming a loose collection of separate organs; and, furthermore, the author is not himself particularly conscious of the disjunction or that he has anything to account for. Then there is the introduction of the bliss of paradise, which the reader may take or leave as he sees fit—I prefer to leave the inflation. But the following clauses are something else again. They contain another disjunction or, more precisely, a false pairing. A man and woman loving each other are paired with genitals fitting perfectly to each other, as if there were some necessary correspondence between emotions and anatomy. Rather it is as if the author were trying to express in strictly physical terms, in terms of the size, shape, and conformation of organs what is a mental or emotional reality. A similar thing is true of the following pair: a man and woman coming together and striving to become one can only be expressed by the author in physiological terms—juices mix together. What can only be expressed adequately by means of the emotions is displaced onto organs again; and human bodies come more and more to seem like machines, a kind of sexual

Mixmaster. The author's intention, of course, is to exalt the sexual, the bodily processes in themselves; but in attributing to them the properties of mental and emotional operations he does nothing of the kind. The general breakdown in his rhetoric is itself demonstration of these contradictions in his purpose. And when in the last phrase he throws in the utterly irrelevant reference to reproduction—irrelevant to the intention of the paragraph and the entire context in which the passage is set—we see that the style has gotten altogether out of his control and that he no longer knows what he wants to say.

Another passage is equally instructive: "So after I had paid visits to some neighbouring friends I thought of leaving, when something detained me. It was a woman again. God bless cunt! Copulation forever! God bless it for all the sweet associations and affections it produces. This act described as filthy, and not to be alluded to, is the greatest pleasure of life. All people are constantly thinking of it. After the blessed sun, surely the cunt ought to be worshipped as the source of all human happiness. It takes and gives and is twice blessed." There is a kind of charming nuttiness in the style of this passage, in the total inappropriateness of the language to the objects it describes. Under the rubric of "let copulation thrive," he speaks of the female genitals in terms that, during the Victorian period, were reserved for the family and the domestic hearth, both of them full of "sweet associations." He has in this passage embroidered a sampler to be hung on the brothel wall. And the final sentence, with its scriptural reference and tone, completes the reversal, a reversal all the more comic because it is so deadly serious. The point is that the material which the author is trying to write about must, if it is to be treated in his sense, be dealt with plainly, with as little style as possible—with no style at all, if that were possible. Other writers have since run into the same difficulties and have attempted equally disastrous solutions—James Joyce in *Ulysses* represents the one unqualified success so far. It must be said for the author of *My Secret Life,* however, that the passages of fancy writing do not occur with obtrusive frequency. Most of the time he is content to do the one thing that he can do well.

It should also be noted that the general style, tone, and method of *My Secret Life* share certain properties in common with the style, tone, and method of pornography itself. And we must finally conclude that in *My Secret Life* we are confronted with a document that is an authentic account of experience that is also at the same time in certain ways pornography. At this stage in history the two modes overlap and are sometimes identical. Certain of the similarities between the writing of *My Secret Life* and pornographic writing are worth considering. There is first the ubiquitous projection of the male sexual fantasy onto the female response—the female response being imagined as identical with the male. In this fantasy, women have orgasms as quickly, easily, and spontaneously as men, and tend to be ready for sexual activity at almost any time. Their sexual needs are as impetuous as men's, if not more so, and there is the usual accompanying fantasy that they ejaculate during orgasm. These fantasies are connected with the focus or concentration upon organs, particularly the genital organs, although no area of the body is excluded from sexualization—indeed the whole fantasy of the highly excited women has as one of its meanings that the woman herself is an organ; with the penis in her she becomes an extension of it, an expansion of it, a reassurance of its continued existence, and a witness to its supreme power. Regarding women as bodies and then finally as organs results in their abstraction and depersonalization. In both *My Secret Life* and pornography, it is often extremely difficult to distinguish one woman from another; finally they are all the same, although the search for variety and the quantitative accumulation of experiences mechanically persists. And there is also in both the final absence of almost all emotions except the aggressive ones.

Both kinds of writing tend to regard the world as a pornotopia. Reality is conceived as the scene of exclusively sexual activities and human and social institutions are understood to exist only insofar as they are conducive to further sexual play. It makes sense, then, that the form taken by the life of the author resembles the form of a typical piece of pornographic literature. Beginning rather simply, it goes on to gradually increasing elaboration and freedom and to a considerable mechanical complexity of combinations. This development is accompanied by the steady emergence of the forbidden and the systematic violation of prohibitions and taboos. The whole process culminates in the desire for totality and the effort to achieve it, either in action or fantasy; in this culminating expression of infantile megalomania, we have the beginning, and the desire to return to the beginning, making itself felt at the very end.

But it is not only the form of the author's life that resembles the form often taken by pornography; the form of his book as well resembles the form of a pornographic work of fiction. It has only an excuse for a beginning, but once having begun it goes on and on and on and ends nowhere; it really has no ending, since one of its cardinal principles of existence is repetition. This endless repetition, this repetition without a real termination, indicates to us again that, on at least one of its sides, this kind of fantasy is both a sad and frustrating mode of either experience or expression. Obsessed with the idea of infinite pleasure, the author does not permit the counter-idea of genuine gratification, and of an end to pleasure, to develop. And this absence helps us further to understand why it is that pornography is so profoundly, and by nature, anti-literature and anti-art. One of the few useful literary definitions is that form consists in the arousal in the reader of certain expectations and the fulfillment of those expectations. But the idea of fulfillment inevitably carries in its train the ideas of completion, of gratification, of an ending—and the pornographic fantasy resists such notions. The ideal pornographic novel, as everyone knows, would go on forever—it would have no ending. If it has no ending in the sense of completion or gratification, then it can have no form; and it is this confinement to the kind of form that art or literature must by nature take which is noxious to the idea of pornography. We see here one more reason for the opposition of pornography to literature.

Nevertheless, we must also observe that in this one sense at least pornography is closer to certain existential realities than art or literature can usually be. For life itself does not end in the way that a work of literature does. It ends in the meaninglessness of non-existence, of nothing (only very rarely does a life occur whose end can be thought of as a completion).[5] And if one takes a work such as *My Secret Life* and strips away the superstructure of sexual fantasies, one discovers directly beneath them the meaningless void, the sense that life is founded on nothing and that there is nothing to hold on to. If it were not for the fact that the activities we are discussing are of a compulsive nature, one would be tempted to regard them as in their way courageous—it takes some courage, after all, to live constantly on the brink of the meaningless. And indeed certain kinds of what we ordinarily think of as free choices appear to take the form of compulsion; it seems that one can be driven to choose certain paths or courses of action. (The contradictory logic of experience here exceeds the logic of rationality.) Among the many extraordinary—and even admirable—qualities of the author of *My Secret Life* is the fact that he had the courage of his compulsions. The considerable achievement of this document, if not of the life that it records, is founded in such paradoxical circumstances.

What we have, therefore, in *My Secret Life* is the record of a real life in which the pornographic, sexual fantasy was acted out. That the writing is both authentic and pornographic at the same time tells us something again about the stage of intellectual and sexual development that Victorian culture had reached. It also suggests to us still one more way of explaining the flourishing or exfoliation of pornography during that age. And it is to that abundant literature that we now must turn.

[5] For an extremely cogent discussion of these and related matters, see K. R. Eissler, *The Psychiatrist and the Dying Patient* (New York, 1955).

Chapter 5: THE WORLD OF FICTION

W E now turn to fiction. I have chosen to discuss four novels. These novels, it seems to me, illustrate the general range and tendencies of pornographic fiction during the Victorian period. They are *The Lustful Turk,* first published in 1828; *Rosa Fielding, or, A Victim of Lust,* which Ashbee dates for us as 1876; *The Amatory Experiences of a Surgeon,* of 1881; and *Randiana,* 1884.

I

The first of these, *The Lustful Turk,* is composed in the form of an epistolary novel. It consists largely of a series of letters written by its heroine, Emily Barlow, to her friend, Sylvia Carey. The novel opens as Emily is about to depart from England. She is bound for India, where she is to stay with a rich uncle; her mercenary parents have forced this visit upon her, and have torn her away from her friend Sylvia and from Sylvia's brother, Henry, with whom Emily is in love. Accompanying Emily as a traveling companion is another young woman, Eliza Gibbs.

They sail from England in June, 1814. When they are three weeks along in their voyage, their ship is attacked by "Moorish Pirates." The Turks board the ship and capture the girls. The pirate ship, we then learn, is "an Algerine Corsair," and its "barbarian" captain is "an English renegade." In due course they reach Algiers, where the renegade captain makes known to the girls his intention of handing them over as a present to the Dey. Horrified, the girls are taken to the harem, "into a most sumptuous chamber, at the far end of which sat the Dey, apparently about forty-five years of age." They are then separated, Eliza being taken away. The Dey approaches Emily and addresses her in "good English." (We later learn that he is fluent in Italian, Greek, French, and Turkish to boot.) He then immediately grapples with her, determines that she is a virgin, and is about to deflower her on the spot when a premature ejaculation forces him to postpone the operation.

Emily is then conducted to private apartments in another part of the harem, is attended to by slaves, refreshed, and dined. One of the slaves speaks English, and after dinner brings in "a parcel of English books" for Emily's perusal in her idle hours. As Emily is undressing for bed, she suddenly hears "a noise by the side of the bed. Ere I could have turned my head I found myself in the arms of the Dey, who was as naked as myself." The deflowering then takes place and is conventionally represented as a rape-murder-sacrifice.

> I quickly felt his finger again introducing the head of that terrible engine I had before felt, and which now felt like a pillar of ivory entering me. . . . My petitions, supplications and tears were of no use. I was on the altar, and, butcher-like, he was determined to complete the sacrifice; indeed, my cries seemed only to excite him to the finishing of my ruin, and sucking my lips and breasts with fury, he unrelentingly rooted up all obstacles my virginity offered, tearing and cutting me to pieces, until the complete junction of our bodies announced that the whole of his terrible shaft was buried within me. I could bear the dreadful torment no longer, but uttering a piercing cry sunk insensible in the arms of my cruel ravisher.

Upon awakening, Emily is forced to go through the whole thing again, including the fainting. Disabled by this experience, Emily is given a week for R and R, at the end of which interval the Dey returns and forces her to undergo a "second martyrdom." This time, however, Emily is transformed into a willing victim, and, in a fashion wholly representative of the genre, is made to love her master and his "grand master-piece," which is also "Nature's grand master-piece," and upon which pages of description and praise are spent.

Having been thus undone and thoroughly broken in, Emily then meets the other ladies of the harem, "one French, one Italian, and one Greek." Two of them then proceed to tell their stories. The Italian, Honoria Grimaldi, comes from Genoa and was "the only daughter of a senator" of that city. Proud, chaste, and independent, she has a lover, Ludovico, "but it was his mind I loved." She has no wish to marry, and only consents to marriage when her father threatens to confine her to a nunnery. Even after marriage, she does not give herself to her husband, her plan being to surrender her delicacy only gradually and by degrees. In these circumstances, they embark on a trip to Corsica, in the midst of which the corsair turns up again and snags himself another present for the Dey—as Honoria remarks, "unfortunate end to all my pure and heroic sentiments!" Presented to the Dey, Honoria makes a mistake. "From the mildness of his speech and manner, I thought I could assume the same authority with him as I had done Ludovico, so would scarcely answer any of his questions." The Dey rises up in mixed excitement and wrath—"How now, audacious slave, do you presume to oppose the will of thy Master?" When she resists his advances, he then calls in "his black eunuchs," and there follows a scene of flogging. This is in turn succeeded by a lengthy representation of her defloration, which is in no way different from the description already rendered by Emily of her own. The proud and dominating Honoria is overcome, dominated, mastered by the Dey; and in the degree that she submits to his power and responds to his desires, in that degree also is the master subdued in the lover. "All the authority of a master which he had so strongly assumed in the morning was now lost in the most passionate and tender regards of a most devoted and even submissive lover—even poor Ludovico could not be more so." Nature is stirred up in her, and she enters into womanhood "smiling at my ignorance when I considered the ridiculous airs I had assumed to Ludovico about my

chastity." Her honeymoon with the Dey lasts for a month. The
Dey then begins to visit her less frequently, to her great regret.
She has now been in the harem for two years and concludes her
account with this remark: "Of Ludovico I have never heard
anything since we parted, and under all circumstances I think it
as well I should not, for it would now be impossible for me to
return to him with anything like satisfaction to myself, so
firmly has the Dey fixed himself in my affections."

Upon the conclusion of this story there follows an odd episode or interlude. Emily learns to her disgust and horror that
the Dey has an inclination for anal intercourse. When he approaches her to satisfy this desire, she repels him and begs him
to spare her "the greatest disgrace I could possibly experience."
He reasons with her at length, but is unable to persuade her out
of her proper Englishwoman's folly, or into the perfect and
"entire submission" that he requires of his women-slaves. He
quits her and refuses to return. She cannot bear the isolation or
his absence and decides to give in. A description of her "second
undoing" is then given. She is "oppressed with mental anguish" by it, and "with mingled emotions of disgust and pain, I
sensibly felt the debasement of being the slave of a luxurious
Turk." After a time she becomes accustomed to these proceedings, "but the only result is, if anything, an augmentation of my
disgust and horror. By my submission I was reinstated in his
affections, and everything proceeds as usual. But the charm is
broken." Her one consolation in her depression is the company
of Adianti, the Greek girl, whom Emily teaches English and
whose story is then told.

It is a story of Greek oppression and Turkish rule. In love
with and betrothed to a youth of her own persuasion, she is
snatched away from him at the very altar by the intervention of
the Turkish local governor. Her lover and father are then
slaughtered before her eyes. She collapses first into "insensibility" and then into a "state of raving delirium, in which I have
been informed I continued for many weeks." During this time,
a complicated series of transactions take place which end in her
being presented to the Dey. She tells him her sad story. "I could

clearly feel and see by his agitation how much my story affected him. The tear of sensibility stood trembling in his eye at the relation of my sufferings." However much this Harley-Willoughby-Dey is affected, he is not to be deterred from pursuing his designs. Gently he approaches her, gently she resists. He promises to preserve her modesty, "but his promise was all deception." He slips her a mickey and, while she is under the stupefying influence of the infusion, robs her of her virginity. When she wakes up and discovers what has happened, he pleads extenuating circumstances; he tells her, she recounts to Emily, that "burning for my enjoyment, and plainly seeing my invincible modesty would oppose the most strenuous resistance to the completion of his desires, he determined, by rendering me insensible to my seduction, to spare my feelings and blushes." It is as if he had literally killed her with kindness. Adianti cannot, however, undo what has been undone, and in jig time—but only after lengthy descriptions of the process—she finds herself happily adapted to her new state. So ends Part I of *The Lustful Turk*.

Part II is less coherent. It begins with an account of the fate of Eliza, Emily's companion and maid. The Dey has presented her as a gift to his friend, the Bey of Tunis, and he in turn writes an epistolary account of her fate. Eliza is made of sterner stuff than Emily; she resists all the way, a regular pornographic Susan Nipper. Her exertions can of course do her no good. She is bound, flogged interminably, and raped peremptorily. Even this does not break her, and at the first opportunity she stabs her persecutor. There, critically wounded, we leave him, forever.

Next comes a letter from Sylvia Carey to Emily. She has received Emily's letter and is disgusted, insulted, and outraged by Emily's "account of the libidinous scenes acted between you and the beast whose infamous and lustful acts you so particularly describe." She is full of judgment and indignation. The Dey decides to settle her hash, and details one of his henchmen to kidnap her from Toulon, where she is now staying.

There then follows a whole secondary and almost independent narrative. It has to do with monastery life in Italy, with the goings on among the monks, priests, abbots, and nuns. In particular, it concerns the fate of Julia, a young novice in an Ursuline Convent. She has been placed there by her parents. She tries to escape, is caught, and is sentenced to be buried alive. She is rescued from this doom by Pedro, Abbot of St. Francis, but must pay the usual price for her rescue. The exaction of this price is described in great detail and is identical with what has gone before. The connection of this narrative with the rest of the story is revealed when we learn that this young girl is also going to be sent along to the Dey, and that the Abbot operates in his spare time a white-slave racket for African clients.

We return to Emily's letters. They are now postmarked from London and dated from 1816, and are addressed to one Maria Williams. They have to be, since their subject is what happened to Sylvia, Emily's morally indignant friend. She is kidnaped according to the Dey's plan and then made the victim of an extended practical joke. The Dey's object is "the subjection of a haughty woman" by "attacking . . . her modesty at once in the most sensible part." He rigs up the following scheme: he has her taken to the slave bazaar, where she is handled, dandled, and humiliated. He then disguises himself as a Frenchman, "first physician in Algiers, also Deputy Consul for that nation," and appears at the bazaar to buy her and save her from slavery. To keep her out of the clutches of the Dey, who he causes her to believe is actively pursuing her, he arranges for a fake marriage performed by a fake English priest. There then follow the scenes of her defloration, of her loss of modesty and gain of sexuality, at the crisis of which the Dey reveals himself to her. Her letter of pride and condemnation has "procured the pleasure you have received in my embraces" and the humiliation that her former state has undergone. She has been the agent of her own undoing and re-creation.

Emily is then revealed to Sylvia, the friends are reunited, and for a time the Dey amuses himself with the two of them alternately, serially, and simultaneously. These enjoyments, and the novel itself, are brought to an abrupt end. A new girl is brought to the Dey, and he subdues her; when he attempts to enter her anally, she whips out a knife and cuts off his penis. He calls upon his physician to complete the castration, and has "his lost members preserved in spirits of wine in glass vases." He then sends for Emily and Sylvia, gives each of them one of the vases, and has both girls shipped back to England.

Since *The Lustful Turk* is the earliest of these novels, it is not surprising that its relation to certain literary forms, styles, and conventions should be more pronounced and elaborate than the relation which is ordinarily to be found in later examples or productions. Pornography as a genre had not yet fully achieved that autonomy from experience or those qualities of self-reference or self-enclosure that characteristically define it in its "pure" or "ideal" state. What is most interesting about *The Lustful Turk* is the way it makes use of certain literary ideas or forms, the way it fuses and adapts them to its own pornographic purposes.

There is, in the first place, the crudely and coarsely skillful use of the epistolary style, which is itself a variant form of a narrative in the first person. Emily's letters often include letters written by other persons, so that within the confinements of a narrative in the first person a variety of different points of view may be introduced, and a single action or event be regarded from different perspectives. In the hands of Richardson or Laclos, this device was put to the most subtle and remarkable uses. In *The Lustful Turk*, however, the device, although it is formally present, is empty of content and must remain so. Multiplicity of perspective creates doubt, ambiguity, uncertainty and increased possibilities of meaning. Such qualities are at cross-purposes with the intentions of pornography and can, within its context, only serve as distractions and excrescences. Another function of the first-person narrative is not, however, opposed to the purpose of pornography. In some primitive way, a story told in the first person may seem closer to actuality, less invented, less a fantasy, more immediate and authentic than a narrative in any other form. Pornography, which is a fantasy, regularly tries to extinguish its awareness of that circumstance, for the most obvious reason—a person engaged in an autoerotic fantasy is not aided in his undertaking if he permits himself consciously to reflect upon his state while he is involved in it. Thus, in the subtitle to this novel we are told that its scenes "faithfully and vividly" depict the full particulars of what happened, "with that zest and simplicity which always gives guarantee for its authenticity." And another subtitle states that this novel is "an interesting history, founded on facts." Pornography has persisted in this simple—not to say simple-minded —convention up until the present.

The Lustful Turk also makes considerable use of the convention of sensibility and of the novels that were its chief literary expression. At the very opening of the novel, Emily gives voice to her feelings at parting: "Poor Eliza did everything in her power on the road to this place to amuse my wounded feelings, but it was beyond the extent of her artless sophistry to remove the weight that pressed upon my heart. Oh, Sylvia! how cruel is the sacrifice exacted in our obedience to our parents, how happy had I been if this uncle of mine had never existed. All I hold dear, my mother, my friend, my lover; all, all, sacrificed to the prospect of possessing this uncle's wealth." One need only recall *Love and Friendship* and the works it parodies to see how closely dependent on this style such a passage is. The emphasis upon excessive feelings, the tyranny of parents, the falseness of social and material values are all components of this style. Even more important, however, in *The Lustful Turk* sexuality is itself largely represented in the language, the diction, of sensibility. The Turk himself ruminates in this style:

> how strange it is . . . that these slaves, whose destinies depend on our will, rarely give that fervent return to our pleasure, so absolutely necessary to the true voluptuous energy of enjoyment. It is true, nature will always exert its power over the softer sex, and they frequently give way to its excitement, but the pleasure they experience is merely animal. Thus it is with Zelia . . . even in the

height of our ecstacies, a cloud seems to hang on her beauteous countenance, clearly indicating that it is nature, not love, that creates her transport.

The key terms here are "nature," "animal," and "love." A hierarchy of values is being acknowledged, with love as the supreme value. That this recognition is in essence an outright contradiction of pornography's purpose is not to the point—and in any event our understanding of such matters has consistently proceeded through the discovery and analysis of just such contradictions. What is of greater interest is the discovery of just how simple, unimpeded, and convenient was the conversion of the terminology of sensibility into the terminology of sexuality, of sexual reverie.

This conversion is demonstrated through the novel. Emily describes the Dey's first assault:

> You may guess the shock it at first gave me, but you will scarcely credit it when I own that my indignation was not of long continuance. Nature, too powerful nature, had become alarmed and assisted his lascivious proceedings, conveying his kisses, brutal as they were, to the inmost recesses of my heart. On a sudden, new and wild sensations blended with my shame and rage, which exerted themselves but faintly . . . in a few short moments his kisses and his tongue threw my senses into a complete tumult. . . .

When one sees the term "nature" being used in this way, one understands a bit better why people were inclined to go into fits and rages whenever it was introduced. Nature here is operating under an idiosyncratic, though familiar, eighteenth-century definition. It slumbers, but can be alarmed; and then it is "too powerful." It is implicitly opposed to moral and social feelings, yet it is somehow connected with the "recesses" of the heart. It makes itself felt through the senses, through "new and wild sensations," and it produces at first not pleasure but disorder, confusion, "a complete tumult." Further on, Emily makes the following reflections: "After he had left me in the morning, and reason had resumed its empire, I was fully sensible of my deviation from strict virtue in the return I made to his pleasure." Here a more traditional opposition is being invoked; nature is opposed to reason. And when reason resumes its "empire," then Emily (and her author) uses "sensible" in the sense of Elinor Dashwood.[1]

Another passage from the narrative of Honoria (it should go without saying that it doesn't matter what part of such a work one chooses passages from; the characters are almost never differentiated enough in their responses to create problems of context) reveals similar matters.

> Never, oh never shall I forget the delicious transports that followed the stiff insertion; and then, ah me!, by what thrilling degrees did he, by his luxurious movements, fiery kisses, and strange touches of his hand to the most crimson parts of my body, reduce me to a voluptuous state of insensibility. I blush to say so powerfully did his ravishing instrument stir up nature within me, that by mere instinct I returned him kiss for kiss, responsively meeting his fierce thrusts, until the fury of the pleasure and ravishment became so overpowering that, unable longer to support the excitement I so luxuriously felt, I fainted in his arms with pleasure. . . . So lively, so repeated were the enjoyments that the Dey caused me to participate with him, I wondered how nature could have slumbered so long within me. I was lost in astonishment that in all the caresses I received from Ludovico he had not contrived to give the slightest alarm or feeling to nature.

Nature and "instinct" are herein allied, and their combined operations work to "reduce" Honoria to a state of "insensibility," which means that her senses have been overcome by the excessive charge they have been made to bear, and not that she is or becomes insensible in the sense of being wooden or of not being able to feel at all.[2] Furthermore, "pleasure" and "ravishment" go together (the women typically experience an "agony of bliss"); that is to say, feelings of pleasure and pain are copresent

---

[1] For an extended discussion of this and related problems, see William Empson, *The Structure of Complex Words* (New York, n.d.), pp. 250–311.

[2] The word "reduce" is also being used in a special sense. The Dey applies himself to women "with an energy the most reducing." The term is taken from the medical practice of the time; certain kinds of treatments or diets were thought of as "reducing" or "lowering" in their effects.

in a state that is larger, more intense, more overwhelming than either could be alone. The analogy of this state with the notion of "the sublime"—and with what an experience of the sublime was said to be—is clear. And, one recalls, one also experienced the sublime by means of "nature."

The idea of sensibility provided a juncture for feelings and emotions on the one hand, and for sensation or sensations on the other; rather, it provided a juncture for two different classes of emotions that were in the late eighteenth and early nineteenth centuries distinguished by the terminology of feelings and sensations. Thus, when the Dey hears Adianti's tale of woe — "The tear of sensibility stood trembling in his eye at the relation of my sufferings." And he takes her maidenhead while she is insensible from the opiate because, she says, he was "determined, by rendering me insensible to my seduction, to spare my feelings and blushes." In such passages, the opposites are fused and unified; such a unification does not, however, lead to a new synthesis. On the contrary, its intention appears to be the obliteration of distinctions—an intention that it shares in common with almost all pornography. For the most part, nevertheless, *The Lustful Turk* maintains the old distinctions even as it emphasizes the juncture of opposites and their clash—as in the following passage: "I was lost to everything but the wonderful instrument that was sheathed within me. I call it wonderful, and I think not improperly; for wonderful must that thing be that in the midst of the most poignant grief can so rapidly dissolve our senses with the softest sensations, spite of inclination, so quickly cause us to forget our early impressions, our first affections, and in the most forlorn and wretched moment of our existence make us taste such voluptuous delight and lustful pleasure." Here the "senses"—in at least two possible acceptations—are dissolved by the power of "sensations"; and "inclination," which is now enlisted on the side of "early impressions . . . first affections" (is one hearing an echo of the "Immortality Ode"?), is along with both overcome. But it will not do to press too hard on the text of this novel. In the

first place, its diction is not that coherent: it does not aim for
coherence, is not concerned with it, and does not achieve it.
Secondly, as the last clauses of the passage I have just cited
demonstrate, the prose of this novel consistently drops into
dead phrases, clichés, stereotypical verbal counters. And in the
third, although a pornographic novel is by necessity a written
work, it exists less in its language than any other kind of literature. Unlike a poem, it cannot even remotely be conceived of as
a verbal structure. Unlike a novel, it cannot be conceived of as
in part a verbal structure, in part a system of relations which
have referents in and must be checked against some larger, su-
pervening external reality. Language is for pornography a
bothersome necessity; its function is to set going a series of non-
verbal images, of fantasies—and if it could dispense with words
it would. Which is why, one supposes, that the motion-picture
film is what the genre was all along waiting for.

What the foregoing discussion does suggest, however, is that
the early critics of the cult and style of sensibility had their
point. They were right to sense that there was something subversive in this new attitude toward the individual self, in this
new valuation of strong emotions and vivid sensations, in this
increased awareness of the antagonism between the claims of
impulse, "nature," and pleasure, and traditional social arrangements and restraints. And they were right to sense that the cult
of sensibility was at its origins connected with sexuality, with
sexual claims and impulses—as the conversion, literally without
modification, of the language of sensibility into the language of
a pornographic work of fiction amply demonstrates. They were
further right in their suspicion that the style of sensibility, if it
were acted upon—or, as we say today, "acted out"—would result in the destruction of certain social, moral, and personal distinctions and in their additional suspicion that this was in fact
sensibility's end in view. What they could not know was that,
along with the subverting and negating influence exerted by
sensibility, something new and of great value was also in the
process of being brought into existence—it was one of the earli-

est moments of what we like to think of today as the modern consciousness.

The same conclusion holds for the other "borrowings" in *The Lustful Turk*. The use made of Byron, for example, is unmistakable. The "English renegade" captain of the Algerine Corsair needs no explanation. And both of the interpolated stories—the histories of Honoria and Adianti—are adorned with Byronic touches. Honoria, with her cicerone-lover, clearly alludes to the Byronic legend as well as to the poems. And Adianti, in her statements about Turkish tyranny over Greece, alludes to the same popular, literate consciousness. Here is her description of her Greek lover, Demetrius: "He was born for a land of freedom, and one might have predicted from his appearance that he was destined to chafe and struggle not a little under the restraints and mortifications which ever fall to the lot of those who show the least spirit of independence. His stature was tall; he carried his head higher than a Bashaw; he was of easy carriage . . . active and graceful in his walk . . . and impatient of insult to the last degree. He was eloquent, poetical, romantic, enterprising, and a lover of the arts." Despite the vulgarity and inconsequence of that last series—one wonders just what "enterprising" means in such a context—the whole passage, along with the other Byronic trappings, demonstrates the cultural-functional nature of Byronism. They make even clearer what was already clear: that the introduction of anything from the corpus of Byronic material could be counted on automatically to release an erotic response. The Dey himself is a Byronic figure, with this important modification—something has been left out. The guilty, remorseful, brooding, doomed, and conflict-ridden part of the Byronic hero has been deleted. The Dey may be blessed with a sensibility, but he is not cursed with a conscience, nor does he suffer from inward conflicts. These deletions may be regarded as necessary, for pornography characteristically envisages a world in which conscience and real conflict do not exist. The freedom it imagines is attained by an act of suspension—half of human nature is put to one side. And its use of literature follows the same course—it adapts by subtraction and is always less than what it takes. In pornography the whole is smaller than the sum of its parts. But then that is the very principle by which pornography exists, and by which it acquires whatever power it exerts. It exists as something less than literature, and it persists because it meets certain needs that literature does not and cannot meet.

The Lustful Turk uses the trappings of the Gothic romance in much the same way as it uses Byron. The Abbots, monasteries, novices, burials alive, illicit relations, etc., all function as parts of a tissue of reference through which the whole of reality is sexualized. Such a circumstance confirms again what has often been suspected. Romanticism, especially in its more popular forms, has often been regarded as a movement from beneath upward, as gestures from the underground, a giving of articulation to what had hitherto been ignored, denied, or constrained. We are doubly confirmed in this notion when we see that Romanticism, once it established itself aboveground, could then with consummate ease feed back into the underground, the real underground, the underworld or underlife of pornography. To my mind, the most distinctive—and slightly spectacular—demonstration of this process is to be found in the third instance of borrowing in *The Lustful Turk*.

After the Dey has deflowered Sylvia Carey, he leaves the exhausted girl alone for a few hours. When he returns, he finds that she is asleep. He kisses her, but she sleeps on and appears to have a dream. "A blush spread itself on her face and bosom . . . her lovely thighs spread of themselves, her breasts heaved rapidly, her whole body was agitated, her arms spread, then of a sudden fell, and then she became motionless as death. Certainly she had tasted in a dream all those joys which the waking sense can know." Watching her, the Dey states that he was "more lost in transport even than she." At length he wakes her, but "the dream still retained some influence over her waking mind." She has been dreaming, of course, of the Dey, but the Dey idealized, and of herself as "less ashamed," as "happy without regret . . . or pain." The Dey then proceeds to transform the real into the ideal, the climax of which is represented thus: "The soft joy had seized upon her senses, her tremblings, heavings, soft shudders, the active movements of her arms and legs, quick breathings, graspings, return of my kisses, all bespoke her dream realized." This is, of course, nothing less than the spelling out of what happens in Stanza XXVI of "The Eve of St. Agnes." And this time it can be said that the pornographer's intention was by no means incongruent with the great poet's—although the poet had other intentions besides. It may be argued that literature resides in just such "other intentions," but here, I believe, we are on less solid ground. That the central moment and climax of an important Romantic poem should find something which resembles its explicit statement, if not its fulfillment, in a work of pornography should help to restrain us from settling for easy conclusions about the relations between the genres.[3]

The chief sexual fantasies represented in *The Lustful Turk* can be rather simply outlined. They have largely to do with the sexuality of domination, with that conception of male sexuality in which the aggressive and sadistic components almost exclusively prevail. Each of the separate stories is in this sense identical with the others. Each begins with a virgin, reluctant, proud, chaste, a young woman in whom Nature has not yet been awakened. She then undergoes a series of violent experiences, which ritually include beating, flogging, and defloration in the form of rape. By means of these sufferings, her pride is subdued, her chastity broken, and in their place Nature—responsiveness—is substituted. This conception of male sexuality is what I have earlier called the historically older or more traditional form, the form of aggressive domination. It is also the form in which male sexuality is represented in the overwhelming majority of pornographic works written during the nine-

[3] It should be observed that this scene of dream, awaking, and then continuation and fulfillment of the dream in reality soon becomes a convention in pornographic fiction. I have noted at least a dozen subsequent instances of it.

teenth and twentieth centuries. It may be that this conception, which naturally is the expression of certain unconscious ideas, is universal and an invariable. We do know, however, that pornography, in the sense that we understand it today, is a historical phenomenon; it begins to exist *significantly* sometime during the middle of the eighteenth century and flourishes steadily —though with periodic fluctuations in intensity—throughout the nineteenth and twentieth centuries. It is at least possible to speculate, therefore, that this conception of male sexuality is also historically influenced or determined, and that it came to be represented with such obsessive frequency and fantastic elaborations only when it had ceased effectively to exist, only when male sexuality had already begun to take on the shape that it has today.

The central part of this conception concerns the penis, which it regards literally as a magical instrument of infinite powers. Emily describes her first experience with it: "If I had wished to remove my hand from its position I could not; and so wonderful was the fascination I felt from the mere touch of this unknown object, I think I could not have removed my hand had it been perfectly at liberty. Without knowing what it was, every throb created in me a tremor unaccountable. I little dreamed the dreadful anguish I was doomed to experience by that which my hand was warming and raising to life." This is animal magnetism with a vengeance. This immense overestimation of the penis has as one of its elements the notion that the penis is a weapon. It rends, wounds, tears, and is capable of killing the object of its attack. Here is another perfectly conventional representation of its power.

In my agony I strove to escape, but the Dey, perfectly used to such attempts, easily foiled them by his able thrusts, and quickly buried his tremendous instrument too far within me to leave me any chance of escape. He now paid no kind of attention to my sufferings, but followed up his movements with fury, until the tender texture altogether gave way to his fierce tearing and rending, and one merciless, violent thrust broke in and carried all before him, and sent it imbrued, reeking with blood of my virginity, up to its utmost length in my body. The piercing shriek I gave proclaimed that I felt it up to the very quick; in short, his victory was complete.

Such passages clearly illustrate the fact that almost all pornography is written by men and for men—that the point of view is entirely masculine. It concentrates upon this organ and what it can do: the organ becomes the person, and the woman ceases to be a woman and is transformed into an object, an object upon which the penis works its destructive yet delightful effects. *The Lustful Turk* consciously elaborates upon this paradox. Emily writes: "You, Sylvia, who are yet, I believe, an unexperienced maid, can have no conception of the seductive powers of this wonderful instrument of nature—this terror of virgins, but delight of women. Indeed there can be no description given of the pure delight, I may even say agony, of enjoyment excited by the excessive friction which the rapidity of its thrusts caused. I was soon taught that it was the uncontrolled master-key of my feelings." Here again the penis becomes the man: it does the thrusting and not the man; it is its own agent. And the final sentence, including the ambiguity in "uncontrolled," sums up the entire notion—power, potency, omnipotence itself is attributed to this magical organ.[4]

From organs and objects it is but one step to machines. This is the general tendency of logic in pornography, and *The Lustful Turk* does not depart from what may be said to be its prescribed course.

---

[4] As in almost all pornography, *The Lustful Turk* is redundant with such representations. Emily wakes in the morning while the Dey is still asleep. "However reduced as it was in appearance, it had the same power of fascination over me which is attributed to the serpent's eye over the bird. I could not withdraw mine from it." She follows this up by touching "what may be termed Nature's grand master-piece." Later on, the Dey adds these reflections: "How magical is the influence of the distinction of our sex over the feelings of the softer one. Shrieks, cries, tears, and resistance accompanied the discovery and my seizing her, when directly she felt its head dividing her lips of life her resistance ceased, and her cries became hushed; as it penetrated her tears became dried [etc., etc.]. . . . Nature had already assumed its sway." The repetitions are formulaic and ritualistic, and serve the same incantatory and invocatory functions for which formulas and rituals are employed.

Stretched almost to suffocation on a rack of pleasure, its point stung her so much that catching at length the rage from my furious driving, she went wholly out of her mind, her sense concentrating in that favorite part of her body, the whole of which was so luxuriously filled and employed. There alone she existed, all lost in those delicious transports, those ecstacies of the senses. . . . In short she was a machine (like any other piece of machinery) obeying the impulses of the key that so potently set her in motion, till the sense of pleasure foaming to a height drove the shower that was to allay this hurricane. She kept me faithful company, going off with the old symptoms. . . . And now in getting off her, she lay motionless, pleasure-filled—stretched and drenched— quite spent and gasping for breath, without any other sensations of life than in those exquisite vibrations that trembled yet on the strings of delight, which had been so ravishingly touched, and which nature had too intensely striven with for the senses to be quickly at peace from.

Pleasure so intense that it is torture and suffocation drives her out of her mind—which means that "sense" departs from her mentally, makes its way downward, and is converted into the "sense" of the body. At this point, she is "lost" and becomes a machine; she is like some clock or spring-driven contraption, which is set in motion by being wound up. The key too is a piece of machinery (metaphorically dramatizing the fantasy that the penis is a detachable appendage that can be thought of as having a separate existence of its own); but a key at least implies a human agent behind it. The imagination of human sexuality in this passage is in large part the imagination of Newtonian mechanics; and the key that sets things in motion is the same key with which *Tristram Shandy* begins. At the end of the passage, we see that the machine is some kind of music box which is now wound down; or perhaps it is some kind of harp or lute.[5]

Machines can run down, but they can be wound up again. They cannot become tired, and they cannot achieve gratification. I have said before that the idea of pleasure in pornography

[5] "And what if all of animated nature/ Be but organic Harps diversely framed." It is Coleridge's notion that the harps are "organic," which of course makes for all the difference.

typically excludes the idea of gratification, of cessation. Pleasure is thought of as endless and as endless repetition. This fantasy is given full expression in *The Lustful Turk;* the different stories of which it is composed are as much alike without being identical as they can possibly be. Indeed, the writer of this novel seems to have been more aware than most pornographers are of certain of the implications of his fantasies. Since the idea of endless pleasure contradicts the idea of an ending, most pornographic novels have no ending—they end nowhere. If the author of *The Lustful Turk* had no adequate idea of gratification, he had at least the wit to see that a situation demanding unlimited repetition could be brought to a conclusion by removing its apparent exciting cause. The castration of the Dey is a coherent way of bringing the novel to a close—it rises out of a particular context and refers meaningfully back upon it.

What we have then in *The Lustful Turk* is an instance of the juncture of literature and pornography. We have an instance of how the conventions of literature and the conventions of pornography operate when they are brought into juxtaposition and connection. They operate according to a kind of Gresham's Law: whenever there is a question of priority, whenever there is a choice to be made, the pornographic convention or mode triumphs over the literary, and triumphs over its reality and reality itself. Thus, although the different women in this novel are introduced as different in character, attitude, and response, they do not persist in their differences. They are essentially plastic, and their plasticity allows them to become simple objects; in their role as objects they are all reduced to a common identity, they are all the same. A similar circumstance obtains in regard to the secondary narrative. It is introduced as being connected with and corollary to the central narrative. But nothing is made of either connection or correlation; both are forgotten and dropped, and the secondary narrative remains wholly without consequence and simply floats about in the middle of the novel. Indeed, whenever some consideration or requirement of the narrative arises, it almost seems as if the purpose of the intervention is to provide an occasion for dispensing with it absurdly. "In short," runs a passage in the secondary narrative, "I was as blessed as youth and voluptuous beauty could make me, until forced to retire from her arms to attend to my monastery duties. They were quickly dispatched, and after refreshing myself with a few hours rest, I returned to my captive with recruited strength for the night's soft enjoyment." Those monastery duties are there solely to be "quickly dispatched"; their reality lies in the idea that they are to be gotten out of the way, and they exist only in order to be negated.

The results of such proceedings are to turn the novel in the direction of pornotopia—that vision which regards all of human experience as a series of exclusively sexual events or conveniences. Under the pressure of this vision, narrative is transformed into unconscious comedy. "The next day [writes Emily] I was sitting on the sofa when the Dey entered my apartment. I tried to frown on him, but could not, for he drew his robe on one side and disclosed that delightful instrument that attunes my heart to harmony. I threw myself on my back, and in a moment His Highness was in the pinnacle of bliss. Thrice did he return my embraces ere he withdrew, then, seating himself beside me on the couch, he began as follows: 'You are no doubt dying with curiosity to know. . . .'" This is the art of the comic strip. Before he can impart any kind of information to her, they must ritually and automatically go through a series of mechanical gestures—like a sexual Punch and Judy, a pornographic Krazy Kat and Offisa Pup. In passages such as this, we can observe how *The Lustful Turk*, though it is still related to literature, moves toward those conditions of autonomy from both literature and actual experience which characterize pornography in its fully developed state.

I I

The Lustful Turk is a pre-Victorian novel. Its narrative mode, prose style, and literary references all belong to the late eighteenth and early nineteenth centuries, as does the relative lack of complication with which its sexual fantasies are elaborated. *Rosa Fielding, or, A Victim of Lust* was published in 1867, and a summary of its narrative indicates how centrally it is connected with the mid- or high-Victorian period.

The story opens in "the small country town called Rutshole." Its central character is Mr. Bonham, a "portly widower of fifty or thereabouts," "rich and respectable," and the owner of "Rutsden Lodge," where he lives with his unmarried daughter, Eliza. Mr. Bonham is a person of "a very staid and even strict outward demeanour"; he prudently aspires to "keep up . . . outward appearances," and is ambitious to maintain "a saintly character among his neighbours and friends." Until now he has restrained "his indulgences within very narrow bounds, and . . . [has been] circumspect and moderate in the enjoyment thereof." This self-denial has proved a double benefit to Mr. Bonham: "among the saints of his acquaintance he was pleasingly conscious that, thanks to his regular but very generous diet, and his habit of self-control (not abstinence) as to the softer sex, he was enjoying what is called a green old age; and was when on the verge of fifty pretty confident that his latent powers when called into action would be found quite equal to those of many a worn out young roué of five and twenty."

Mr. Bonham enters a hosier and glover's shop in Rutshole High Street, and there sets eyes upon Rosa Fielding, "a pretty girl of sixteen," who is employed in the shop, and whose "remarkable grace and modesty had already attracted numerous young squires, young farmers, and officers from the neighbouring garrison town, as real or pretended customers." The portly widower of fifty is simultaneously "struck with Rosa's beauty," and with "a bright idea." He questions the owner of the shop about Rosa and discovers that she is the daughter of respectable farmers who live about three miles from the town. Next morning "the model gentleman" rides out to Elm Tree Farm and proposes the following scheme to Rosa's parents: "namely, that Rosa should be placed in a first-rate school in the neighbourhood of London; that all the expenses, including her equipment, should be borne by him; and that in twelve or eighteen months, if Rosa had been well-behaved and steady, as there was every reason to suppose she would, he, the speaker, would make her Mrs. Bonham and mistress of Rutsden Lodge." The parents are astonished and delighted, Rosa is at once outfitted for her new prospects in life, and Mr. Bonham conveys her in his carriage to London. "Rosa enjoyed the ride immensely. Her guardian, as she took to calling him, was so kind and affectionate . . . that she considered herself a very fortunate girl." For his part, Mr. Bonham regards Rosa "already as my wife, morally speaking," and pursues the implications of such remarks. Rosa is altogether complaisant, and only escapes losing her virginity on the road to London because of Mr. Bonham's incontinence, which was, we are told, brought on by overexcitement and protracted "tension." He leaves her "happily situated" at a school in London.

Meanwhile, back in Rutsden Lodge, Eliza, Mr. Bonham's daughter, "a tall, dashing-looking young lady, with dark eyes and raven hair," has not been idle. She has caught wind of her father's scheme, which he has tried to conceal from her, and is busily engaged in undoing it. As we first see her, Eliza is engaged in writing a letter to her cousin and betrothed "Captain Alfred Torrant, 51st Dragoons, Baboonfield Barracks." She is aghast at the prospects of such "a mother-in-law!—a vulgar, uneducated country girl, about sixteen or seventeen years old." She confides to Alfred that they have misunderstood her father: "you see my dearest cousin, that somebody else can fuck besides you, and as sure as that stupid old party, my respected father, marries a young fresh country girl, he'll get her with child. . . . And then my inheritance will be lessened at his death, or perhaps cut away altogether." Eliza has, however, already thought of a way out: "You see if you or some of your brother officers could get access to this girl, give her a good rogering and get her with child, or turn her upon the town, it would settle the question at once." She suggests that Alfred "get a few days leave and come here on some pretext or other and we will have a consultation on the subject," and then adds that "I rather think that I want something else besides a consultation . . . so if you do come you had better take the precaution of bringing a dozen preventatives in the shape of French letters in your pocket."

Alfred arrives, the lovers meet, and while they are doing so, a subplot is developed. Alfred sends his manservant, Robert, on a reconnoitering tour of the countryside to see what he can discover about Rosa. On his way to the Fieldings' farm, Robert has some casual sexual adventures on his own behalf; having arrived at the farm, he is made welcome by Mrs. Fielding, who plies him with ale. Under the influence of the alcohol, and apparently out of purely boyish high spirits, he concocts for Mrs. Fielding a fantastic tale. It concerns a mythical major from his regiment and how he seduced a maiden lady from the town of Rutshole in Little Bethel Chapel, beneath the very eyes of the Reverend Brother Stiggins while he was ranting out one of his sermons. Robert further develops his tale by stating that after the event occurred, Stiggins came to the barracks and tried to blackmail the mythical major for ten pounds. "Upon this," he continues, "the Major informed him, that he, the saintly Stiggins, had been discovered in a pig-pen, rogering a young sow, that he, the Major, had half a dozen witnesses quite ready to prove it, and that if he annoyed him . . . with his blackguard lies, he would have him up before the magistrates for bestiality." He then, according to the tale, has Stiggins kicked out of the barracks. Mrs. Fielding is shocked by the story, and the reader is informed that she is sure to spread the gossip about Stiggins around the town.

Robert then returns to his master to make a progress report.

Alfred and Eliza are delighted by the mischief, and the following scenes represent a variety of sexual activities among the two lovers and Robert and Lucy, Eliza's maid. These performances are brought to a halt by the return from London of Mr. Bonham, and the next morning Alfred returns to his barracks. Once there, he tells his fellow officers about Robert's story, and they all prepare to welcome the Reverend Stiggins, who is certain to come there in outrage when once he hears the malign story that is circulating about. He soon turns up, is treated with perfect coolness by the officers, is insulted, then is gotten dead drunk and passes out. He is then tarred and feathered, "placed on a wheelbarrow," and trundled into town, where he is deposited on the doorstep of "Miss Larcher's Temperance Coffee-House"—Miss Larcher is the lady whom the mythical major is supposed to have seduced during holy services. Miss Larcher is at first aghast—"oh my, what a state for a babe of grace, a minister of the word," she exclaims, on seeing the woebegone Stiggins—but she is soon distracted by the attentions of one of the dragoons officers. He conducts her back inside the temperance hostel, effortlessly seduces her, and then gaily leaves her "to take what pride she could in the idea that if she were not a married woman, she was at any rate no longer an old maid."

The scene then switches to London, where Rosa is a "parlour boarder" at Mrs. Moreen's establishment. In a series of extraordinarily conventional episodes, Rosa is introduced to homosexual play by her fellow boarders, some of whom then tell their own stories. Rosa takes to it all uncommonly well. These activities are interrupted by a visit from Mr. Bonham; on this occasion he does succeed in his design of deflowering Rosa. After having achieved his goal, he strolls "towards his club in Pall Mall," and to his surprise runs into Alfred Torrant. His prospective son-in-law has his own purposes to pursue, and after a suitable interval offers to show Mr. Bonham "a scene or two of London life known only to a few of the initiated." In the company of one of Alfred's fellow officers, they repair to a fancy brothel where they propose to pass the night. Two girls are assigned to provide for "the delighted Bonham," and we see him "shown into a most luxurious chamber, feeling more like a he-goat or a young bull than a sanctimonious elder of the chapel which he patronized." In the morning, he wakens to a new revelation: "what a novice I have been, and what a number of delightful and comparatively innocent pleasures, I have in my ignorance debarred myself from," he cries in wonder. This is what Alfred had been waiting for. He recommends to his uncle the enjoyments of "a comfortable, bachelor-like, legitimate way" of life as far superior to the prospects offered by another marriage; "you might have a pretty villa at Richmond or Twickenham, with a pretty mistress keeping house for you, and you, yourself at liberty to visit your club, take dinners at Greenwich, or pay a visit to our esteemed hostess, Mrs. Goater, or to inspect her cabinet of choice curiosities by a way of a change, whenever you felt disposed." Mr. Bonham has, however, been there before his nephew: "a new vista in his career was opening to him . . . [and] as for marriage, or any such moral proceeding, that faded from before his eyes."

The purposes of both parties now coincide. Mr. Bonham now recognizes that "to get rid of his daughter was absolutely necessary, before entering upon any of his newly hatched schemes of felicity." He thereupon supplies Alfred with enough money to purchase a Majority that is about to become vacant, and with more than enough to set up the young couple in a respectable establishment. Alfred, for his part, brings matters to a conclusion in the following way. Under the guise of being an emissary of his uncle's, he calls for Rosa at Mrs. Moreen's, saying that he has been sent to escort her to a dinner party. Their destination is "Great Poke-hole Place," and on the way there, in the carriage, Alfred seduces the always complaisant Rosa and just about brings her up-to-date on developments in Rutshole. At Great Poke-hole Place they enter the house of the Earl of Longbowles, where a party is in progress—one of the Earl's regular orgies. They all take part in the proceedings, which are described with aimless good humor, and the novel is brought to a close with these arrangements: the Earl is much pleased with Rosa, and she with him, and so she consents to becoming one of his kept women, considering "that the offer of a handsome income from his Lordship was worth more than the prospect—rather an uncertain one—of becoming Mrs. Bonham." Mr. Bonham gets his "neat little villa at Twickenham" and keeps up his visits to Mrs. Goater's establishment. Alfred "was happily married to his cousin Eliza, and was almost as faithful a husband as could be reasonably expected from one of his natural character, and exposure to such temptations as were to be found in the attractions of the Earl of Longbowles' establishment and Mrs. Goaters'." Q.E.D.

Rosa Fielding is related to literature, but its relation is of a different kind than that which exists in *The Lustful Turk*. The first thing to be noted about it, in this connection, is the use to which it puts Dickens. The hosier and glover's shop in which Mr. Bonham first meets Rosa is owned by a widow named Trabb. Mrs. Trabb is a confidante of Mr. Bonham, and it is from her shop that Rosa is also fitted out when Mr. Bonham takes her to London. The name of Trabb was bound to be familiar to the readers of *Rosa Fielding*. It occurs, of course, in *Great Expectations,* which was published in 1861. Mr. Trabb is the tailor in the town of Pip's birth, and it is to Mr. Trabb's shop that Pip resorts when he is about to go up to London at the request of his "guardian" (Rosa refers to Mr. Bonham as her guardian), to come into his great expectations. The comic parallels between Pip's expectations and Rosa's are self-evident, although it seems more likely that what would be set in motion by these allusions are recollections of that marvelous character, Trabb's boy, and his deathless confrontations on the street with Pip.

Mr. Bonham is also "a philanthropist," and in the course of his private conversations with Mrs. Trabb he discloses

a case of soul-harrowing destitution among the Fukkumite Islanders recently converted to Christianity.

The interesting females had not the wherewithal to cover their bare bottoms, but used to display those wellrounded features to the unhallowed gaze of the unregenerate sailors of whale ships calling at the islands. Now the missionaries considered that if any bottoms were to be displayed by their precious converts, the exhibition should be made in private to their spiritual advisers. And to end the story, the benevolent gentleman, by way of advancing the moral and physical comforts of the Fukkumite ladies (to say nothing of the missionaries) asked Mrs. Trabb if she would like to contract for the supply of say to begin with one thousand pairs of frilled pantalettes.

There then follows an extended discussion of the articles of dress in question. There were, to be sure, other places than *Bleak House* in which the projects issuing from such sources as Exeter Hall were exposed to satire, but within the present context it seems clear that the author had in mind—and expected his readers to follow him—Mrs. Jellyby, Mrs. Pardiggle, the banks of the Niger, Borrioboola-Gha, the Tockahoopo Indians, and all such related matters. But the author has not simply taken over Dickens's satire—he has, in a slightly mad way, extended it and turned it upside down. Not only has he, like every writer of pornography, discovered the secret sexual nucleus within every human action, but he discovers as well that the missionaries are no missionaries at all. Mrs. Trabb remarks to Mr. Bonham that "woman's pants are made, to speak plainly, with openings at the front and rear, corresponding to her natural openings"; as a result, "the garments proposed are no obstruction whatever to a man who is determined to violate a woman." Mr. Bonham replies that this is all very well, "but then of course the women should have opportunities for performing their natural functions conveniently; and then our self-sacrificing brethren, the missionaries, they must have facilities for their comforts." So, the missionaries dress the natives only to undress them more thoroughly, put pants on the women to ensure a more comfortable violation of them. The missionaries are not misguided; they are cynical frauds—but so is everyone else. And since everyone seems to be enjoying what he is doing, there is no cause for anger, concern, or alarm, and satire is thus converted into footless comedy.

In a similar way, the style in which Mr. Bonham is represented is also adapted from Dickens. Mr. Bonham is a kind of indiscriminate combination of characteristics annexed from Mr. Pickwick, Fagin, Pecksniff, Chadband, and heaven knows who else. He proceeds down High Street "leisurely, but with the usual solemnity on his countenance," an expression that he considers both "dignified and respectable." He is referred to as "the artful old gentleman," and "the model gentleman." When he speaks, he does so in the role of "the moralist"; and when he inserts "the first two fingers of his right hand in Rosa's tender orifice," he does so in the capacity of "the moral gentleman." He is also called "the venerable Philanthropist," and can, when he chooses, reply "without moving a muscle of his face." What the author has appropriated from Dickens here—apart from most of the phrases themselves—is the deliberate, ironic use of current conventional terms of approbation. (In particular one should note the use of the word "moral"; as Dickens's career progressed he came to be virtually unable to use the word, or its variants, in any but an ironic sense.) The author's attitude toward that which he is ironically representing, however, is, as we shall see, something very different from Dickens's.

Some of the borrowings are slight and casual. At one point, a country girl who has gotten into trouble is mentioned: her name—Susan Flipper. And here is a passage that is supposed to render the speech of an angrily excited man: " 'Go to magistrates—bring action—defamation c'racter—spectable lady member cong-g-ration, Miss Larcher, thousand pounds damages!' " This is of course the author's recollection of the speech of Alfred Jingle. In point of fact, the levy of borrowings from *Pickwick Papers* is rather high. The Reverend Stiggins, with his "mountebanking, his prayers and howlings, and damning everybody except himself, up hill and down dale," has its origin in that novel. And when Stiggins is gotten drunk and taken off in a wheelbarrow, the author is fusing the character of Stiggins with an episode in which Mr. Pickwick is the victim. This oc-curs in Chapter XIX of *Pickwick Papers*. On one of the hunt-ing expeditions, Mr. Pickwick gets drunk on milk punch and subsides into a wheelbarrow and into sleep. Discovered in that state by the irate landowner, he is wheeled off to the Pound, where he awakens to gaze with "indescribable astonishment on the faces before him." He is then pelted with vegetables by the villagers. Stiggins is deposited, as I have indicated earlier, on the steps of the Temperance Coffee-House and hotel—in this context an adequate enough variation.

The author's annexations from Thackeray are of a similar order. The life in the barracks of H. M.'s 51st Dragoons is taken directly from *Vanity Fair*. " 'Well, madam,' said Robert gravely, 'we don't generally call the barracks a den of iniquity; you see, perhaps our gentlemen might not understand what that meant, but it's commonly known by the name of Hell's Blazes; and Mrs. Mantrap, the Colonel's lady—his wife's at Cheltenham—calls it Little Sodom. But that's neither here nor there.' " The cool tone is typically Thackerayean, as is the inclu-sion of a bit of ritual nostalgia for the Regency: " 'Pray allow me to . . . offer you a slight refreshment,' " says one of the officers; " 'It was considered a valuable stomachic by that model of all the monarchs—the late George the Fourth—named Prince's Mixture, in his honour when Regent.' " The author has even aspired to take over one of Thackeray's narrative de-vices. "Leaving then these friends of ours so comfortable," he writes, "we will return to Rutsden Lodge, and entering a small room where a tall, dashing-looking young lady, with dark eyes and raven hair is writing a letter, we will take the privilege of narrators who are ex-officio invisible and ubiquitous, and peep over a round white shoulder." Although it cannot be said that this novelist "knows everything," it cannot be denied that he knew his Thackeray.

What can we learn from these borrowings; what do they suggest to us about this novel and its audience? In the first place, they reveal a certain depth of common assumption—the author was able to assume that his audience would catch on to his allusions and would share in his knowledge of the literature which he was humorously working up. It is difficult to determine just what audience the author had in mind (if I were forced to make a choice, I would say that the ideal reader of this novel would have been a latter-day version of young James Crawley, the Reverend Bute Crawley's sporting son). What can be said, however, is that the author assumed something like a universal knowledge of Dickens and Thackeray to exist in his audience. To assume that Dickens and Thackeray were universals is the same as saying that these two novelists were thought of as providing a common culture, even for such a specialized and limited audience as this novel would naturally reach. Such a possibility confirms in its own way what has often been suggested about the depths to which the great Victorian novelists informed the consciousness of their time.

Yet these two popular novelists were also among the chief critics of Victorian society, of the cant, falsehood, and hypocrisy that they saw being practised on a vast organized scale in the world about them. The author of *Rose Fielding* was self-consciously aware of this circumstance, and at first sight his novel appears to follow the satirical, critical example of his two "masters." The portrait of Mr. Bonham, for instance, might seem to be a satirical treatment of middle-class Victorian respectability, a parody of benevolence, philanthropy, and piety. The Reverend Stiggins is a stock character from the period's satire: the ranting, canting Dissenting minister and his flock at Little Bethel are extremely familiar images. Miss Larcher, who runs the Temperance Coffee-House, but who is happy to give herself on the sly to a young dragoons officer, is no less familiar a figure. Handsome Miss Eliza, outwardly chaste, demure, and delicate, but in reality very sharp and very sexy, is quickly recognizable as well—merely consider how many novels by Trollope contain some version of her. And Rosa, young, innocent, darling, but in fact game for anything—she too is readily to be found in the literature of the age. But in reality, and with the possible exception of Stiggins, none of these characterizations is either satirical or critical. The author of *Rosa Fielding* is neither opposed to the attitudes held by his characters, nor is he critical of their behavior. He is in fact in favor of both their activities and the hypocrisies and double-dealings that condition those activities and make them possible. What we are confronted with in *Rosa Fielding,* therefore, is a confusion and possibly a contradiction between the satirical, critical form—which the author has adapted from the Victorian novel—and the inner content of that form, which in this instance may be regarded as coincident with the author's intention. This disparity appears with singular distinctness in the novel's prose.

The reader will have noted that the diction, syntax, and rhythm of the prose of *Rosa Fielding* are unexceptionably Victorian. Another difference between this prose and the prose of *The Lustful Turk* is that in *Rosa Fielding* the prose is, so to speak, more conscious of itself. It is conscious of itself as a work of pornography, and it is further aware that the conventions of pornography and the conventions of the Victorian novel differ. Here, for example, is the description of Alfred's arrival at Rutsden Lodge: "But the gallant young officer had not driven over from the barracks for nothing, and begged to assure his beautiful cousin that in his present state of mind and body it would be quite impossible for him to give proper attention to any serious business, until his burning love for her received some temporary gratification (the plain English of this being that he had a tremendous cock-stand, and felt that if it was not allayed pretty quickly that he must burst). . . ." Such a passage contains the awareness that at least two different kinds of language have developed. There is, on the one hand, the public language of Victorian life and of its literature; and on the other, there is the language of sex or of pornography. One is elaborate, genteel, and periphrastic; the other is "plain," direct, and violent. The two dictions do not readily consort with one another. When they are juxtaposed, they produce an effect which is slightly ridiculous, although it is regularly intended to be funny. Furthermore, brought together in such a context, the validity, the reality, of both kinds of language tend to be canceled: neither of them alone is adequate; together they are impossible; and one has the sense after reading an accumulation of such passages that, for the state of consciousness represented by this condition of language, no satisfactory or integrated way of describing such events, and therefore of ultimately experiencing them, was possible.

The speech of the characters demonstrates an analogous division. Here is Rosa in reply to Mr. Bonham.

> I shall be very glad, my dear guardian, to do anything to contribute to your comfort or to show my gratitude for the kindness you have done me; but I do, I certainly do think that this thing, this part of your person (I hardly know what to call it), is far too large to go into the slit between my thighs—which just now you called my cunt. Of course, you have a right to do as you please with me, and are perfectly welcome; but I fear you will hurt me dreadfully, even if you do not actually split my belly open, or extend my little orifice as far back as my bottom hole.

And Mr. Bonham replies in kind. Later on, when Rosa is thoroughly accommodated to her new experiences, she speaks like this: "'I am very glad to contribute to his pleasure, and he fucks me very charmingly and tenderly, and I am sure I try to meet him half way, don't I, Alfred?' continued the laughing girl, 'but his cock is devoted henceforth to a more legitimate business, and Miss Bonham would half murder me if she knew how often and what lengths he has pierced into my person.'" It is safe to say that no person in life or character in literature (outside of pornography itself) has ever spoken in this way. The most striking thing about such a prose is its quality of dissociation; it is dissociated from itself, from experience, from literature. The split or divided consciousness, whose working we observed in the writings of Acton and Ashbee, we can now observe again, within pornography itself. The dissociation is to be found not only in the dialogue of the characters but in the relation of the prose to the objects it purports to represent. Mr. Bonham asks Rosa to expose herself to him, and Rosa "did as she was requested and made a splendid exposure of her secret parts immediately." The dissociation here is between "splendid" and "exposure," between the descriptive adjective and the noun-event it is supposed to modify. One does not know what meaning should be attached to the modification, or from what point of view one ought to take hold of it. "Splendid" may be intended as vague, general praise; it may be meant ironically; or it may carry with it the meaning of being dazzling and impressive through brilliance or luster. Or it may mean all three or none. In all events, such passages leave the reader with a sense of radical disjunction between word and object, rhetoric and event, image and emotion. We are in the presence of a severe dislocation in language which corresponds to and expresses a dislocation in experience.

If we return to the author's handling of his characters and their attitudes, we find a similar situation. After Mr. Bonham and Rosa's first experience in the carriage, he tells her to take care of herself. "So by his advice, Rosa wiped herself dry, and he looked as fatherly and demure as he could; and from his long practice in what we hardly choose to call hypocrisy but something very like it, succeeded very well." The implication is that hypocrisy is a very good and very useful thing indeed. Miss Eliza's speech and epistolary style reveal a variation of this conception. " 'There was a baby-faced girl in a shop here,' she writes to her cousin, 'and the old idiot, I fear, has seen her and fancied her. If he would only give her a fucking and a five pound note' (this was the style the young lady wrote in), 'there would be no harm done.' " This is, of course, intended to be a parody of the genteel style of a young Victorian lady; but it is more of a reversal than it is a parody. It is a reversal in several senses. This is what young ladies are really like, it implies. Or, alternatively, this is what young ladies *should* be like. Furthermore, the author's attitude constitutes a reversal of our conventional moral expectations of him. Whether ladies and gentlemen are really like this, he suggests, or whether they only ought to be like this, this is what they all would secretly like to be, this is the way I describe them, and this is good.

Such reversals are characteristic of pornography in general. They also define its limits on one side. At best, pornography may be subversive in the sense that it reveals the discrepancy which exists in society between openly professed ideals and secretly harbored wishes or secretly practised vices—it may act indirectly to "unmask" society's official version of itself. It never, to my knowledge, is capable of taking the next step of subversion: it cannot supply a vision that either transcends or transvalues what passes for current reality. On the contrary, pornography is perfectly and happily at home with hypocrisy, cant, injustice, and all kinds of social malevolence; it may even be regarded as dependent upon them for its existence. It is itself part of the present order of things, and one of its central unvoiced intentions is that the present order of things should continue to exist as it is, if possible more so. Its reversals are thus self-contradictions, and pornography persists in this condition because in it—as in the mind of a child—no distinction is made between thought and deed, wish and reality, between what ought to exist, what one wants to exist, and what does in fact exist. It is a fantasy whose special preconditioning requirement is that it deny, delay, and stave off for as long as possible the recognition that it is a fantasy. Recognition dispels the dream of omnipotence and returns one to oneself, alone and palely loitering on the cold hill's side.

Considerations such as these help to explain the peculiar tone of *Rosa Fielding* and of many other pornographic novels. This tone may be described as both unreal and good-humored at the same time. Alfred and Eliza arrange for an assignation; she speaks first.

> There is a convenient little house of retreat, you know, among the bushes at the end of the serpentine walk, and there you know, although it is not a very genteel place for the purpose, you can—"
>
> "Of course I can, darling," interrupting her with a graceful kiss, "what a capital manager you are!"

"Then mind, sir, that you are a good manager too," replied the
young lady. "And don't hurt me any more than Robert did Lucy."

"I shan't hurt you at all, pet," was the reply. "Robert was rather
rough and piercing; I shall be very gentlemanly, only mind you
bring a small pot of cold cream with you. A privy or a water
closet is a capital place for such an encounter, as my injection
might produce all the effect of a warm clyster."

It is not so much the fantasies as the tone in which the fantasies
are represented which is of interest here. It is cool, canny, witty,
dead-pan, and tongue-in-cheek. It is quite aware that it is
spoofing certain genteel conventions of behavior and speech,
yet the spoofing is less real than that which it spoofs. In part,
this unreality is a result of the fact that the introduction into a
Victorian work of fiction, even a pornographic work of fiction,
of all those details—privies, water closets, sex, buggery—which
Victorian fiction universally excluded could not be managed
convincingly within the unmodified form itself. For one thing,
as we have already seen, the language, the diction, of Victorian
fiction had no way of accommodating to itself the specialized
and isolated diction of sex. In part, however, the unreality is the
result of other things. At night, Alfred "made pretty certain of
two matters; first, that his respected uncle was in bed and sleeping the first sleep of the just, and secondly, that notwithstanding his delightful encounters with his lovely cousin, in the
course of the day, he was perfectly able to do her as much jus-
tice as she could possibly desire in the fucking department."
Once again the prose is quiet, witty, dislocated, aware of its dislocation—and dead. Its deadness consists in the absence from it
of all those emotions that are normally associated with and appropriate to the actualities of "the fucking department." These
emotions are elicited by the presence of another person, but
since in pornography there is no "other person," only oneself,
the emotions—even the lust that one feels toward an actual living object, in contradistinction to the abstract and self-
referential lust of fantasy—which might be expected to accompany a representation of sexual activities between two persons
have no real place there and no real way of being expressed.

Instead, what is substituted for those emotions is a kind of light-hearted, good-humored, genteel smilingness, a bemused blandness of wit, a mild, tolerant amusement. Everything in the novel, from the hypocrisy of Bonham and Stiggins to the wild orgy at the Earl of Longbowles, is represented in this light, good-humored, distant, and slightly incoherent manner. There is a kind of pleasant, sweet meaninglessness to it all, and at moments the novel is almost conscious of this circumstance—that it is, within the context of the terms that it itself proposes, meaningless. At such points the novel teeters on the edge of explicitly acknowledging its unreality, its silliness; and in the degree that it approaches awareness of its childishness (about to enter a woman by surprise, Alfred is typically represented as "chuckling to himself with the glee of a mischievous school-boy"), it comes to resemble another peculiar Victorian phe-nomenon, nonsense literature. Both are childish; both elaborate extremely distorted, hallucinated, and self-enclosed visions of human experience; both are written in code; both have an es-sentially mechanical view of things, and describe relations among human beings as a series of mechanical combinations of varying degrees of intricacy. But pornography, if it is to remain pornography and not transform itself into something else, must stop short of full explicitness in this regard. It cannot explicitly state that it is only a bit of fantasy; it must remain within its self-enclosed universe, wherein it repeats, reconstructs, and spins out yet once again those immemorial fantasies which it cannot relinquish.

The sexual fantasies represented in *Rosa Fielding* are not set down with any systematic or obsessive regularity of purpose—this regularity, by the way, constitutes the real formal structure of most works of pornography. In *Rosa Fielding,* some of the fantasies are familiar and conventions of the genre; some of them, at least in their accent and coloration, seem distinctly Victorian. Notice should be taken of certain instances of both kinds.

When Alfred first comes to Eliza, "the gentleman was in that state of lust that two or three judicious rubs from the hand of his fair cousin would have released his evacuation." In such a passage we have reconfirmed for us what we have observed earlier in Acton's official view of sexuality: how deeply conditioned by the conception of anality the conception of genitality can become, how indeed the genital organization can be modeled upon the earlier anal system. The consequences of such a notion (if one expands the metaphor one begins to see that the penis then might be either a fecal column or the lower end of the alimentary tract out of which fecal matter is to be expelled, the woman's body, particularly her genitals, becomes a toilet, etc.) for one's view not only of the relations between men and women but also for one's view of life itself need not be gone into any further. Another fantasy that *Rosa Fielding* shares not only with the sexual writings of its time but with pornography that is being written today concerns female ejaculation. I have already discussed this fantasy and, at this point, will only add that its universality and persistence indicate how unflagging is the need among men to deny the existence of two sexes. Another form of this fantasy concerns the clitoris; when Rosa is at school in London, she is told by her schoolmates that "only one woman in fifty . . . has her clitoris prominent enough to produce the desired effect upon another woman's cunt"—which, for a work of pornography, is virtually a repudiation. Connected with these ideas is the superstition that a woman can be impregnated only if she has an orgasm and ejaculation simultaneously with her partner. "For his beautiful antagonist met his attack so grandly and discharged her battery so promptly in reply to his, that if the latter had not been retained by the discreet covering, very serious consequences to the lady would have almost inevitably made themselves apparent in nine months time or thereabouts." The unconscious beliefs that are being revealed in this notion are, it seems to me, another form of the same cluster of fantasies.

In the latter part of the novel, when the sex begins to get

communal, a different series of fantasies are brought into play. The most important, because most widely recurrent, of these has to do with the idea of two men entering a woman at the same time. The underlying and pervasive current of homosexual impulses in pornography finds articulation in these images. To which it must be added that this particular fantasy is usually the final threshold in pornography: it is the last form in which male homosexual play is still disguised in heterosexual activities. Customarily this is either the fantasy that a pornographic work of fiction will end with, or else it will be followed by direct representations of male homosexual activity. Behind all these fantasies, however, is a further one, expressed in the desire of the Earl of Longbowles "to enjoy a perpetual cock-stand." As I have suggested earlier, the chief importance of this notion is not to be found in the image of pleasure it refers to, since the pleasure it conceives is a pleasure without climax, or release, or gratification in the sense of completion, and rest. Rather, this fantasy of enjoying "a perpetual cock-stand" acts as do all the other fantasies I have just discussed. It acts as a reassurance. To have a perpetual erection is the one way of being continually reassured that one really does have a penis, that one's penis is always there, that it has not gone or been taken away. This, it seems to me, is the central organizing purpose which most of the fantasies in pornography serve. They are in the literal sense of the term self-serving.

One thing more remains to be pointed out. The reader will have noted that this novel contains certain references to contraception. Eliza says to Alfred: " 'You must really cover your beautiful instrument with that sheath, or condom, or whatever you call it. I have no notion of having a pretty white belly bow-windowed before marriage!—indeed I shan't particularly care about it after marriage!' " The reader is entitled to wonder why, in the midst of this fantastic symphony, such a note of reality should be struck. The answer, I believe, is not to be found within this novel itself, but within the genre as a whole. Such a device, or maneuver, or figure is a regular occurrence in pornographic novels. Sometimes, amidst the incessant barrage of sexual activities, it will be the fact of menstruation that is brought in, and when it is brought in it almost invariably brings those activities to a temporary halt. Sometimes it is the fear of venereal disease, and sometimes it is pregnancy. Usually only one such circumstance is introduced, and just as usually that circumstance turns out to be the single instance of the recognition of sexual reality in the novel. These instances, it seems to me, have the function of maintaining one last link with, one final toehold in, reality. It is as if the pornographic novelist were almost aware that there was some danger in cutting himself entirely loose from the earth, of precipitating himself completely into the open space of fantasy. The single link with reality, then, may serve the novelist unconsciously as a kind of control; it protects him from finally and ultimately identifying his universe of fantasy with the real world. It is his way of reassuring himself that he is in fact sane.

I I I

The Amatory Experiences of a Surgeon was written by Ashbee's acquaintance and colleague, the pseudonymous James Campbell. It is less than one hundred pages long and is told in the first person. The narrator is born a bastard, the son of "a nobleman of the first rank." His mother "was of that disgraced and neglected race, a discarded mistress." After this "toy" and "plaything" had been thrown off by her lover, she dies; but unlike Maypole Hugh or Hyacinth Robinson, his counterparts in the higher walks of fiction, the illegitimate son is not abandoned by his father. He is sent to "a boarding school, and at the age of fourteen had grown a tall, well-made and genteel looking youth." He is initiated into sex by his schoolmates and is then prepared to leave school. He obtains "the permission of my noble parent to study for the medical profession," goes to London, "and after several years studious application at the hospitals, I received my diploma from the Examiners at Surgeon's Hall, or in modern parlance, from the Royal College of Surgeons." He then settles into "a small practice, at the village near which my paternal patron had his principal estate . . . my lord's patronage was quite sufficient to bring me plenty of practice, and within a time I became the fashionable doctor of the district."

His sexual career now begins in earnest. His father, who is still a bachelor, keeps both his residence and a new mistress "in the locality." The son, in his "capacity as medical adviser to the family . . . had frequently seen and spoken to this lady." With her, his "fancy soon found a resting place, and full of notions of revenging Lord L——'s desertion of my mother, I allowed myself to cherish ideas of putting in practice a signal retribution." The project is accomplished speedily and without effort. Two months pass, and then one day the narrator finds the lady in the company of the butler, "greatly relishing the assault of her huge antagonist." He makes himself known to the pair, and then leaves "resolving in my own mind that, as my father's place was so well filled by his butler, it was no longer necessary for his son to try to compensate his fiery mistress for that which he could only administer in insufficient doses, not enough to satisfy the craving appetite of his fair protégé."

His next adventure concerns the daughter of "an opulent resident in the town." He had of late observed in her "those usual indications of approaching puberty, that disturb the imagination of young girls"—the onset of menstruation and of sexual desire. He asks her to come and visit him, and she describes her distress and alarm.

> I entered fully into the particulars of her case. I found as expected, that she was experiencing the full force of those sensations which were never intended to be borne without relief. . . .
>
>   I told her of the cause of her own symptoms. I gradually explained their effects, and without shocking her modesty, I contrived to hint at the remedy. . . . I broke off into a warm condemnation of that state of society which allowed such complaints

to blast in secret the youth and beauty of young girls like herself.

I went on to hint at the evident necessity there was for the medical man supplying those deficiencies which society left in the education of young ladies.

Her education is soon completed, but at this point a bit of reality is permitted to enter: although "Julia had often received the entire length of my large member in her little cunt . . . that was the sum total of our bliss; to emit there was more than I dared." The young woman, however, is not content to stop short, and seduces the narrator into ejaculating while he is in her. She becomes pregnant—"the prolific juice had taken firm hold"—and the narrator-physician is forced to perform an abortion. As a result of the operation, she begins to fail in health. The narrator recommends a change in air, and her father takes her to Baden, where after a few months two things occur: "the roses again revisited her cheeks," and she "became the wife of a Russian prince."

After this termination he gives himself up "without reserve to the pleasures of love. All my patients who showed the least susceptibility were overcome by my potent argument, and vigorously fucked. I varied my pleasures in every possible way. Nothing which could enhance the enjoyment did I scruple to call into action." He begins to read "curious amorous works" to stimulate his fantasies, but satiety and boredom soon overtake him. In his plight, he turns to longing

for an unripe beauty, a young girl, a child even—to caress, to lie with, to suck. I found a lovely little girl of thirteen years of age, who had been under my care for a spinal affliction, in the treatment of which complaint I had been for a long time acknowledged a successful practitioner.

She had been an inmate of my house in order to be more fully under my care. Her friends were resident in another country, and had such confidence in my discretion that I believe had I even proposed to have slept with their niece they would have thought it was only part of my system.

There follow a number of scenes that anticipate scenes in *Lolita* and that culminate in the deflowering of the young girl. Matters proceed smoothly, with this single exception: because of her spinal complaint, the girl has "to keep still, and my gentle movements when I fucked her, only seemed to excite without giving her that full satisfaction which she instinctively felt could only be obtained by giving full license to all our desires by a perfect abandon of voluptuousness in those extatic conjunctions. . . ." She implores the narrator to "fuck me with real energy, if only for once; do let me feel what the extasies of sexual conjunction are really like; let me die of love for once, if I am never able to bear it again." The narrator consents to gratify her desires upon one condition; he proposes to tie her down to a "couch . . . a veritable battleground of Venus, having been made for my special use, according to ideas I furnished to my upholsterer." The tying down is effected, the orgy takes place, and is "afterwards repeatedly given by special request of my little loving Mary." The episode is brought to a close with this comment: "Another extraordinary thing I ought to mention, is that the fucking, etc., had such a salubrious effect upon my young patient that she eventually quite got the better of her spinal complaint, and was married at the age of eighteen." Things were never like this in Hecate County.

The novel ends with two abbreviated further episodes. One concerns the daughter of a local clergyman who is raped by her betrothed, the squire's son. The other has to do with a horse dealer, his frigid wife, and how the narrator manages to cure her indisposition. Both episodes are treated along lines identical with those I have already sketched.

The only literature with which *The Amatory Experiences of a Surgeon* has any significant relation is pornography itself. Like some fifth-rate novel, or short story in a woman's magazine, or Grade B film, it must be understood as one among a large number of slightly differentiated variations within a highly conventionalized form. We must understand it in this way first, if we are to understand at all its relation to experience, if we are to understand the transactions it envisages as taking place between human beings.

The first thing to be noted in this regard is this novel's prose. It is written, almost literally, with a dead hand. "I carefully raised up her clothes. As I proceeded, I unveiled beauties enough to bring the dead to life, and losing all regard to delicacy, I threw them over the bosom of the sweet girl. . . . Everything now lay bare before me, her mossy recess, shaded by only the slightest silky down, presented to my view two full pouting lips of coral hue, while the rich swell of her lovely thighs served still further to inflame me." It is no exaggeration to say that every single phrase in this passage is a cliché—it is a little miracle of formulaic gesturings, of rigid, stereotyped moribundities. "Beauties enough to bring the dead to life," for example, occurs in countless passages of other pornographic works. By the time one runs across it here, one realizes that it is no longer referring to anything that might possibly have happened or happen. It is referring primarily to other literature and secondarily to the author and his readers—who, one suddenly recognizes, are in reality the dead who have to be brought to life. In a similar way, "sweet girl" has nothing to do with the nature of the imaginary object before the narrator; it is an epithet, a single unit of meaning, plucked out of a closet full of similar phrases, to do service in any context at all. When we come to "mossy recess" and "silky down," I will content myself with remarking upon the tautological character of the representation and will permit the reader to puzzle out for himself just what the author is trying to describe. The prose as a whole may be regarded as an interesting combination of stale eighteenth-century euphemisms and some kind of mid-Victorian anticipation of Mickey Spillane—"pouting lips" and "the rich swell of her lovely thighs" are almost pure Mike Hammer. In the nineteenth-century underworld of literature the detritus of the eighteenth century was already fermenting with the future.

Another quality of this prose is revealed in its adjectival insistence; "the soft voluptuous languor in her humid optics was far more expressive than words of the amorous storm within that tumultuous bosom." The point about these adjectives is not only that they are interchangeable; they are interchangeable without any loss of meaning. On the one hand, such words function as non-specific abstractions—they can all be filled with the same general content. On the other, to the extent that they become verbally non-referential, they express an important tendency in pornography. Pornography, as I have mentioned earlier, moves ideally away from language. In its own way, and like much modern literature, it tries to go beneath and behind language; it tries to reach what language cannot directly express but can only point toward, the primary processes of mental energy. This is a partial explanation of why pornography is also the home of the forbidden, tabooed words. These are the stubborn, primitive words of the language; they undergo the least evolution and retain their original force. Their primeval power has much to do with the fact that in our minds these words are minimally verbal, that they are still felt as acts, that they have not been dissociated from the tissue of unconscious impulses in which they took their origin.[6] The very deadness of much of the language of pornography, even its clichés and meaninglessness in a verbal sense, demonstrate to us that its meaning is to be found in some other area. This area is beyond language, although we have only language to show us where it is.

This tendency is further revealed in certain verbal distortions. The narrator describes himself: "I sank upon her almost fainting with delight, my prick panting and throbbing in her belly." This is a familiar figure, a combination of animism and synecdoche, in which the part is substituted for the whole, or the whole is seen only as an extension or magnification of the part. Although this figure is formally a metaphor, it has no specific metaphoric or verbal value. It does not fuse or identify similar characteristics from disparate objects with the aim of increasing one's command over reality—and the objects in it—by magically exercising one's command of the language through which reality is identified and mediated. Its intention is, rather, un-

[6] See Sándor Ferenczi, "On Obscene Words," *Sex in Psychoanalysis* (New York, 1956), pp. 112–130; and Leo Stone, "On the Principal Obscene Word of the English Language," *International Journal of Psycho-Analysis* XXXV (1954), 30–56.

metaphoric and literal; its aim is to *de-elaborate* the verbal structure and the distinctions upon which it is built, to move back through language to that part of our minds where all metaphors are literal truths, where everything is possible, and where we were all once originally supreme.

If everything is possible, peculiar things are certain to occur. Describing his specially made sexual couch, the narrator remarks that "could my readers but have the experience of that sofa, instead of this partial scrawl, they would indeed have a repletion of luscious adventures, *ad nauseam.*" It is hard to know whether the writer simply didn't understand what he was putting down, or whether some sort of unconscious truth was being confessed. For the most part, however, the prose proceeds smoothly, with a kind of dreamy monotony of rhythm. Sentence after sentence begins with the word "I"; the reader's attention is lulled; his own fantasies are liberated; and the content of what he is reading becomes irrelevant. In its own way, a pornographic work of fiction is truly a bedtime story.

The Amatory Experiences of a Surgeon is an instance of that kind of pornographic novel which is constructed upon a gimmick. The narrator is a physician, and the sexualization of all reality is achieved through the metaphor of his medical practice. In other novels, the same thing is done through making the narrator an attorney, a hotel manager, a traveling salesman —almost anything will do. This sexualization is attained by various other means. Some of these have already been discussed. One that has not been mentioned, but that is used with considerable frequency, turns up in this novel. This has to do with certain interventions on the narrator's part. Here is the way an episode is typically concluded: "What an orgy of lust we enacted that night! It seemed to me heavenly at the time, and even now as I write these lines my old cock stands at the remembrance of it." The possibilities suggested by this device, and the assumption of identity it makes between the author and his readers, do not require further discussion.

This general tendency and the vision it strives for I have already called pornotopia—the imagination of the entire universe beneath the sign of sexuality. Several further and extreme instances of it occur in this novel. At one point the narrator observes two persons having sexual intercourse: "As the huge yard moved in and out of its moist sheath, it literally glistened in the sunlight, while the beams of old Phoebus were full upon them. (What luscious sights old Sol must often enjoy, and he deserves it too, as but for his enlivening warmth we, poor mortals, should be little fitted for the pleasures of coition.)" The sun warms us; and its purpose in doing so is to fit us for the pleasures of coition. In return he is granted those "luscious sights," which he deserves, and which, it is suggested, are adequate recompense for his continuing to shine.[7] If we move down from this cosmic landscape into the privacy of inward contemplation, we meet the same thing. Here is the narrator alone: "One evening in early spring, a little after dark, I was sitting in my easy chair in the surgery, in a state of revery, my brain revolving all the luscious scenes of my experience, my prick at the moment actually at full cock, and almost ready to go off itself. . . ." When a man is by himself there is only one thing he can think of. And if sexuality is omnipresent, then it is also omnivalent. The narrator reads *Justine* and describes it as "the celebrated work of the Marquis de Sade, over which it is said that extraordinary man went out of his mind." The confusion and reversal of cause and effect suggested by this statement are remarkable; among several possibilities, it seems to imply that the Marquis de Sade wrote *Justine,* and, having written it, was then driven mad by it. Or it may also mean that the Marquis de Sade was driven mad by the writing of *Justine.* The one thing it cannot mean is that

[7] Keats seems to have flirted with this fantasy in his early years:
> . . . but who, of men, can tell
> That flowers would bloom, or that green fruit would swell
> To melting pulp, that fish would have bright mail,
> The earth its dower of river, wood, and vale,
> The meadows runnels, runnels pebble-stones,
> The seed its harvest, or the lute its tones,
> Tones ravishment, or ravishment its sweet
> If human souls did never kiss and greet?
> (*Endymion,* I, 835–842)

the Marquis de Sade was mad and in his madness wrote his "celebrated work."

A further fantasy that is constitutive of pornotopia concerns the seminal fluid. *The Amatory Experiences of a Surgeon* is richly furnished with instances of this idea. The narrator describes himself as "drench[ing] her little stomach and thighs with almost a supernatural flood of sperm." When he rises, he carefully removes "the reeking traces of victory." On another occasion, "I could say no more, but with a violent drive forward I sank spending on her belly; my prick fairly buried in her up to the hair, and the semen spouting from me in torrents." When the woman who has been thus inundated gets up, "a heavy pattering sound announced the return of the fluid which fell in large drops upon the carpet, and ran in rills down her beautiful thighs." There is something comically Homeric about such representations: the narrator seems to imagine himself as a kind of physiological Jupiter Pluvius. And indeed he does speak of himself as emitting "a most plentiful shower of semen." The psychological meaning of such fantasies is not difficult to determine. In the first place, as we have already observed, they are in part a reaction against and the mirror image of those fantasies which imagine the emission of semen as a loss, as a "spending." The plenitude represented in these images, however, is not limited to the anal-economic system alone. Semen becomes a metaphor for all the fluids of the body, including that original one by which we were nourished. This is demonstrated most clearly in that image which I take to be the final, or most inclusive, form of this particular notion: a man and woman, reversed upon each other, sucking away, "spending," and swallowing each other's juices. This fantasy may be an immemorial one, but it is also peculiarly apposite to the eighteenth and nineteenth centuries. It imagines nothing less than a perfect, self-enclosed economic and productive system. Intake and output are beautifully balanced; production is plentiful, but nothing is lost, wasted, or spent, since the product is consumed only to produce more of the raw material by which the system is sustained. The primitive dream of capitalism is fulfilled in the primitive dream of the body.

Yet this obsessive fantasy is also a bit of stock in trade, a convention of the genre. It turns up with only the slightest variations in novel after novel. This relatively undisguised coming together in pornography of psychological obsession and literary convention has, I believe, a heuristic value. It permits us to observe the formation in process of a literary convention; we see what is behind that convention, what it expresses and conceals, and what perpetuates it. Most studies of literary conventions—I am thinking in particular of work done in the dramatic literature of the sixteenth and seventeenth centuries—tend to regard conventions as autonomous forms or configurations that are passed along like beads from one writer to another. Such studies do not as a rule inquire into why some conventions— such as the tragedy of revenge or the figure of the boasting soldier—survive while others do not; nor do they normally try to discover the meaning of a particular convention. It seems to me virtually self-evident that every formal literary convention has behind it the sustaining energy of some fantasy or obsession and that one way of studying the highly conventionalized literature of the European past would involve the analysis of the formal elements of structure and composition in just such terms.[8]

One of the early episodes in this novel provides a useful instance of these operations. The narrator determines to revenge his mother's desertion by his father by seducing his father's current mistress. Since this woman occupies exactly the same position as the narrator's mother, the situation as a whole represents a classic re-enactment of the Oedipus fantasy. The narrator does succeed in his design and carries on an affair of several months with this woman. When he discovers her together with his father's butler, he takes advantage of the occasion to break off connections with her. One must first remark that this kind of

---

[8] One may remark that such work has been begun in the writings of Ernst Robert Curtius and Erich Auerbach.

episode is also an extremely conventional one. Pornography exists in order to violate in fantasy that which has been tabooed; and incest occurs in it with about the same frequency as marriages occur at the end of English novels. Incest is customarily represented or dealt with in one of two ways. It is described as great fun, and thereupon everyone available is enlisted in the goings on. Or, it is described as great fun, and then someone like the butler is introduced in order to get the episode out of the way. In the second alternative, what is particularly clear is the writer's impulse to avoid the logical and psychological consequences of the dramatic situation he has imagined. It is as if by instinct the writer understood that there was no pleasure to be gotten from either further extension or examination of this theme. This inconsequent, irrelevant, but perfectly conventional, narrative intervention helps to preserve intact the convention of the happy incestuous affair. In this instance, we see how the literary convention not only expresses certain fantasies but how it also works as a defense or screen against the unpleasant implications of the very ideas it is expressing. One might even suggest that in literature the success of many conventional devices depends upon this double capacity—the ability of a certain figure, turn, or image both to suggest certain exciting and dangerous possibilities and to guard us against their consequences. Aristotle seems to have had something like this in mind when he described the workings of tragedy.

A similar circumstance obtains in respect to the explicit moral statements made in this novel. *The Amatory Experiences of a Surgeon* undertakes to represent the ordinary everyday world of Victorian England by reversing it—this much is already familiar. Thus, although "it is one of the requirements of society that the feminine portion of it should wear, at least to outward gaze, the semblance of virtue, yet there is nothing in female human nature which is more difficult to do." And it regards women as either "sacrificed on the altar of mock modesty for fear, lest the disgrace of the only natural cure for their complaint should blast their character" or as making use of "expedients . . . to allay those raging fires which in too many cases prematurely exhaust the constitutions of our young women . . . designs to cheat society of its whimsical requirements." In this passage, we see that the writer is simultaneously subverting and endorsing the official view of things. The morality may be arbitrary, false, and hypocritical, but the sexuality is in any event lethal: whether the outcome be abstinence or indulgence, the organism is burned up, exhausted by its own raging energies. In another place, the novel discusses masturbation and states that it is as good as universal, among females as well as males. And then there is the part about the young girl's spinal ailment being cured by uninhibited sexual activity. Such simple reversals are qualified, however, in those passages of the novel in which the narrator speaks of the "purpose" of his writing. "It is really surprising, how many married women actually pass through life without ever feeling the real pleasure of coition. I consider that medical advisers ought to catechise young married ladies on the subject, and that it is their duty to enlighten the fair but cold innocents to the joys they lose, by simply submitting to the marriage-rites as a necessity, and not entering into the spirit of the fun." It might appear that Mr. Acton is now standing on his head. Putting to one side the feeble-minded and rationalizing character of such a statement, we can make out an "intention" analogous to Acton's. Through a proper disposition of sexuality, the Victorian family will be preserved; if men and women "enter into the spirit of the fun," hearth and home will be snugger and cozier than ever. If there is something disturbing about the fact that this palpably phony conclusion to a Victorian pornographic novel is identical with the advice handed out in countless sex and marriage manuals published today, we have only ourselves and our expectations and fantasies to look to, to call to account.

But all these considerations fall to the ground when we consider the general circumstances in which such a work of fiction was consulted. The growth of the novel as a major form of representing experience was coincident with those vast changes in society that go under the names of urbanization and industrialization. One of the momentous effects of such alterations in social arrangements was the development of a whole new realm of privacy, of private experience or, as sociologists say today, of privatization.[9] The novel is that form of art which both expressed and answered the needs of this new order of experience. It depicts, as no other kind of art had before, the inmost private experience of human beings; and it is generally read in conditions of silence and solitude. If this is true of the novel as a whole, what must one conclude about pornographic novels? They represent solitude raised to another power; they are read not merely in the privacy of one's study or closet, but behind locked doors, and are kept in locked drawers or cupboards; they are consulted in a silence beside which the unmoving air of a library reading room is as the din of market places. In a world of private experiences, they represent a further withdrawal into the arcane, and the only thing more secluded and secret than they is the inside of one's head. Such protests as they utter are muffled by the circumstances in which the utterances are heard, and the secrecy that is the condition of their existence is also the condition of their assent to the world they appear to be protesting against. It is difficult to think of another kind of literature whose content and circumstances are more thoroughly contradictory of one another or that is, in the foundations of its existence, as self-nullifying. Yet those very contradictions and self-nullifications are themselves the local expressions of the larger conditions in society or culture out of which pornography springs.

IV

Randiana, or Excitable Tales; Being the Experiences of an Erotic Philosopher (1884) presents little that is new or that deserves much discussion. It is, rather, a potpourri, a mixture of episodes

[9] See Ian Watt, *The Rise of the Novel* (Berkeley, 1957), pp. 174–207.

drawn together from various sources. It too is told in the first person, and consists of twenty-four small chapters which recount nine or ten pornographic stories. Apart from being chronologically ordered, these stories have no inner connection or coherence. Largely as a result of the random character of their narratives, many pornographic novels are reputed to have been written by several hands. *Randiana* does not share in this reputation, although its disorganization is impeccable. It is my opinion, moreover, that many of the works which are rumored to have been written collectively were written by single persons, and that their incoherence owes more to their authors' mental state than it does to general circumstances of composition.

Randiana naturally relates "only that which is strictly true," and it is therefore logical that it should begin with a lie. "Up to the age of twelve," the narrator begins, "I had remained in perfect ignorance of all those little matters which careful parents are so anxious to conceal from their children. . . ." His ignorance is dispelled by the housemaid, who invites him to visit her in her room at night. His initiation is interrupted by the sound of his father's approaching footsteps. The narrator hides under the bed while his father continues where the son had left off. He is discovered when his father has to use the chamber-pot, but his punishment is delayed by the sudden, unexpected entrance of his mother, who conks her husband over the head with "a little bed-room poker." This brings to an end a rather Chaucerian overture.

The story then jumps some twenty years. We find the author "emerging one summer's evening from the Café Royal, in Regent Street, with De Vaux, a friend of long standing." They in turn run into "Father Peter, of St. Martha of the Angels." This priest is a famous sensualist, flagellant, lecher, *bon vivant,* and buggerer. He lives in Kensington, where he offers prodigious dinners followed by assorted orgies. The two clubmen accompany Father Peter to his house; dinner is eaten, names are dropped, "The History of Flagellation Condensed" is further condensed, and a virgin—who is Father Peter's illegitimate daughter—is flogged and deflowered. All ends happily.

We next meet the narrator in the Inns of Court, where he is living on an income of £7,000 a year. On this stipend he is able to give a number of bachelor's dinners in his rooms. Next door to him lives an impecunious young barrister, and it is upon the sister of this young man that the narrator next goes to work. Lady Fanny Twisser comes down from the country to visit her brother. The narrator gets her alone, plies her with food and drink—"a bijou supper in five courses"—and tops it all off with a dash of aphrodisiac, whose effect was "really magical." Lady Fanny is immensely pleased by what follows, and in due course discloses to the narrator that "my old husband never did such a thing; he always uses a beastly machine, shaped like that which is in me now, but made of guttapercha, and filled with warm oil and milk." Nine months following "that blissful evening," we learn, Lady Fanny presented her husband with a "son and heir"; and three months after that latter event, she had separated from her husband, "the old man, not believing in miracles, could scarcely altogether credit the dildo with" such powers.

The author next seduces the illegitimate daughter of his charwoman, keeps her in a cottage in Kew for a few months, and then finding that she is unfaithful to him gives her £100 and throws her over. He now goes down into the country with his friend De Vaux for a spot of grouse shooting at the estate of one Leveson. While he is there, he seduces the unseduceable Mrs. Leveson along with her maid. There follow several minor adventures interspersed with little essays on a variety of topics.

The narrator now runs down to Folkestone "for a brief holiday, and was staying at the Lees." He meets an old General with "a young wife and a grownup daughter." They all befriend each other. The narrator learns that the old man can no longer impregnate a woman, and offers the young wife his services—if she bears a son, he reasons with her, her income will be secured when the General dies. This argument, in addition to some of the ever handy aphrodisiac, seems to work. The pair are silently discovered by the daughter, who then persuades the narrator to let her in on the action, and these two are in turn discovered by the stepmother. Nothing but more good comes of this.

The penultimate adventure in the book is an account of how by mischance the narrator winds up in bed with his sister. All's well that ends well. The novel ends when the narrator, now in ripe middle age, meets up with three of the women he has previously seduced. They are living together, their "Sapphic tastes" having been somehow aroused; "we are three loving communists," they say, "each one's secrets are sacred as if our own." They take the narrator home, administer some of his own aphrodisiac to him, and, when they find him still not quite up to the mark, flagellate him into readiness. With this representation of the "community of love in the Cromwell Road," the novel leaves off, its tail in its own mouth, like an animated cartoon, everything wound up and going on forever, everyone in, around, and between everyone else.

The reader can see that *Randiana* is a kind of miscellany—it contains something for everyone. There is a bit of incest, flogging, defloration, lesbianism, communal sex; and there is even some ordinary fornication—or, as they say in the London market nowadays, "straight perv." The tone of the novel is humorous, light, and pseudosophisticated, a true vulgar clubman's tone. The novel is almost as concerned with fashion and fashionable names as it is with sex, though its snobbish pretensions are as feeble as its sexual equalitarianism. It is equally interested in food, and that interest serves two functions. On the one hand, it works along with the snobbery; on the other, it has a sexual meaning. The food is always sexually stimulating, and it is, in addition, always followed by a liberal dose of aphrodisiac. The fantasies that are involved here have to do again with fluids and bodily substances; they regard those things that are taken into the body as magical, energizing substances. One of the corrolaries of this notion is the belief that one's sexuality, one's potency, comes not from within oneself but depends upon some outside agent, some energizer, which can be taken at will and mechanically. As a result, human sexuality is again regarded mechanically, and human sexuality is again ideally represented as the functioning of machines. We see this not only in the interest in the aphrodisiac, but also in the enlisting of the dildo (which is filled with "warm oil and milk"). And we see it as well in the author's idea of physiology: the effect of the aphrodisiac is described as "electrical," and a woman's sexual excitement is called "the natural effect of the electro-biology." The mechanical view of the universe which is at work here is not so much Newtonian as it is simply childish. It undertakes to control sexuality by mentally splitting off the sexual apparatus from the sexual emotions. This tendency is unchanging in pornography; and yet, one must remind oneself, what else in 1884 could a writer have done, what alternatives were then open to him?

This vision of a grim, gray, and spiritless universe is common to pornography. Nevertheless, the tone of this novel—like the tone of the majority of pornographic works of fiction—is lighthearted, humorous, harmless in intention, and slightly scatterbrained. It is only when one goes beneath the surface that one finds the mechanical grimness, the frenzied repetition, the impotent quest for omnipotence. This is true of pornography in general, but it seems to me no accident that the genre should have flourished most strongly in Victorian England. The contrasts it presents belong as much to the age whose underworld it adorned as they belong to that underworld itself.

Chapter 6: A CHILD IS BEING BEATEN

My title is from Freud. My text is the vast literature of flagellation produced during the Victorian period. Despite the immense number of works published and titles listed, this literature consists in the elaboration of a single fantasy. This fantasy is presented in an astonishing variety of forms, all of which repeat the same unvarying idea. It is a literature extremely difficult to describe because of its radical incoherence. Compared to it, the pornographic novels that I have just discussed are models of logical exactitude and consequence.[1]

This circumstance is in itself something of a paradox, since the literature of flagellation is on its surface a much more sophisticated kind of writing than ordinary pornography. It makes use, for example, of a wider range of literary forms. It appears not only in novels and as novels, but also as stories and tales, as formal dialogues, and sometimes as lectures. It is often gotten up in dramatic form, and the fantasy is presented as plays and playlets, skits, comic operettas, farces and burlesques. It avails itself of verse; some of the dramatic pieces are written in verse, blank and rhymed; and there are a large number of short "lyric" pieces on the subject, as well as narrative and dramatic poems of considerable length. There are, in addition, any number of works of historical or documentary presumption— histories of flagellation, punishment, torture, discipline, "the use of the rod," etc.; authentic exposures of the goings on at schools in the form of memoirs, confessions, and round-robin

---

[1] This chapter owes much to Freud's two essays on the subject, "A Child Is Being Beaten" and "The Economic Problem of Masochism." I should also like to acknowledge Gertrud Lenzer's "Sacher-Masoch and Masochism," which deals with the topics covered in this chapter in a systematic way: I have freely applied many of the conclusions reached in that essay.

letters; accounts of whipping academies and clubs in London and the provinces; medical tracts describing the salubrious effects of beating on the human frame and constitution; lists of compendia of both the great and the obscure who have been addicted to such practices. For all this show of a secondary kind of interest, almost none of these works sustains itself with the degree of consistency or consequence required by even the simplest literary form. They regularly break down into small, disconnected units, and the natural form, so to speak, of this genre is the anecdote.

The audience to which this literature was directed was clearly limited. It was restricted in the first place, of course, to those men to whom this perversion appealed; but it was further and even more rigidly restricted in point of social class. The literature of flagellation in Victorian England assumes that its audience had both interest in and connection with the higher gentry and the nobility—that this assumption may itself be laden with fantasies is not at this moment to the point. It further assumes that its audience had the common experience of education at a public school. Many works are set at school—"Birchminster," for example—and the anonymous authors style themselves "Etonensis" or "An Old Boy." Indeed, for this literature perversity and social privilege are inseparable marks of distinction. We are regularly told, for instance, that "the lower order of mankind are not such slaves to this passion as people in high life." In one story, a schoolmistress remarks that "one doesn't flog a servant who is detected in a robbery. One sends for a policeman, and gives her in charge." To which exclusion, in another story, a servant responds, "Ah, me! I wish I was a lady to be whipped like one of you. I would not mind the pain a bit." The narrator of "Revelations of Shrewsbury House" remarks of his cast of characters that "it would be vain for me to attempt particular description: about them all there was a marked patrician air." If the recipients of these beatings are thus distinguished, so are those who hand out what is to be received.

Know then . . . there is a manner in handling this sceptre of felicity that few ladies are happy in: it is not the impassioned and awkward brandish of a vulgar female that can charm, but the deliberate and elegant manner of a woman of rank and fashion, who displays all that dignity in every action, even to the flirting of her fan, that leaves an indelible wound. What a difference between high and low life in this particular! To see a vulgar woman, when provoked by her children, seize them as a tiger would a lamb, rudely expose their posteriors, and correct them with an open hand, or a rod more like a broom than a neat collection of twigs elegantly tied together; while a well-bred lady coolly and deliberately brings her child or pupil to task; and when in error, so as to deserve punishment, commands the incorrigible Miss to bring her the rod, go on her knees, and beg, with uplifted hands, an excellent whipping . . . who, all the time, with tears and entreaties of the sweetest kind, implores her dear mother or governess to pardon her; all which the lovely disciplinarian listens to with the utmost delight, running over with rapture, at the same time, those white angelic orbs, that in a few minutes she crimsons as deep as the finest rose, with a well-exercised and elegantly-handled rod!

The reader ought to know, I believe, that this passage is not merely typical—it is one out of literally thousands exactly like it. And before we smile over its vapidity, we might momentarily contemplate its sadness and poverty.

We learn of the great who loved to be whipped: Charles II, the Duc d'Orléans, Voltaire, and of course Rousseau are among those repeatedly mentioned. And the women who tell us about them in this literature are also aristocratic ladies—Lady Termagent Flaybum, Lady Bumtickler, the Duchess of Picklerod, Lady Maria Castigate, Madame Birchini, Lady Harriet Tickletail, the Countess of Greenbirch are among the chief adornments of this world. Legendary figures from the real world and the "aristocracy" of schoolboy farces and japery absurdly consort. And just as paradoxically, we are told that, although these practices are confined to the privileged preserves of high life, the addiction is at the same time spreading like wildfire: "Lovers of the birch, ladies and gentlemen, are almost as com-

mon as the lovers of Venus." The writers of this literature, like
some propagandists for homosexuality, need to reassure themselves that their affliction is simultaneously exclusive and universal. (The adolescent who masturbates and tries to alleviate
his sense of guilt by saying to himself that everyone does the
same thing is following the same procedure.)

The *mise en scènes* of the anecdotes vary. Sometimes they are
located at home, most often in the nursery, occasionally in the
governess's or housemaid's room, sometimes in mother's bed-
room, and sometimes in the schoolroom. Stories about life at
school occur frequently, girls' schools, surprisingly, appearing
with greater frequency. Sometimes the setting is a fantasied
meeting of fashionable ladies, who come together for the purpose of exchanging stories about their whipping propensities, or
for the purpose of exercising those propensities, or for both. Yet
wherever the setting may be placed, what goes on is always the
same.

A person is accused of some wrongdoing. This person is most
often a boy; sometimes he is a man acting as or impersonating a
boy; sometimes he is a boy or a man dressed as a girl; sometimes he is supposed actually to be a girl. The misconduct he is
charged with is sometimes unspecified; on occasion he is supposed to have wet the bed; sometimes he is accused of general
disobedience, insubordination, or impertinence; in a few instances he is supposed to have been caught at some kind of
childish sexual misbehavior. The accuser is almost invariably
some surrogate for his mother: stepmother, governess, schoolmistress, housekeeper, ladies' maid, aunt, occur with regular
frequency. A kept mistress or courtesan posing as any or all of
these will do as well. Only rarely is the accuser the mother herself. An adult male figure, father or schoolmaster, occurs very
infrequently—I have come across only a few instances.

The confrontation may take place between these two persons
alone; or other auxiliary figures, who multiply the number of
mother-surrogates in the scene, may be enlisted. The accusation
or admonition is delivered in ritual form, accompanied by dire

threats. The antiphonal response is either defiance or supplication; if it is defiance it soon gives way to supplication. These pleas for mercy go unheeded. The immense female figure swells up with anger and excitement; her eyes sparkle; her bosom heaves; her brawny yet dazzling white arm twitches expectantly. The instrument of punishment is then fetched or summoned to be brought forth. This is usually a bunch of birch twigs, invariably called "a rod" or "the rod." It is described in great detail. Often it is decorated with a ribbon. If other instruments are used, as they occasionally are, they too are described at length. The accused is then seized. He is either placed across the lap of his accuser, tied down to a bed, horsed upon the back of one of the auxiliaries, or bound to some article of furniture especially made for the purpose, a block, horse, or trestle as they are severally named. His clothes are then lowered or raised, as the case may be, in order to expose his buttocks, and the whipping takes place. It is invariably accompanied by talk, usually dialogue. Here is a typical sample:

"Is it possible," said Mrs. Trimmer, pulling his breeches down to his heels, "that your mistress suffered this tyrannical gentleman to insult her in the manner she has represented?" "No indeed, ma'am, I never insulted my mamma, upon my honour, I did not," roared the youth. "Indeed, Mrs. Trimmer," replied the nurse, "there's not so bold a boy in the parish." "So, so, so, so, so, so, so, so I understand!" said the mistress (making him caper as high as young Vestris at every stroke of the rod). "Yes, yes, yes, yes, yes, I can see you are a wicked young rascal!" "Oh, dear mistress, I'm not indeed! for pity's sake! Oh mistress! mistress! I'll never offend my mama! Oh my a . . . e! my a . . . e! Oh, my dear nurse, beg me off!" "No, no, Sir, I'm desired to see you well whipped, and I think you never got into such excellent hands before." "I'll convince him of that, I assure you, before I have done! . . . The young gentleman thought, I dare swear, there was no one could break him of those crimes, but I'll whip this bold backside of his till I strip every bit of skin from it, or I'll work an amendment in him." "Try me this once, my dearest mistress! Oh, gracious! try me! Oh, I'm killed! let me down! let me down! let me down! nurse! nurse! nurse!" "You may roar, and cry, and kick, and plunge, and implore, my pretty gentleman, but all will not do; I'll whip you till the blood runs to your heels! You shall feel the tuition of this excellent rod!" [2]

The figure who performs the whipping is said to experience unalloyed pleasure. The person who is whipped is represented as experiencing a mixture of pain and pleasure, or of pain succeeded by pleasure. The scene ends either with forgiveness of the culprit or with a prelude to repetition of the whole. And this too is called pornography.

These fantasies seem to fall into two principal phases. In one, a little boy is being beaten by a woman; in the other, a figure represented as a little girl is being beaten, also by a woman. But in fact no such distinctions really obtain, on either side of the transaction. In this literature, anybody can be or become anybody else, and the differences between the sexes are blurred and confused. There is, in the first place, an enormous amount of conscious acting or role playing throughout the literature; everyone is impersonating someone else. "She embraced me," runs a typical passage, "and pressing my hand with transport, begged I would suffer her to represent my niece." Or, "I instantly got up [and] put on an air of austerity and passion." The play-acting is frequently undertaken simultaneously by both parties. "She instantly, by desire, *assumed the character* of Flirtilla's Governess, and having stretched her, with some *seeming* reluctant struggles on the part of Flirtilla, on the bed, she uncovered to the waist the plumpest, fairest, and most beautiful posteriors that ever charmed mankind. Clarissa herself stood entranced at the lovely view, and suspended the rod, till Flirtilla, impatient for the delightful combat, cried out *like* a terrified child . . ." [my italics]. It often happens in this literature that the reader loses track of who is who, along with who is doing what to whom. Point of view is inconsistent and unsustained, sometimes switching several times within a single page —the degree of mental concentration in these fantasies is so uncertain that even the shortest anecdote often cannot be carried through coherently.

[2] One should compare this typical passage with the account given by the author of *My Secret Life* of a similar scene. See Chapter 3, pp. 124–128, above.

The figure of the female who is doing the whipping is, as I have said, almost always a surrogate for the mother. She is also unmistakably the terrible mother, the phallic mother of childhood.

> Martinet meanwhile had taken off her loose morning wrapper, and armed herself with a rod, formed, not of canes and cuttings like the rest, but of stout birch stems with innumerable branches, like a tree in miniature.
>
> With this weapon in her hand, how terrible she appeared! Juno deprived of the apple might have looked like her. Her splendid arms and neck were bare, her cheeks flamed, her huge breasts were heaving. Speech was too weak, the graces of birching were ignored, nothing short of savage *beating* could satisfy her present need of vengeance.

Such a representation needs little analysis. The gigantic size of these figures suggests its own explanation. They are always armed with a rod or symbolic phallus; but in this instance the form taken by the rod calls to mind a more complex symbolic configuration, something on the order of Medusa's head. Furthermore, these women are not merely supplied with detachable appendages. Even as in their feminine wrath they are idealized, they are endowed with certain additional masculine characteristics. "What a magnificent creature she is! superbly scornful, and sitting her steed as if it were a part of herself. Her broad shoulders and bust were set off by the tight fitting jacket; and, notwithstanding the mass of auburn hair, her aquiline nose, keen eyes, and square cut chin, seemed those of a handsome man, when surmounted by the hat." Muscular biceps and hairy arms and thighs are also commonplace, as are faint hints of hair on the upper lip and cheeks. It is difficult to escape the conclusion, therefore, that fused with and peeking out from behind this figure of the violent, phallic mother is a representation of a male person, of a father. The way in which the mother is gotten up in these fantasies serves both to conceal or censor and to express this idea. Indeed the literature is itself remarkably explicit in this matter. "Fear and shame were both gone; it was as though I was surrendering my person to the embraces of a man whom I so loved I would anticipate his wildest desires. But no man was in my thoughts; Martinet was the object of my adoration, and I felt *through the rod* that I shared her passion." Assertion and denial rapidly succeed one another; they continue to coexist, without contradicting one another, by means of "the rod," which mediates, fuses, embodies, and yet screens, what is actually being proposed.[3]

The sexual identity of the figure being beaten is remarkably labile. Sometimes he is represented as a boy, sometimes as a girl, sometimes as a combination of the two—a boy dressed as a girl, or the reverse. The actual sex to which this figure belongs appears at first not to matter. The ambiguity of sexual identity seems in fact to be part of the pleasure that this fantasy yields.

> What a treat in this seminary for the idolators of the posterior shrine! To see in the course of a day a number of b . . s blushing under the rod, exercised by a woman of supereminent charms!
>
> It must be the sublime of felicity indeed, said Miss T., and almost equal to what I tasted from the hand of Lady *** a few days ago.
>
> I know, said Mrs. W., her ladyship is charming in the extreme with a rod in hand. Pray let us hear how she captivated you.
>
> I happened to pay her a visit in my military habit, which so pleased her that she proposed to take the rod in hand and whip me for endeavouring to rival her, my step-mother, by dressing in such alluring habiliments.

Yet one cannot hold for long with the conclusion that the sex of this figure is a matter of indifference. We know from the actual circumstances of this perversion, from the circumstances in which this literature was produced—its writers and the audience who made up its market—and from the internal circum-

---

[3] As, even more flagrantly, does the following passage:
"'Have you made the rod, as I desired you?'"
"'Yes, ma'am, made it the same day; it's in my box, shall I fetch it?'"
"'Do so. . . .'"
"Mrs. Van had apparently been weeping. At sight of the rod she started and murmured a faint remonstrance against its size. Kathleen, enthroned in sullen state, did not deign to turn her head. Her bust was shrouded by the sable locks, from forth which her eyes, fierce as a panther's, glared. . . ."

stances of the literature itself that the figure being beaten is originally, finally, and always a boy.

We see this, for example, in such details as naming: girls, but not boys, in this literature are often named ambiguously —"Georgy" and "Willie," for instance, keep turning up all the time. We see it as well in the dialogue, which, when it is not hopelessly arch or childish, is unmistakably the language of the public school. What has happened in the fantasy to which this literature gives expression is that the erotic zone has been shifted away from the genitals and onto the area of the buttocks. This literal regression of interest helps to account for the fact that in this literature, which was after all written to arouse its readers, the genitals are virtually never mentioned, nor are the usual tabooed words used—these latter being of course ordinarily associated with genital activity. The first phase of this fantasy, in which a boy is being beaten by a woman on to whom masculine characteristics have been grafted or imposed, is fairly straightforward in its significance. The heterosexual situation is retained, although the figure of the mother is supplied with male attributes, and the boy being beaten is in a passive and feminine relation to her. The second phase (which Freud, in his essays, did not take account of, since he had apparently never come across any instances of it) is of greater interest. Here the heterosexual relation has been abandoned and a homosexual one substituted for it—the little boy has transformed himself into a girl. Yet this transformation is itself both a defense against and a disavowal of the fantasy it is simultaneously expressing. That fantasy is a homosexual one: a little boy is being beaten—that is, loved—by another man. And we must conclude, I believe, that the entire immense literature of flagellation produced during the Victorian period, along with the fantasies it embodied and the practises it depicted, represents a kind of last-ditch compromise with and defense against homosexuality.

That the homosexuality is constantly breaking through is evident in the passages I have already cited. Here is another example.

The next time on my maid, Ladow:
  A strong-back'd wench, who takes delight
In horsing naughty boys and girls!
I whipt upon her back last night
  A French Duke, and two English Earls:
The first of which, with frock and sash,
  I drest just like a full-grown Miss;
Then gave him many a vig'rous lash,
  For giving footman John a kiss;
I taught this fancied Miss a dance—
  I made him caper to the ceiling:
He swore no Ma'emoiselle in France
  Convinc'd him more that he had feeling!
And you shall feel, before I've done,
  What I can do with rod in hand;
I never had so bold a son—
  I'll whip your A . . e while I can stand!
I've thrown your Breeches now aside:
  Your half-whipt bum, tho' seeming sore,
With all the glowing prospect wide,
  Pants for a vigorous encore!
Here, kiss the Rod, you wicked Elf;
  And kiss the lovely Hand and Arm!
I'll have you often by myself,
  And this bold A . . e I'll often warm!

Today the homosexual undertones of such a passage seem unmistakable. What we cannot be certain of is the degree to which the Victorians were themselves conscious of these implications. We do know that homosexuality was practiced, and that it caused in particular a great deal of alarm and trouble at schools. We know as well that sado-masochistic activities were engaged in—indeed they were institutionalized—but it is impossible to ascertain how widespread such practices were. We know further that there is almost no literature of a homosexual kind surviving from the period and that as far as can be determined very little was produced (I rule out the homosexuality represented in the kind of pornographic novels already discussed; there it is part of a general pansexualized vision). And we know that, on the contrary, sado-masochistic literature, in particular the literature of passive flagellation, was produced in great quantities, and that therefore the fantasies represented in this writing, if not the activities themselves, were widely distributed—at least among a certain class of Englishmen.

The conclusions such evidence permits us to advance must be slender and tentative in the extreme. Homosexuality is qualitatively different from the other perversions. It seems likely that a different and higher threshold of resistance must be overcome before homosexual fantasies reach consciousness—the social and cultural taboos against them being correspondingly stronger than those that act against the heterosexual deviations. Once that threshold has been passed, however, it is possible that the psychic distance to be traversed between conscious fantasy and action has been considerably shortened. Hence it may be that the virtual absence of a homosexual pornographic literature from the period testifies to the possibility that once homosexual fantasies emerge into consciousness they are enabled, by the same force of energy that overcame the agencies which opposed their emergence, to proceed to action (other explanations are of course possible as well). Conversely, we know that a great many more men experience and confess to sado-masochistic fantasies than go on to experience the activities represented in their fantasies. The existence of a large body of sado-masochistic literature is itself a further confirmation of this finding—one of the few reliable generalizations about this topic being that there is roughly an inverse relation between written fantasy and activity. Thus, although there is no doubt that sado-masochistic activities took place in Victorian England, the efflorescence of a large body of literature concerned with these practices—just as the efflorescence of pornography itself during the period—indicates not merely a general disturbance of sexuality, but what is technically known as a dysfunction. Literature is, after all, as much a deflection of impulses as it is a represrentation of them and of action. We cannot let it pass as an accident that this great age of concerted and organized social growth and social action should also have produced the literature we have been discussing, a literature that may, among other things, demonstrate part of the price we pay for social advancement.

So much for our discussion of literature. With this very brief account of the writings concerned with flagellation, our survey ends: these anecdotes and stories, along with the pornographic novels discussed in the foregoing chapter, constitute the two chief subclasses of such writing in Victorian England. If pornography in general amounted to a reversal of Victorian moral ideals, then the literature of flagellation represented a reversal of Victorian ideal personal standards for men. The striking features of this literature are its childishness, extreme incoherence, absence of focus, confusion of sexual identity, and impulse toward play-acting or role playing. These qualities stand in marked contrast to the Victorian ideals of manliness, solidity, certitude of self, straightforwardness, sincerity and singleness of being. Yet by now, I think, it would be something of a surprise if we were to find that such ideals were not, in a culture, accompanied somewhere by their opposite—the very strength with which those ideals were enforced and striven for tended to ensure, or even to necessitate, the existence of such formations as the literature of flagellation.

The conclusions that such a phenomenon as this literature prompts one to make may be put forward in the form of questions. They are properly the matter for further researches. What, for example, does the steady, high production of this kind of writing throughout the Victorian period signify? [4] What, if anything, does it signify about the social character of the class of men to whom it was addressed? How was it connected with the experience of school? The few summary written efforts to account for this practice assert that beatings at school were the essential cause of this later deformation. It is more likely that experiences at school acted as triggering devices which set in motion earlier processes which had until then remained latent. How did these devices operate, and what was there in the structure of family life among the nineteenth-century English upper and middle classes that gave to those processes the form they subsequently took? Why is it that this

[4] That literature continues being produced today—in immense quantities.

literature is overwhelmingly masochistic rather than sadistic in its coloration? [5] In what ways may this tendency be connected with the reformation in manners and general social behavior that was going on throughout the nineteenth century? During the eighteenth century, the English higher social classes were thought of throughout Europe as the grossest and coarsest of their species. When they ate, they gluttonized; when they drank, they swilled; their sports and games were bloody and brutal. Some of these habits persisted through the nineteenth century, but it is not to be doubted that a general gentling and civilizing of English behavior were taking place. Can social or cultural changes of this order produce alterations in sexual character or affect the form of sexual choices and the direction of sexual impulses? If they can, what intermediate modifications have to be posited in order to establish a believable, or at least a possible, series of connections?

If this literature represents a compromise with and a defense against homosexuality, how successful was that defense, and how well did that compromise work? Did it work as well as that other Victorian compromise, which was said to have preserved England safe from the social upheavals that shook the Continent throughout the century? Why was the compromise necessary, and was there anything new about it? And why did it take the peculiarly weak and childish form that it finally did? We began our study with an examination of the writings of William Acton. In them we saw that sexuality itself had come to be regarded as problematical. It is fitting that we close with a discussion of the literature of flagellation. This literature existed for sexual purposes; yet sexuality as it is represented therein is so muted, so incoherent, so defracted and so infantile that it is virtually at the point of extinction. Here too, sexuality has become problematical, but it is sexuality in its specific heterosexual form that is being threatened. Mr. Acton, with his offi-

---

[5] There are, however, several examples of sadistic literature in the period, the most notable of them being *The Mysteries of Verbena House,* the first part of which, at least, seems to have been written by G. A. Sala.

cial view, is at one end of the scale; the literature of flagellation, in all its bizarre aberrancy, occupies a place at the other end. The extremes do not meet, but they tend to converge. In between there stretches the whole range of writing about sexuality that was produced during the Victorian era. The issues raised in this writing, the fantasies played out in it, the conflicts which it tries to evade and the problems with which it struggles, have, as I have tried to show, come down to us. They are part of our civilized legacy.

Chapter 7: CONCLUSION: PORNOTOPIA

THERE is a passage in one of Max Weber's great essays on the methodology of the social sciences which is pertinent to our discussion. In it Weber is struggling to define with absolute rigor and clarity his difficult notion of the "ideal type." He is trying to demonstrate that this notion or analytical construct "has no connection at all with *value-judgments*," and that further "it has nothing to do with any type of perfection other than a purely *logical* one." To illustrate the distinction he has in mind, Weber states that "there are ideal types of brothels as well as of religions"; and he goes on to say that there are even "ideal types of those kinds of brothels which are technically 'expedient' from the point of view of police ethics as well as those of which the exact opposite" holds true. The writer or scholar who undertakes to discuss pornography has in effect made a contract to construct an ideal type of a brothel—and he has in addition contracted to maintain the distinctions that Weber established. This is not a simple task, as Weber himself was quick to recognize. On the one hand, he states, we must guard ourselves against such "crude misunderstandings . . . as the opinion that cultural significance should be attributed only to *valuable* phenomena. Prostitution is a *cultural* phenomenon just as much as religion or money." At the same time, and on the other hand, he continues, prostitution, religion, and money "are cultural phenomena *only* because and *only* insofar as their existence and the form which they historically assume touch directly or indirectly on our cultural *interests* and arouse our striving for knowledge concerning problems brought into focus by the evaluative ideas which give *significance* to the fragment of reality analyzed by those concepts." Weber's strained and circling syntax attests to the difficulty of keeping these two fields of discourse distinct. Our interests and our values inevitably dictate our choice of subjects—the significance we attribute to any fragment of reality that we subject to analysis has its point of origin and reference in a realm external to the analysis itself. Nevertheless, in the course of analysis we must dissociate ourselves, as much as possible, from those very values that informed our choice of a subject to begin with. This is not altogether possible, in practice if not in logic—although I believe it to be logically impossible as well. Which is to say that in the social sciences, as much as in literary criticism, the problem of judgment remains central, unyielding, and full of impossible demands. That these demands are impossible in no way rules out the necessity that they be fulfilled.

Our difficulties seem to be further compounded if we examine another part of Weber's long definition-discussion of this heuristic idea or device. An ideal type, Weber remarks, is not "an average" of anything. It is formed rather by "the one-sided *accentuation* of one or more points of view and by the synthesis of a great many diffuse, discrete, more or less present and occasionally absent *concrete individual* phenomena, which are arranged according to those one-sidedly emphasized viewpoints into a unified *analytical* construct." In substance, he states, "this construct is like a *utopia* which has been arrived at by the analytical accentuation of certain elements of reality." And he goes on to add that "in its conceptual purity, this mental construct cannot be found empirically anywhere in reality. It is a *utopia*." The writer who tries to take the next step beyond the analysis of specific works of a pornographic character, who extends his discussion in order to reach some synthetic or theoretical conclusions, is compelled to deal with utopia on two fronts. In summing up, sorting, and ordering the material he has already dealt with, he is employing the logical method of the ideal type —by abstraction, accentuation, suppression, emphasis, and rearrangement, he attains to a hypothetical or utopian conception

of the material which earlier he had analytically dispersed. At
the same time, however, in the instance of pornography that
material itself inclines to take the form of a utopia. The literary
genre that pornographic fantasies—particularly when they appear in the shape of pornographic fiction—tend most to resemble is the utopian fantasy. For our present purposes I call this
fantasy pornotopia.

What is pornotopia?

Where, in the first place, does it exist? Or where, alternatively, does it take place? The word "utopia," of course, means
"not place," or "not a place," or "no place." More than most
utopias, pornography takes the injunction of its etymology literally—it may be said largely to exist at no place, and to take
place in nowhere. The isolated castle on an inaccessible mountain top, the secluded country estate, set in the middle of a large
park and surrounded by insurmountable walls, the mysterious
town house in London or Paris, the carefully furnished and
elaborately equipped set of apartments to be found in any city
at all, the deserted cove at the seaside, or the solitary cottage
atop the cliffs, the inside of a brothel rented for a day, a week,
or a month, or the inside of a hotel room rented for a night—
these are all the same place and are identically located. These
places may be found in books; they may be read about in libraries or in studies; but their true existence is not the world, or
even the world as it exists by special reference in literature.
They truly exist behind our eyes, within our heads. To read a
work of pornographic fiction is to rehearse the ineffably familiar; to locate that fantasy anywhere apart from the infinite, barren, yet plastic space that exists within our skulls is to deflect it
from one of its chief purposes. A representative nineteenth-
century novel begins, "In the town of X——, on a warm summer's day . . ." By the time we have finished with such a novel
we have learned an astonishing number of things about that
town and its weather, about its inhabitants, their families, how
they go about making their livings, what their opinions may be
upon a variety of topics, what they like and dislike, how they

were born and how they die, what they leave behind and what they set up in store for the future. A representative pornographic novel may also begin with the town of X—— and a summer's day, but it does not proceed from that point, as the novel does, by elaboration and extension. What typically happens is that after having presented the reader with some dozen concrete details—by way of a down payment on credibility, one assumes—the novel then leaves this deposit of particularities behind and proceeds by means of abstraction to its real business, which is after all largely irrelevant to considerations of place. In the century of national literatures, pornography produced a body of writing that was truly international in character. It is often impossible to tell whether a pornographic work of fiction is a translation or an original—one need only change the names, or the spelling of the names, of characters in order to conceal such a novel's origin. The *genius loci* of pornography speaks in the *lingua franca* of sex. One need not inquire very far to find sufficient reasons for pornography's indifference to place: in the kind of boundless, featureless freedom that most pornographic fantasies require for their action, such details are regarded as restrictions, limitations, distractions, or encumbrances.

Utopias commonly have some special relation to time, and pornotopia is no exception to this rule. Some utopias are set in a distant past, some are located in a distant future; almost all seem to be implicitly conceived as taking place at some special juncture in time, where time as we know it and some other kind of time intersect. Although utopias are often furnished with novel means of measuring and counting time—such as new kinds of clocks or calendars—it is sound to say that most of them are outside of time. So is pornotopia, although the special ways in which it represents its exemption need to be specified. To the question "What time is it in pornotopia?" one is tempted to answer, "It is always bedtime," for that is in a literal sense true. Sometimes a work of pornography, following the example of the novel, will establish an equivalence between time and the duration of a single life-span or personal history. In pornography, however, life or existence in time does not begin with birth; it begins with one's first sexual impulse or experience, and one is said to be born in pornotopia only after one has experienced his first erection or witnessed his first primal scene. Similarly, one is declared dead when, through either age or accident, one becomes impotent—which helps to explain why in pornotopia women are immortal, and why in pornographic novels there are so many old women, witches, and hags, and so few old men. In another sense, time in pornotopia is without duration; when the past is recalled, it is for the single purpose of arousing us in the present. And the effort of pornography in this regard is to achieve in consciousness the condition of the unconscious mind—a condition in which all things exist in a total, simultaneous present. Time, then, in pornotopia is sexual time; and its real unit of measurement is an internal one—the time it takes either for a sexual act to be represented or for an autoerotic act to be completed. (These last two distinctions depend upon whether one chooses to emphasize the author's or the reader's sense of time—in a considerable number of instances the two seem to coincide.)

On a larger scale, time in pornotopia is determined by the time it takes to run out a series of combinations. Given a limited number of variables—that is, persons of both sexes with their corresponding organs and appendages—and a limited number of juxtapositions into which these variables may be placed, time becomes a mathematical function and may be defined as however long it takes to represent or exhaust the predetermined number of units to be combined. This is why *The One Hundred and Twenty Days of Sodom* represents one kind of perfection in this genre. Pornography's mad genius, the Marquis de Sade, with psychotic rigidity and precision, and with psychotic logic, wrote his novel along strict arithmetical lines: so many of this and so many of these and those, doing this, that, and those to them in the following order or declension; to be succeeded on the following day, after all have changed hands or places by . . . et cetera, et cetera. Although it is commonly believed that Sade did not finish this novel, since large parts of it exist only in outline, such a conclusion is not acceptable. Having completed his outline, Sade had in effect written his novel—the rest is only filling in. The truth of this suggestion may be demonstrated by a reading of the novel: I can for myself find no essential difference between the filled-in parts and those that exist only in outline. Form and content are perfectly fused in the outline, and the filling-in or writing-out is largely a matter of adornment—a circumstance that both anticipates and points to certain distinctions which have to be made in considering pornography's relation to literature. It also serves to suggest that a pornographic novel might be written by a computer. If one feeds in the variables out will come the combinations. I have no doubt that one day this kind of literature will be produced, and I must confess to a sense of relief when I recognize that I will not be around to read it.

So much for the coordinates of space and time. We next may turn to the actual external world as it appears in pornotopia. How, for example, is nature represented? It is represented as follows. It is usually seen at eye-level. In the middle distance there looms a large irregular shape. On the horizon swell two immense snowy white hillocks; these are capped by great, pink, and as it were prehensile peaks or tips—as if the rosy-fingered dawn itself were playing just behind them. The landscape then undulates gently down to a broad, smooth, swelling plain, its soft rolling curves broken only in the lower center by a small volcanic crater or omphalos. Farther down, the scene narrows and changes in perspective. Off to the right and left jut two smooth snowy ridges. Between them, at their point of juncture, is a dark wood—we are now at the middle of our journey. This dark wood—sometimes it is called a thicket—is triangular in shape. It is also like a cedarn cover, and in its midst is a dark romantic chasm. In this chasm the wonders of nature abound. From its top there depends a large, pink stalactite, which changes shape, size, and color in accord with the movement of the tides below and within. Within the chasm—which is roughly pear-shaped—there are caverns measureless to man, grottoes, hermits' caves, underground streams—a whole internal and subterranean landscape. The climate is warm but wet. Thunderstorms are frequent in this region, as are tremors and quakings of the earth. The walls of the cavern often heave and contract in rhythmic violence, and when they do the salty streams that run through it double their flow. The whole place is dark yet visible. This is the center of the earth and the home of man.

The essential imagination of nature in pornotopia, then, is this immense, supine, female form. Sometimes this figure is represented in other positions and from other perspectives; sometimes other orifices are chosen for central emphasis. Whichever way it is regarded, however, this gigantic female shape is the principal external natural object in the world we are describing. Although I have in part composed this catalogue of features with a humorous intention, I should add that every image in it is taken from a work of pornography, and that all of these images are commonplaces—they really are the means through which writers of pornography conceive of the world. As for man in this setting he is really not part of nature. In the first place, he is actually not man. He is an enormous erect penis, to which there happens to be attached a human figure. Second, this organ is not a natural but a supernatural object. It is creator and destroyer, the source of all and the end of all being—it is literally omnipotent, and plays the role in pornotopia that gods and deities play elsewhere. It is the object of worship; and the nature that we have just finished describing exists—as does the universe in certain cosmogonies—for the sole purpose of confirming the existence of its creator. Finally, we should take notice of the gigantic size of these figures. This is not simply another aspect of their godlike characters; it suggests to us as well in what age of life the imagination of pornography has its grounds.

As for external nature as we ordinarily perceive it, that exists in pornotopia in an incidental yet interesting way. If a tree or a bush is represented as existing, the one purpose of its existence is as a place to copulate under or behind. If there is a stream, then the purpose of that stream is as a place in which to bathe before copulating. If a rainstorm comes up, then the purpose of that rainstorm is to drive one indoors in order to copulate. (When D. H. Lawrence dragged in a rainstorm in order to drive his lovers out of doors, he was doing something that no right-minded pornographer would ever dream of.) Nature, in other words, has no separate existence in pornotopia; it is not external to us, or "out there." There is no "out there" in pornography, which serves to indicate to us again in what phase of our mental existence this kind of thinking has its origins.

These attributes of nature in pornotopia are in turn connected with others, which have to do with the richness and inexhaustibility of life in this imaginary world—pornotopia is a pornocopia as well. Pornotopia is literally a world of grace abounding to the chief of sinners. All men in it are always and infinitely potent; all women fecundate with lust and flow inexhaustibly with sap or juice or both. Everyone is always ready for anything, and everyone is infinitely generous with his substance. It is always summertime in pornotopia, and it is a summertime of the emotions as well—no one is ever jealous, possessive, or really angry. All our aggressions are perfectly fused with our sexuality, and the only rage is the rage of lust, a happy fury indeed. Yet behind these representations of physiological abundance and sexual plenitude one senses an anxiety that points in the opposite direction. Pornotopia could in fact only have been imagined by persons who have suffered extreme deprivation, and I do not by this mean sexual deprivation in the genital sense alone. One gets the distinct impression, after reading a good deal of this literature, that it could only have been written by men who at some point in their lives had been starved. The insatiability depicted in it seems to me to be literal insatiability, and the orgies endlessly represented are the visions of permanently hungry men. The Marquis de Sade once again

took the matter to its logical conclusion; when his orgies include the eating of excrement, and then finally move on to murder with the purpose of cannibalism, he was bringing to explicit
statement the direction taken by almost all works of pornography. Inside of every pornographer there is an infant screaming
for the breast from which he has been torn. Pornography represents an endless and infinitely repeated effort to recapture that
breast, and the bliss it offered, as it often represents as well a
revenge against the world—and the women in it—in which
such cosmic injustice could occur.

Relations between human beings also take on a special appearance in pornotopia. It is in fact something of a misnomer to
call these representations "relations between human beings."
They are rather juxtapositions of human bodies, parts of bodies,
limbs, and organs; they are depictions of positions and events,
diagrammatic schema for sexual ballets—actually they are
more like football plays than dances; they are at any rate as
complicated as either. As an example of how such relations are
represented, I will quote some passages from *The Romance of
Lust*. This novel was published during the 1870's. It is in four
volumes and runs to six hundred pages, every one of which is
devoted to nothing other than the description of persons in sexual congress. This novel comes as close as anything I know to
being a pure pornotopia in the sense that almost every human
consideration apart from sexuality is excluded from it. The passages I quote were chosen almost at random.

We ran off two bouts in this delicious position, and then with
more regulated passions rose to form more general combinations.
    The Count had fucked the Egerton while we were engaged
above the divine Frankland. Our first pose was suggested by the
Egerton, who had been as yet less fucked than any. She had been
also greatly taken with the glories of the Frankland's superb body,
and especially struck with her extraordinary clitoris, and had
taken the curious lech of wishing to have it in her bottomhole
while riding St. George on my big prick. We all laughed at her
odd choice, but agreed at once, especially the Frankland, whose
greatest lech was to fuck very fair young women with her long

and capable clitoris. A fairer creature than the lovely Egerton could not be found. The Frankland admitted that in her inmost heart she had longed thus to have the Egerton from the moment she had first seen her, and her delight and surprise at finding the dear Egerton had equally desired to possess her, fired her fierce lust with increased desire. I lay down, the Egerton straddled over, and feeling the delight of my huge prick when completely imbedded, she spent profusely with only two rebounds. Then sinking on my belly she presented her lovely arse to the lascivious embraces of the salacious Frankland. . . .

The Count next took the Benson in cunt while I blocked the rear aperture, and the Frankland once more enculed the Egerton, who dildoed herself in cunt at the same time; all of us running two courses. We then rose, purified, and refreshed. When our pricks were ready it was the Egerton who took me in front and the Count behind, and the Benson, who had grown lewd on the Frankland's clitoris, was sodomised by her and dildoed by herself. The Egerton still suffered a little in the double stretching, so that we ran but one exquisite bout, enabling us, whose powers began to fail, to be re-excited, and to finish with the double jouissance in the glorious body of the Frankland.

Before proceeding any further, I should like to direct attention to certain qualities in the prose of these passages. First, this prose manages to combine extreme fantasy with absolute cliché —as if the fantasy, however wild and excessive it may seem, had been gone through so many times that it had long since become incapable of being anything other than a weary and hopeless repetition of itself. Second, the whole representation takes place under the order of "regulated passions." That is to say everything in it—the movements and responses of the imaginary persons—is completely controlled, as things are in autoerotic fantasies but as they never are in the relations of human beings, and even, one might add, as they never are in the relations of human beings as these are represented in literature. Third, the relations between the persons in these passages are intricate and mechanical; the juxtaposition of organs and apertures is convoluted yet precise, and it is impossible to know the players without a scorecard. In this connection, one should also note the tendency to abolish the distinction between the sexes: clitorises

become penises, anuses are common to both sexes, and everyone
is everything to everyone else. Yet this everything is confined
strictly to the relations of organs, and what is going on may be
described as organ grinding.

The Romance of Lust continues, after a short hiatus, as
follows:

> So to five women we thus had six men, and eventually a very
> handsome young priest, debauched by the others, joined our
> party, and we carried on the wildest and most extravagant orgies
> of every excess the most raging lust could devise. We made chains
> of pricks in arseholes, the women between with dildoes strapped
> round their waist, and shoved into the arseholes of the man before
> them, while his prick was into the arsehole of the woman in his
> front. . . .
>   Our second double couplings were, myself in my aunt's cunt,
> which incest stimulated uncle to a stand, and he took to his wife's
> arse while her nephew incestuously fucked her cunt. The Count
> took to the delicious and most exciting tight cunt of the Dale,
> while her son shoved his prick into his mother's arse, to her un-
> speakable satisfaction. Ellen and the Frankland amused them-
> selves with tribadic extravagances.
>   This bout was long drawn out, and afforded inexpressible ex-
> tasies to all concerned. And after the wild cries and most bawdy
> oaths that instantly preceded the final extasy, the dead silence and
> long after enjoyments were drawn out to a greater length than
> before. After which we all rose and purified, and then took re-
> freshments of wine and cake, while discussing our next arrange-
> ments of couples. . . .
>   I then took my aunt's arse while the lecherous Dale was under-
> neath gamahuching and dildoing her, and by putting the Dale
> close to the edge of the bed, the Count stood between her legs,
> which were thrown over his shoulders, and thus he fucked her,
> having taken a lech to fuck her cunt, which was an exquisite one
> for fucking; her power of nip being nearly equal to the Frank-
> land, and only beaten by aunt's extraordinary power in that way.
> We thus formed a group of four enchained in love's wildest sports
> together.
>   The Frankland was gamahuched by uncle while having
> Harry's prick in her arse, Ellen acting postilion to Harry's arse
> while frigging herself with a dildo.
>   The closing bout of the night was the Count into aunt's arse,

my prick into the Frankland's arse, Harry enjoying an old-fashioned fuck with his mother, and Ellen under aunt to dildo and be gamahuched and dildoed by aunt. We drew this bout out to an interminable length, and lay for nearly half-an-hour in the annihilation of the delicious afterjoys. At last we rose, purified, and then restoring our exhausted frames with champagne, embraced and sought well earned sleep in our separate chambers.

The relations between persons set forth in such passages are in fact combinations. They are outlines or blueprints, diagrams of directions or vectors, and they must be read diagrammatically. They are, in other words, sets of abstractions. Although the events and organs they refer to are supposed to be concrete, one may observe how little concrete detail, how few real particularities, these passages contain. Persons in them are transformed into literal objects; these objects finally coalesce into one object —oneself. The transactions represented in this writing are difficult to follow because so little individuation has gone into them. In a world whose organization is directed by the omnipotence of thought, no such discriminations are necessary.

With this relentless circumscription of reality, with its tendency, on the one hand, to exclude from itself everything that is not sexual and, on the other, to include everything into itself by sexualizing all of reality, pornography might appear to resemble poetry—at least some power analogous to metaphor appears to be always at work in it. This possibility brings us again to the question of the relation of pornography to literature. The subject is extremely complex, and I do not intend to deal with it systematically. I should like, however, to make a number of elementary distinctions.

Since it is written, printed, and read, and since it largely takes the form of fictional representations of human activities, pornography is of course, in a formal sense, literature. Furthermore, it is impossible to object theoretically to its purposes. There is, on the face, of it, nothing illegitimate about a work whose purpose or intention is to arouse its readers sexually. If it is permissible for works of literature to move us to tears, to arouse our passions against injustice, to make us cringe with

horror, and to purge us through pity and terror, then it is
equally permissible—it lies within the orbit of literature's functions—for works of literature to excite us sexually. Two major
works of literature may be adduced which undertake this
project—part of the undertaking being, at least to my mind, a
conscious intention on the author's part to move his readers sexually. *Madame Bovary* and the final section of *Ulysses* seem to
me to have been written with such an intention. They also seem
to me to have been successful in that intention. I will go one
step further and assert that anyone who reads these works and
is not sexually moved or aroused by Emma Bovary or Molly
Bloom is not responding properly to literature, is not reading
with the fullness and openness and attentiveness that literature
demands.

Literature possesses, however, a multitude of intentions, but
pornography possesses only one. This singleness of intention
helps us to understand how it is that, in regard to pornography, the imponderable question of critical judgment has been
solved. Given a work of literature whose unmistakable aim is to
arouse its reader, and given a reader whose range of sexual responsiveness is not either altogether inhibited or aberrant, then
a work of pornography is successful *per se* insofar as we are
aroused by it. Keats's hope for literature in general has been
ironically fulfilled: pornography proves itself upon our pulses,
and elsewhere. Its success is physical, measurable, quantifiable;
in it the common pursuit of true judgment comes to a dead
halt. On this side, then, pornography falls into the same category as such simpler forms of literary utterance as propaganda
and advertising. Its aim is to move us in the direction of action,
and no doubt Plato, in *his* utopia, would have banned it along
with poetry—which to his way of thinking exerted its influence
in a similar way and toward similar ends. There remains an
element of truth in this radical judgment.

Despite all this, we know as well that pornography is not
literature. I have, at earlier and separate points in this work,
tried to demonstrate how this negative circumstance operates,

but it might be useful to bring several of these demonstrations together and quickly repeat and recapitulate them. First, there is the matter of form. Most works of literature have a beginning, a middle, and an end. Most works of pornography do not. A typical piece of pornographic fiction will usually have some kind of crude excuse for a beginning, but, having once begun, it goes on and on and ends nowhere. This impulse or compulsion to repeat, to repeat endlessly, is one of pornography's most striking qualities. A pornographic work of fiction characteristically develops by unremitting repetition and minute mechanical variation—the words that may describe this process are again, again, again, and more, more, more. We also observed that although pornography is obsessed with the idea of pleasure, of infinite pleasure, the idea of gratification, of an end to pleasure (pleasure being here an endless experience of retentiveness, without release) cannot develop. If form in art consists in the arousal in the reader of certain expectations and the fulfillment of those expectations, then in this context too pornography is resistant to form and opposed to art. For fulfillment implies completion, gratification, an end; and it is an end, a conclusion of any kind, that pornography most resists. The ideal pornographic novel, I should repeat, would go on forever; it would have no ending, just as in pornotopia there is ideally no such thing as time.

In terms of language, too, pornography stands in adverse relation to literature. Although a pornographic work of fiction is by necessity written, it might be more accurate to say that language for pornography is a prison from which it is continually trying to escape. At best, language is a bothersome necessity, for its function in pornography is to set going a series of non-verbal images, of fantasies, and if it could achieve this without the mediation of words it would. Such considerations help us to understand certain of the special qualities of pornographic prose. The prose of a typical pornographic novel consists almost entirely of clichés, dead and dying phrases, and stereotypical formulas; it is also heavily adjectival. These phrases and formulas

are often interchangeable, and by and large they are interchangeable without any loss of meaning. They tend to function
as non-specific abstractions, and can all be filled with the same
general content. Nevertheless, to the extent that they become
verbally non-referential, they too express the tendency of pornography to move ideally away from language. Inexorably
trapped in words, pornography, like certain kinds of contemporary literature, tries desperately to go beneath and behind
language; it vainly tries to reach what language cannot directly
express but can only point toward, the primary processes of
energy upon which our whole subsequent mental life is built.
This effort explains in part why pornography is also the reposi-
tory of the forbidden, tabooed words. The peculiar power of
such words has to do with their primitiveness. They have undergone the least evolution, and retain much of their original
force. In our minds, such words are minimally verbal; they
present themselves to us as acts; they remain extremely close to
those unconscious impulses in which they took their origin and
that they continue to express. The language of pornography
demonstrates to us that the meaning of this phenomenon is to
be found somewhere beyond language—yet we have only language to show us where that is.

Even in its use of metaphor, pornography can be seen to
differ from literature. Although the language of pornography
is highly metaphoric, its metaphors regularly fail to achieve
specific verbal value. Metaphor ordinarily fuses or identifies
similar characteristics from disparate objects; its apparent aim,
both in literature and in speech, is to increase our command
over reality—and the objects in it—by magically exercising our
command of the language through which reality is identified
and mediated. In pornography, however, the intention of language, including metaphor, is unmetaphoric and literal; it
seeks to *de-elaborate* the verbal structure and the distinctions
upon which it is built, to move back through language to that
part of our minds where all metaphors are literal truths, where
everything is possible, and where we were all once supreme.

Taking their origins in the same matrix of impulses, pornography and literature tend regularly to move off in opposite directions.

The third way in which pornography is opposed to literature has also been mentioned. Literature is largely concerned with the relations of human beings among themselves; it represents how persons live with each other, and imagines their feelings and emotions as they change; it investigates their motives and demonstrates that these are often complex, obscure, and ambiguous. It proceeds by elaboration, the principal means of this elaboration being the imagination of situations of conflict between persons or within a single person. All of these interests are antagonistic to pornography. Pornography is not interested in persons but in organs. Emotions are an embarrassment to it, and motives are distractions. In pornotopia conflicts do not exist; and if by chance a conflict does occur it is instantly dispelled by the waving of a magic sexual wand. Sex in pornography is sex without the emotions—and this we need not discuss any further: D. H. Lawrence has already done the job.[1]

[1] That pornography is almost entirely written by men and for men was demonstrated to me by a reading of one or two of the few works of pornographic fiction known definitely to be written by women. In these stories, there is no focus or concentration upon organs; much more attention is paid to the emotions, and there is a good deal of contemplation, conscious reverie, and self-observation.

I should like, at the close of this discussion, to remind the reader once again that pornotopia does not exist and is not anywhere to be found. It is an ideal type, an instrument to be used for comparison and analysis. None of the works that I have discussed—and none that I have ever read—is actually a pornotopia, though several approach that extreme limit. If the theoretical model which I have constructed is an adequate one, then the reader should be helped in making certain discriminations. It should be possible to apply the idea of pornotopia to concrete, existing works, and to determine in what ways and in how far such works are or are not pornographic. I do not at all mean that this device can be a substitute for critical judgment, but that it can act as an aid to judgment and as one more instrument of analysis.

A concrete illustration may prove useful. In the last few years, much has been written about *Fanny Hill*. Almost every article about this book that I have read seems to me to have been—with the best will in the world—mistaken and misguided. *Fanny Hill* is of course a pornographic novel; it contains, however (as does every other work of pornography), a number of non-pornographic elements, qualities, or attributes—it may even contain these to a more substantial degree than other or subsequent pornographic works of fiction. One does not,

Finally, something should be said about the historical circumstances of pornography. Although the impulses and fantasies with which pornography deals are trans-historical, pornography itself is a historical phenomenon. It has its origins in the seventeenth century,[2] may be said to come into full meaningful existence in the latter part of the eighteenth, persists, develops, and flourishes throughout the nineteenth century, and continues on in our own. To ask what caused such a phenomenon to occur is to ask a stupendous question, since the causes of it seem to be inseparable from those vast social processes which brought about the modern world. A few matters may, however, be briefly referred to. The growth of pornography is inseparable from and dependent upon the growth of the novel. Those social forces which acted to contribute to the rise of the novel—and to the growth of its audience—acted analogously in contributing to the development of pornography. Like the novel, pornography is connected with the growth of cities—with an urban society—and with an audience of literate readers rather than listeners or spectators. These considerations are in turn involved with the development of new kinds of experience, in particular with the development of private experience—sociologists call the process "privatization." If the novel is both evidence of and a response to the needs created by the possibilities of increased privacy and private experience, then pornography is a mad parody of the same situation. No experience of reading is more private, more solitary in every possible way.

As an urban, capitalist, industrial, and middle-class world was being created, the sexual character of European society un-

---

it must be emphasized, need a device like pornotopia to arrive at such a judgment; but the device may nevertheless be used in the analysis of that novel, in the effort of demonstrating just how it goes about achieving its pornographic purposes, how it may at certain points be deflected from such purposes, or how in fact other purposes may be included within its larger or overall design.

[2] My own researches and those of David Foxon, referred to in the Introduction, p. xv, above, agree in this conclusion. I regret that this is not the place to make a demonstration of these findings, but I refer the reader to Mr. Foxon's essays.

derwent significant modifications. The sexual character or roles attributed to both men and women changed; sexual manners and habits altered; indeed the whole style of sexual life was considerably modified. Among the principal tendencies in this process was a steadily increasing pressure to split sexuality off from the rest of life. By a variety of social means which correspond to the psychological processes of isolation, distancing, denial, and even repression, a separate and insulated sphere in which sexuality was to be confined was brought into existence. Yet even as sexuality was isolated, it continued to develop and change—that is to say, human consciousness of sexuality continued to change and to increase. Indeed that isolation was both the precondition of and the vehicle through which such a development occurred. The growth of pornography was one of the results of these processes—as, in another context, was the development of modern romantic love. Pornography and the history of pornography allow us to see how, on one of its sides, and under the special conditions of isolation and separation, sexuality came to be thought of in European society from the end of the seventeenth to the end of the nineteenth century.

Matters came to a head during the middle and latter decades of the nineteenth century. During that period, pornographic writings were produced and published in unprecedented volume—it became in fact a minor industry. The view of human sexuality as it was represented in the subculture of pornography and the view of sexuality held by the official culture were reversals, mirror images, negative analogues of one another. For every warning against masturbation issued by the official voice of culture, another work of pornography was published; for every cautionary statement against the harmful effects of sexual excess uttered by medical men, pornography represented copulation *in excelsis,* endless orgies, infinite daisy chains of inexhaustibility; for every assertion about the delicacy and frigidity of respectable women made by the official culture, pornography represented legions of maenads, universes of palpitating females; for every effort made by the official culture to

minimize the importance of sexuality, pornography cried out—
or whispered—that it was the only thing in the world of any
importance at all. It is essential for us to notice the similarities
even more than the differences between these two groups of
attitudes or cultures. In both the same set of anxieties are at
work; in both the same obsessive ideas can be made out; and in
both sexuality is conceived of at precisely the same degree of
consciousness. It was a situation of unbearable contradiction.
And it was at this point that the breaking through began.

This breaking through was made in three areas. First and
most important was the invention or discovery of modern psychology, most centrally of course in the work of Freud. For the
first time in human history it became possible to discuss sexuality in a neutral way; for the first time a diction and a set of
analytic concepts or instruments were established through
which men could achieve sufficient intellectual distance from
their own sexual beliefs and behavior so as to be able to begin to
understand them. And it may even be added that for the first
time human sexuality achieved a meaning, using the word
"meaning" in the sense put to it by philosophy and the social
sciences. The work of retrieving human sexuality had begun,
but what would be retrieved was in the nature of the case a
different thing than what had earlier been set apart.

The second breaking through took place at about the same
time. In the work of the great late nineteenth-century and early
twentieth-century avant-garde artists, and in particular among
the novelists, the entire fabric of modern society came in for
attack. The focus of their assault was the sexual life of the bour-
geois or middle classes, as those classes and the style of life they
conducted had come to be the prevailing social powers. The
difficulties, agonies, contradictions, double-dealings, hypocrisies, inequities, guilts, and confusions of the sexual life of the
middle classes were for these novelists not only bad in themselves; they were symbolic of general circumstances of injustice,
unpleasantness, demoralization, and malaise which for these
artists characterized the world they inhabited. They endorsed a

freer sexual life as a good in itself; and they depicted the sexual anguish of modern persons and the sexual hypocrisies and contradictions of modern society not merely for the sake of exposure and sensationalism (although there was that too), but in order to outrage and awaken the society which had imposed upon itself such hideous conditions of servitude. Society being what it is, they were often punished for their efforts, but the work of awakening had been furthered, the work of bringing back into the central discourse of civilization that sexual life upon which it is built and through which it is perpetuated.

The third breaking through followed upon the other two, and is still happening. I refer to the general liberalization of sexual life and of social attitudes toward sexuality that is taking place in our time. It seems likely that what we are witnessing today will be as important, momentous, and enduring as that other revolution in sensibility, manners, and attitudes which occurred in England during the latter part of the eighteenth and first part of the nineteenth century. One of the more interesting recent developments in this social drama is that pornography itself is now being openly and legally published. We need not inquire into the motives of those who publish and republish such works—and I feel constrained to add that I would indeed be troubled if I came across my small son studiously conning *Justine*. Nevertheless, this development was inevitable and necessary, and on the whole, so far as we are able to see, benign. It suggests to me, moreover, that we are coming to the end of an era. We are coming to the end of the era in which pornography had a historical meaning and even a historical function. The free publication of all the old pornographic chestnuts does not necessarily indicate to me moral laxness, or fatigue, or deterioration on the part of society. It suggests rather that pornography has lost its old danger, its old power—negative social sanctions and outlawry being always the most reliable indicators of how much a society is frightened of anything, how deeply it fears its power, how subversive to its settled order it conceives an idea, or work, or act to be. (What will happen to sexuality itself if this goes on long enough is a matter upon which I hesitate to speculate.) As I have said, the impulses and fantasies of pornography are trans-historical—they will always be with us, they will always exist. Pornography is, after all, nothing more than a representation of the fantasies of infantile sexual life, as these fantasies are edited and reorganized in the masturbatory daydreams of adolescence. Every man who grows up must pass through such a phase in his existence, and I can see no reason for supposing that our society, in the history of its own life, should not have to pass through such a phase as well.

Index